THE TRAGEDY OF KING LEAR

The Tragedy of King Lear

WILLIAM SHAKESPEARE

EDITED BY E. A. HORSMAN
THE UNIVERSITY OF OTAGO
NEW ZEALAND

THE BOBBS-MERRILL COMPANY, INC.

INDIANAPOLIS · NEW YORK

First Printing

Copyright © 1973 by The Bobbs-Merrill Company, Inc.

Printed in the United States of America

Library of Congress Catalog Card Number 72–160789

ISBN Numbers

0–672–51127–4

0–672–61102–3 (pbk.)

Designed by Joseph P. Ascherl

Cover and Title Page Illustrations by Edward Gorey

The Bobbs-Merrill Shakespeare Series

is under the General Editorship of

Ian Watt, Stanford University

CONTENTS

Introduction

KING LEAR: FROM FOLK TALE TO TRAGEDY

There is an extreme contrast between the origins of the story of King Lear and the work in which Shakespeare refashioned it to explore a wider range of suffering and of attitudes toward suffering than in perhaps any other tragedy.

The story ultimately originates in folk tales of the Cinderella type such as those collected by Coxe[1] in which the heroine is disowned by her father. In a number of the variants discussed by Perrett, the reason for disowning the heroine is that, when her father asks how much his three daughters love him, the heroine can outbid the pleasing answers of her sisters only by saying she loves him like salt. Before the father can learn that this response is not an insult, the heroine is disowned, takes menial work, and marries the prince who has fallen in love with her while she was a servant. When the father discovers the value of salt by being served unsalted food, he and the heroine are reconciled.

It was Geoffrey of Monmouth who first told such a tale of a King of Britain named Leir. Geoffrey, writing his *History of the Kings of Britain* in Latin during the twelfth century, seems to have used the tale to help fill the huge gap left in the legendary record between the founding of Britain, about 1100 B.C., by Brutus, a descendant of Aeneas, and the coming of Julius Caesar. To justify the telling of the story at all, the father has to be a king of Britain; the question how much his daughters love him is asked because he wishes to divide his kingdom, giving a larger

[1] A list of abbreviations is given in Appendix G. Other references can be found in Appendix F.

share to the one who seems on this test the most worthy. Of the elder sisters, Gonorilla (or Goronilla or Gorenilla) claims that she loves her father better than her own life; Regau (or Ragau), that she loves him better than all created things. The youngest, Cordeilla, surprised that anyone should undertake to love a father more than as a father, claims always to have loved him as her father and still to do so; if pressed, she will say only that he is worth as much as he has and that so much is the measure of her love. Cordelia is more brusque but just as tactless in I.i.82–102. Angered, Leir divides half the kingdom between the two elder daughters. They are to marry the Duke of Cornubia (Cornwall) and the King of Albania (Scotland) respectively and to share in addition, after Leir's death, the half of the kingdom which he still retains. Leir refuses Cordeilla all prospect of being married with the same honor as her sisters, but he allows Aganippus, King of the Franks, to marry her without a dowry. Subsequently the other sisters, with their husbands, rebel against Leir, seize his part of the kingdom, and humiliate him so that he flees to Cordeilla. With the help of Aganippus he regains his kingdom and reigns for three years. Then both Leir and Aganippus die; hence Cordeilla inherits the kingdom of Britain. After five years her sisters' sons rebel, capture her, and imprison her; there she kills herself.

Many succeeding writers in English, French, and Latin retold the tale, until during Shakespeare's lifetime it appeared in the four works to which he appears to be directly indebted: the 1574 additions by John Higgins to *The Mirrour for Magistrates*, Holinshed's *Chronicles of England* (Book II, chapters v–vi), Spenser's *Faerie Queene* (Book II, canto x, stanzas 27–32), and a play published in 1605 but written and possibly performed earlier, *The True Chronicle History of King Leir, and his three daughters, Gonorill, Ragau, and Cordella*. Relevant sections of the last three of these works appear in Appendix B.

In these versions Lear is eventually restored to his kingdom. The old play stops at that point, while the others go on to the despair and suicide of Cordella—who becomes Cordell for the sake of the rhyme in *The Mirror for Magistrates,* and Cordelia, for the same reason, in Spenser (p. 217 below). Despair and suicide are plainly inappropriate for the role which Shakespeare allots to Cordelia and he retains them in relation to her only in the report which was to have been circulated after she was murdered (V.iii.251–2). Instead it is Goneril who accepts the knife from Despair. But there can be little doubt that the heroine's death in these two versions and in Holinshed had some part in turning Shakespeare's mind toward the extreme types of suffering which may lead to the possibility of suicide.

Lear, too, is forced to face such a possibility. For this aspect of the plot, for an important part of the physical setting (Act III) and for the varying views of the governing powers to which he makes the whole give rise, Shakespeare is indebted to Sidney's *Arcadia.* His obligation is clearest in the subplot of Gloucester and his sons, as can be seen from Appendix B; but this story, which Sidney offers as "worthy to be remembered for the unused examples therein, as well of true natural goodness, as of wretched ungratefulness," interacts in Shakespeare's mind with that of the main plot. Hence the persecutors become both more inhuman and more intelligent and the persecuted acquire a degree of moral awareness which, for the audience, sinks pity in admiration. The light in which Shakespeare views the action has clearly been affected by other parts of the *Arcadia,* for instance by the verse dialogue on the death of Erona (only two chapters after that from which the Edgar–Edmund subplot is taken) with its rebellious questioning of the heavens:

> What greater ills have now the heavens in store . . . ?
> Plangus doth live, and must Erona die?
> Erona die? O heaven (if heaven there be)
> Hath all thy whirling course so small effect?
> Serve all thy starry eyes this shame to see?
>> (ed. Feuillerat, I, 227–8)

The admonitory answers to these questions seem to have affected

Shakespeare less, except for the phrase about men "with inward tempest blown / Of minds" (ed. cit., p. 229), which describes the bewildered mental activity of these verses and of Lear in Act III. The selection and grouping of ideas in such passages as IV.vi.171–6 seem also to have their origin in Sidney:

> Like players placed to fill a filthy stage,
> Where change of thoughts one fool to other shows,
> And all but jests, save only sorrow's rage.
> The child feels that; the man that feeling knows,
> With cries first born, the presage of his life. . . .
>
> (ibid., p. 227)

In Book III, chapter 10 the arguments about providence contain views comparable to those in IV.i.36–7: "to think that those powers (if there be any such) above, are moved either by the eloquence of our prayers, or in a chafe by the folly of our actions; carries as much reason as if flies should think that men take great care which of them hums sweetest, and which of them flies nimblest" (ibid., pp.406–7). Something very much like the two views of Nature presented by *King Lear* is also found in Sidney: on the one hand there is "a Nature, as we speake of the fire which goeth upward, it knows not why: and of the nature of the Sea . . ."; on the other, "a right heavenly Nature [which] as it were unnaturing them, doth so bridle them," "a Nature of wisdom, goodness, and providence, which knows what it doth . . ." (ibid., pp. 408–9). Finally, the indictment of Pyrocles and Musidorus toward the end of *Arcadia* opens a vision of lawlessness, in which "man's nature infinitely rangeth," so that we may be glad to "find any hope that mankind is not grown monstrous" (ed. cit., II, 195–6), which may be compared with IV.ii.48–50.

This kind of debt is made all the more striking, as W. R. Elton has shown (*King Lear and the Gods*, pp. 63–71), by the contrast with the pious confidence of King Leir in the old play:

> There lives not any under heaven's bright eye
> That can convict me of impiety.
>
> (1600–1)

The heavens are guiltless of such heinous acts.
(1627)

Ah, my true friend in all extremity,
Let us submit us to the will of God:
Things past all sense, let us not seek to know;
It is God's will, and therefore must be so.
(1655–8)

It may have been the publication of this play in 1605 which kindled Shakespeare's interest, although it is always possible that he knew it in manuscript or that it had been performed much earlier; certainly a play 'kinge leare' was performed in 1594 at the Rose theater (see Henslowe's *Diary*, ed. Foakes and Rickert, 1961, p. 21). In 1594, too, a "chronicle historye of Leire Kinge of England and his Three Daughters" was entered in the Stationers' Register (see p. xxvi below), although it was not published. The extant play was entered in the Register on 8 May 1605, at first as a "Tragedie" (whereas its title page, like the 1594 entry, calls it a "Chronicle History") and then, by emendation, as a "Tragecall historie." This change has led to the suggestion that the clerk was confusing the play with Shakespeare's tragedy and hence that the latter had already been performed by 1605. (The Quarto of Shakespeare's play was not entered until two and a half years later, on 26 November 1607.) What has hardly been in doubt since Greg's article, *The Library* XX (1940), 377–400, is that Shakespeare made some use of the old play, whether before or after its publication. Muir (*Sources*, p. 142) draws particular attention to the close resemblance between the terms used in reproaching Goneril in IV.ii.60–7 and in *Leir*, 2581–2:

> thou monster, shame unto thy sex;
> Thou fiend in likeness of a human creature.

This speech is followed by an episode in which Ragan snatches and tears the letters implicating her in a plot against her father's life, as Goneril attempts to do with the incriminating paper of V.iii.152–4; the question put in each case is almost the same:

"Know'st thou this paper?" (V.iii.157) and "Knowest thou these letters?" (2586). The echoing of words or of pieces of stage business like this makes Shakespeare's debt plain: a reading of Appendix B, 1 will show how persistent it is: sometimes a rhythm has caught his ear, as with "Upon the radiant splendor of the sun" (516) beside "For, by the sacred radiance of the sun" (I.i.104); sometimes a phrase, as with Cordelia's "I cannot" (277 and I.i.86). But the tone and aim of the old play are transformed.

The interpretation of the action forms an important part of this change. Here Shakespeare is indebted not only to Sidney but also to the skeptical and humane French essayist Montaigne, whose work went through four editions between 1580 and 1595. An English translation by John Florio was published in 1603, although entered in the Stationers' Register in 1600. According to Taylor's study of Shakespeare and Montaigne, the debt in *King Lear* is second only to that in *Hamlet*. Some of the detailed evidence is convincing, for instance when a phrase like "Necessity's sharp pinch" (II.iv.205) is compared with Florio's "Necessity must first pinch you by the throat"; the sheer number of similarities, even though not many of them are as close as this one, is suggestive to say the least.

Shakespeare adds, too, much detail of contemporary demonology, a subject on which King James had written a book. Theobald first showed that Shakespeare used a famous exposure of sham demoniacs and their exorcists by Samuel Harsnett, first published in 1603, *A Declaration of Egregious Popish Impostures*. The debt goes beyond the names of Edgar's demons, as Muir demonstrates. The connection of particular sins with animals in III.iv.82–3, for example, is taken from Harsnett.

A final book which many critics find underlying the whole play is the Book of Job. Some passages, like 19:14–19, seem to epitomize Lear's plight, while the major tendency of Acts IV and V—redoubling the afflictions of Lear, Gloucester, Edgar, or Cordelia, precisely when humility, repentance, or forgiveness might seem to justify relief—is clearly parallel to the course of Job's sufferings, as John Holloway has emphasized (*The Story of the Night*, pp. 88–9).

KING LEAR AND THE CRITICS

Unlike the Book of Job, however, Shakespeare's play manages to call in question everything except men's power to endure suffering and to give service. In order, it seems, to accentuate such powers, he exaggerates the challenge to them by showing evil as intensely active while good is seen as curiously inhibited. Thus Edgar, while going with his father to Dover, makes no attempt to reveal himself or to offer comfort, any more than Kent does for Lear; or Edmund, when suddenly reformed, seems unable—until it is too late—to attempt to countermand his orders for the murder of Lear and Cordelia. The resulting action includes such extremes of human suffering and joy that, as with life itself, there has been no agreement as to whether it shows or does not show the working of divine providence. At the same time Shakespeare draws attention to the varied opinions which may be held about the governing powers: compare, for instance, Gloucester and Edgar on the gods at IV.i.36–7 and V.iii.167–8, or the view of Nature taken by Edmund in I.ii.1ff. and implied by Lear in I.i.206–7. It is not surprising that the play has been subject to much interpretation in theological terms.

Dr. Johnson was troubled by the death of Cordelia "in a just cause," but he placed the emphasis of his criticism not upon the metaphysical problem which her death raised (and which was solved on the stage in his time by the happy ending of Tate's version) but upon the plot, "the artful involutions of distinct interests, the striking opposition of contrary characters, the sudden changes of fortune, and the quick succession of events" (*The Plays of William Shakespeare*, 1765, VI, 158–9). Romantic critics, on the other hand—Coleridge, Lamb, or Hazlitt, followed in many ways by A. C. Bradley—were much more interested in what "agitates our passions" than in what "interests our curiosity" (to use Johnson's words). To them the play was not an exciting sequence of events, but an exhibition of the "character, passions, and sufferings" of Lear and others: "a world's convention of agonies . . . All external nature . . . all moral nature convulsed," says Coleridge (*Lectures and Notes on Shakespeare . . .*, ed. Ashe, p. 341); the passion "like a sea, swelling, chafing, raging, without bound, without hope, without beacon, or anchor," says Hazlitt (*Works*, ed. Howe, XVIII, 332)—both echoed by Bradley when he writes about "the vastness of the convulsion both of nature and of human passion" (*Shakespearian Tragedy*, Lecture VII).

Coleridge, Lamb, and Bradley find the stage inadequate to present all these features. Bradley stresses the defects of the plot, claiming that the play "as a whole is imperfectly dramatic," that "there is something in its very essence which is at war with the senses, and demands a purely imaginative realisation." He admits, however, that he writes at a time when *King Lear* is "the least popular of the famous four . . . the least often presented on the stage, and the least successful there" (ibid.). By contrast, in the last thirty years there has been an extraordinary number of outstanding productions of *King Lear*. Yet criticism has been slow to learn from the theater: critics have tended to concentrate on the play as poetry and upon the action only in so far as it contributes to the building of "a deeply metaphysical metaphor, or myth, about the human condition" (Maynard Mack, *King Lear in Our Time*, p. 115).

Such criticism may place the play in the tradition of the Moralities, with their allegorical interplay of personified abstractions like Youth, Charity, Riot, or Pride. On the other hand, it may emphasize the images in the language of the play as if it were a modern symbolist poem. Those who, like Bernard Spivack or Maynard Mack, find the morality plays apposite, can point to the grouping of the characters into good and bad, a grouping which Bradley noticed and related to a tendency in *Lear* for Shakespeare's imagination "to analyse and abstract, to decompose human nature into its constituent factors, and then to construct beings in whom one or more of these factors is absent . . ." (Lecture VII); in a performance, on the other hand, he claimed we see "mere particular men and women." But the productions of the last twenty years have shown how the actor may individualize a part while still observing the restraints which a play subject to this kind of stylization imposes.

The action itself is stylized. It is common in Shakespeare for one part of the action to be echoed in another, but here we have an elaborate system of correspondences: the parallel plots of Lear and Gloucester; the adoption of disguises by both Kent and Edgar—in the case of the latter not once but thrice, or four times if the trial by combat is counted; the trial conducted by Lear of his daughters' love in I.i., followed immediately by a similar testing of the love of Burgundy and France for the disinherited Cordelia; the first of these trials is answered by the imagined trial of Goneril and Regan in III.vi. which is followed in turn by the trial "without the form of justice" of Gloucester in III.vii; in IV.vi.145–63 Lear's mind is preoccupied with the doing of justice and in V.ii. there is the trial by combat. Such rhythms in the action have their origin not in "character," but in the demands of the imagination which shapes the whole action; inevitably they invite us to relate them to similar repetitions in the language of the play.

Bradley had seen the importance of the "incessant references to the lower animals;" Caroline Spurgeon emphasized "the continuous use of verbs and images of bodily and generally anguished motion." These allusions add to our awareness of the action; the elaborate explication of Robert Heilman (*This Great Stage*) shows us more of this repetition than we would suspect from watching the play, but he adds interpretations which carry us away from the action. It is true that Heilman's examination of key notions in the play like "sight" or "smell" does bring to light repeated references which are there and in places where the plot does not always require them. Shakespeare's imagination, in fact, seems to hold the entire action before him at once so that any one part is seen in relation to many others. What is important is that each of Heilman's "patterns of imagery" originates in an action conceived for the stage and that the stage-action must control our view of their significance; they do not exist for philosophical purposes that transcend the bounds of the action and turn the play into "an inquiry into the nature of man and the framework of reality within which he acts" (Heilman, p. 133). Such a view encourages attempts to sum up the play in abstract terms. L. C. Knights, for instance, argues that *Lear* presents "the complete endorsement of a particular quality of being," namely love, which he characterizes as a "self-forgetful concentration . . . upon the true being of 'the other' " and as "that without which life is a meaningless chaos of competing egotisms . . . the condition of intellectual clarity . . . the sole ground of a genuinely self-affirming life and energy" (*Some Shakespearian Themes*, p. 118).

Statements like these divert attention from the more specific— and moving—"service" which certain characters give to others (as Jonah Barish and Marshal Waingrow have stressed) and from the sober duty and compassion which have a muted triumph at the end of the play. The action is concerned with the utmost intensification of misfortune caused by the hero's initial misjudgment of a daughter: the death of this daughter, after she has become the dearest of all to him, and in a war which, but for his misjudgment, might never have occurred. The gods or Nature (in at least two senses) are repeatedly either believed to be active or asked to act; but actual good is achieved only through human agency, in particular the agency of those who have been wronged—Cordelia, Edgar, and Kent. Indeed if the action is to involve the utmost intensification of suffering, nothing must be allowed to interfere with "the worst," namely that those who undergo most suffering—Lear and Gloucester—should have the greatest responsibility for the events which cause it. It is this, not any speculative theology, which makes it impossible that "the gods" should "defend" Cordelia. Those critics who labor to show that the play is written either to assert or to question eternal providence disregard the action which makes the play what it is. References to religious or metaphysical speculation, whether to astrology or to the justice of the gods, are to be seen in relation to the particular point in the action at which they come and to the place in the action of the character who makes them, for, as Maxwell points out, each character has a religion appropriate to his predicament. No one of these references, not even any one group, can be taken as containing the final significance of the whole work, since the action of *Lear* places them in relationships to each other that differ from the argumentative relations of theology or philosophy. There can be no doubt of the Christian quality of the charity and forgiveness exchanged between Lear and Cordelia in IV.vii., of the regenerate character of the hero in this scene compared with his pride and wilfulness in I.i., or of the specific references to the end of the world in IV.vi.131–2 and V.iii.260–1. But these examples are insufficient to turn the play— as O. J. Campbell or R. W. Chambers would have us do—into anything like a "Divine Comedy." In the catastrophe which overtakes Lear, these gifts are lost; understanding nothing, he dies with his wits quite gone, but with his attention fixed on Cordelia. For the observer of the action, if not for the speculative theologian, this is enough. Shakespeare is not writing to justify the ways of God to men, but to interest us in the human consequences of a mistaken choice—particularly one which divides a kingdom. He is not troubled by any theological inconsistency between having Lear call Cordelia "a soul in bliss" in IV.vii.46 and having him cry at her death that she will come no more. From neither case can we reason that he wanted his play to exemplify a certain view of the universe. Now one view, now another is expressed or assumed as Lear moves toward "the worst."

The poetry in its vigor and range makes many parts of the play seem to reverberate far beyond the demands of the action; if the work were an allegory, these reverberations would be its reason for existing. But it is not an allegory: the action is important for itself. Even if the poetry seems to prompt us to take what happens as typical of the general human situation, what happens remains none the less highly unusual. And this the poetry repeatedly emphasizes. It is the poetry (in the ceremony of its balanced movement and the conventional richness of its diction), for example, that opposes the vision of an opulent realm at peace

> With shadowy forests and with champaigns riched,
> With plenteous rivers and wide-skirted meads . . .
> (I.i.59–60)

to Cordelia's single negative in line 82, echoed and reechoed at once and later (see I.ii.31, note, p. 24) so that it becomes the groundwork of the whole invention. Consequently, Herbert Blau is not entirely wrong in building a "subtext" of the play upon "nothing." Through the poetry we ourselves suffer the unusual assaults of the action. For instance, the violent verbs—"Singe," "Strike," "Crack," "Gallow," "Rive" in III.ii.6–8, 42, 56, "Stretch" in V.iii.312—are again and again placed first in the line so that the speech rhythm is at odds with the strict metrical beat in which the first syllable is unaccented. More important, perhaps, than local effects of this kind is the larger one by which ordinary words come to assume extraordinary power as they are echoed in the rhythms of the stylized action—so that at the end, "Pray as you undo this button" (V.iii.306) has a strange resonance caught from "unbutton here" (III.iv.96–7), and the related divesting images from I.i.44 ("we will divest us . . . of rule") to IV.vi.166 ("pull off my boots"). But the implications of such images must not be allowed to override their particularity within the action—the macabre clowning of IV.vi.166, the humble and courteous request for service in V.iii.306. Furthermore, the implications must be brought to bear upon Lear's extraordinary case and not turned into pious platitudes which the action does not support, such as: "In proud array, Lear failed; uncrowned, half-naked, he is saved." (Heilman, p. 86).

It would of course be extremely strange if, in an action dealing with service and suffering, Shakespeare could write without reference to common attitudes toward these things, particularly those encouraged by a religion like Christianity which is centered on them. But at every point it is not the general or theological application of the reference, but rather its function in a particular part of the action, which demands attention. Pitying Lear and appalled at Cordelia's death, Kent asks, "Is this the promised end?" (V.iii.260)—meaning, is this one of the calamities announcing the end of the world? But as this "end" does not follow in the action, the implication is not exhausted by a mere reference to such calamities in Mark 13 or Luke 21. The inference seems to be that the horrors in the play are not unique, like those before "the promised end," so that there is no reason why they will not continue. Yet, on the other hand, this is not to be taken as complete "pessimism," for the calamities of the play are of such a nature that they can be avoided in future ages: they have followed in particular from the very misfortune which James I had prevented, namely the division of the kingdom, including the division of Albany, or Scotland, from the rest.

The end of the action must be related to the beginning, every part to every other part, especially in a play with the scope of *Lear*, which repeatedly provokes the director and the critic into emphasizing one part at the expense of the others. After the theater of the absurd, to take a final instance, it has become possible for Marowitz ("*Lear* Log") to pronounce, "The plot is as Beckettian as anything out of *Molloy*. . . . the scene, a metaphysical farce which ridicules life, death, sanity and illusion. . . . The world of [Peter Brook's] *Lear*, like Beckett's world, is in a constant state of decomposition" (p. 104). This is to overlook all the positive things in the action. It is wholly consistent that Marowitz, when Peter Brook asked him "what, in practical terms, I thought to be the play's greatest problem," should answer "the character of Edgar"; for not only does Edgar become "a madly-capering Bedlam beggar," he also defeats Edmund, finishes up as King, and pronounces upon the action in terms which would be quite out of place in "Beckett's world". Edgar's part in the action allows Kolve to see the middle section of the play as "a superlative example—progenitor if you like—of the theater of the absurd: it uses madness to communicate truth" (p. 181). But Kolve also sees that this is not the whole play. However difficult it may be to apprehend *King Lear* as a whole, nothing less will do.

KING LEAR IN SHAKESPEARE'S THEATER

We shall not see the play whole unless we see it as the work of a man of the theater. The company presenting the play is named in the title page of the Quarto as "his Majesty's servants playing usually at the Globe." Shakespeare was one of them, an actor as well as the writer of the plays which gave the King's Men their preeminence. His experience with this particular company (formerly the Lord Chamberlain's), at the Globe since its erection in 1599, and in theaters of similar design before that, had accustomed him to presenting certain kinds of action for a certain range of players of known abilities, in the expectation that it would be performed in certain ways.

Not all the details of the theater or its company are known, but sufficient information is recorded, or can be inferred, for most of the distinguishing features of an early seventeenth–century performance to be clear. The names of the principal actors are known—like those of Richard Burbage who played the great tragic roles, or Robert Armin who took the Fool's part in *Lear* (see III.iv.103, note, p. 112). Boy actors took the women's roles. Costume was contemporary, modified for particular purposes, but never with the aim of historical accuracy—and it continued to be so until the eighteenth century.

In principle the theater was an enclosed yard open to the sky, with a stage occupying perhaps as much as a third of the area of the yard. In the case of the Fortune theater of 1600, for which we have a builder's contract specifically mentioning the Globe as the model, the yard was 55 feet by 55 feet and the stage 43 feet wide by 27½ feet deep. The "wooden O" of the Globe (as it is called in the Prologue to *Henry V*, line 13) was probably circular —or at any rate polygonal—and may have had a yard of similar width, with the platform reaching to the middle of it. The platform was raised, perhaps four, perhaps five feet, above the yard. Around the yard stood the roofed "frame" containing three gal-

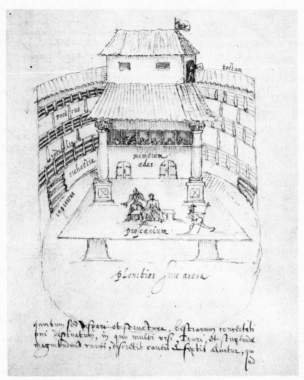

The Swan Theater, from an early copy of a drawing made
by a visitor to London, Johannes de Witt, about 1596.

Notice the rounded shape of the building, the yard marked *planities
siue arena*, the projecting quadrangular stage marked *proscaenium*
(properly the space in front of the *scena* "or forepart of a theater
where players make them readie" according to Florio's *Dictionary*,
1598), the three tiers of galleries round the yard, one marked *orchestra*
for spectators of highest rank (with seats marked *sedilia*) and two
above it marked *porticus*, the top one roofed (*tectum*). Openings to
right and left of the stage, one of them marked *ingressus*, show steps
leading to the lower gallery. At the back of the stage is the tiring-
house, marked *mimorum aedes* or actors' house. It has a raised gallery,
perhaps divided into boxes, accommodating spectators. Below this gallery are two double doors for entry on to the stage. The stage is partly
sheltered by a pent-house roof with a hut rising above it. From the
roof of the hut a flag has been raised to show that the theatre is open
for a performance and a trumpeter is sounding for the beginning of
the play.

leries, one above the other, for those spectators who were prepared to pay extra for shelter and seating. The only surviving contemporary picture of the interior of such a theater, the Swan (reproduced above, p. xxi), shows these features and others, including the canopy, supported by pillars, built over part of the stage, and the actors' tiring house at the back, in the upper part of which is a gallery or balcony. Two wide doors give access to the stage. It is possible that at the Globe there was a third door between these (although *King Lear* does not need it) and that the "heavens," as the canopy was called, were supported from the frame without the use of pillars, as they certainly were at the Hope, built in 1614.

The theaters to which most of us are accustomed today, or have been until recently, are, by contrast, rectangular, with the stage occupying one of the shorter sides and separated from the audience by a proscenium arch. The wings offer the actor the means of almost instant entry both upstage and down (that is, to the parts of the stage nearest to as well as those furthest from the audience). The whole is roofed and artificially lit, giving opportunities for realistic illusion on stage. Shakespeare's stage, on the other hand, juts out among the auditors and permits a closer relationship between them and the actors, especially marked in the case of soliloquies and asides. The stage is open to daylight; there is a minimum of scenery, perhaps a painted back-cloth in some cases, or a tree in others (both are recorded in a 1598 inventory of properties belonging to Henslowe, owner of the Rose Theater). This arrangement makes the maximum appeal to the audience to imagine the surroundings of the action or to forget them in their attention to the actors. The actors make most of their entries from the tiring house at the back of the stage through the doors (which are repeatedly mentioned in stage directions; for instance, see III.i. headnote, p. 95); they need time to reach the area downstage where they are in greatest contact with the audience, and time to get off again. The effect of this fact can be seen repeatedly in the dialogue at the beginning and end of scenes in *King Lear* or at V.i.37, where there is time for Edgar to enter as the others are moving towards the doors to go off.

There were other means, besides the doors, of getting on and off stage. For instance, there were trapdoors in the platform for certain unusual kinds of entry and exit, as in IV.vi.263. Another possibility was entry from one side of the yard; an actor could come into the yard directly from the tiring house or, as Nicol has suggested, through the lower gallery and down the steps marked *"ingressus"* (way in) in the Swan drawing. This method was probably used in V.ii. (see headnote, p. 181). Entry could also be made onto an upper level, as is clear from stage directions in many plays. These directions could conceivably refer to the balcony, although action there might be difficult to see and hear; a booth with a rigid and firmly supported top, set up between the doors, might serve much better. Edgar may just possibly make an appearance "above" in II.i., although this is not absolutely necessary.

In all cases, it is the actors who determine, by what they say and do, the place of the action (see headnotes to II.iii. and III.vi., pp. 77; 118) and, where necessary, its time. There is little problem of scene changing, since the occasional property is carried on or off quickly by stagehands; the action moves swiftly without the sharp break between the scenes to which our printed texts have accustomed us. Indeed scenes are not marked in the editions printed in Shakespeare's lifetime and sometimes not in the Folio of 1623. These divisions have not been given prominence in the present edition: the action must be thought of as continuous.

The staging of *King Lear* is extremely simple. Even the second acting level is not absolutely necessary and Oswald's body could be easily disposed of in IV.vi. without the use of a trap. Musicians, required in IV.vii., might play from the balcony or perhaps within a second gallery above it, but they might equally well be in full view of the audience. The noises offstage are of the simplest kind: the storm would need only the devices which Jonson mentions in the prologue to *Every Man in his Humour* as common in the public theater. (The revised version of this play, with the prologue added for the first time, may have been played in the same year as the first performance of *King Lear*.) He speaks of the "rolled bullet heard / To say, it thunders," that is a cannon-ball rolled along the floor—or else the "tempestuous drum / Rumbles, to tell you when the storm doth come" (lines 18–20). The play is admirably suited to performance by the company in places other than their own theater, whether at court or on tour in the provinces.

SHAKESPEARE'S TEXT AND THE PRESENT EDITION

Shakespeare's plays have come down to us in the First Folio edition of 1623 (commonly abbreviated F) and in a number of quarto (Q) editions most of which appeared during his lifetime. The Folio is a large book made from sheets about 20 by 15 inches, each folded only once to make four pages 15 by 10 inches. Its publication was supervised by John Heminge and Henry Condell, who were not only friends of Shakespeare but fellow actors. The sort of text they would allow to be printed may be presumed to have its origin in the theatre; evidence of the kind mentioned in Appendix E supports this assumption for *King Lear*.

The smaller editions which had preceded the Folio comprise nineteen separate plays; all are printed on sheets of about the same size as the Folio, but each sheet is folded a second time—hence in quarto—to make four leaves to a sheet, or eight pages of 10 by 7 ½ inches. Some of these quartos were printed, without the permission of the company of players who collectively owned the manuscript, from surreptitious copy—obtained, say, by theft or stenography. Naturally these present very bad versions. Other quartos, some of them issued to replace these bad ones, give us unmutilated versions. Some even preserve passages which F omits. The first quarto of *King Lear*, printed "for Nathaniel Butter" and issued in 1608, is in an intermediate position between the good and the bad quartos. It prints some 300 lines which the Folio does not, but at many points throughout the play it seems to rely on someone's memory of the lines rather than on following a copy. It is carelessly printed. Some of its errors have been corrected after proof reading, but corrected and uncorrected sheets have been bound up at random so that a surviving copy will contain some of each.

In 1619, only a short time before work began on the Folio edition of *King Lear*, there was an attempt to publish a quarto collection of at least ten plays called Shakespeare's. Three were not by him but the rest were, among them *King Lear*. The players were apparently able to stop the publication of this collection. At any rate on May 3, 1619 the Court of the Stationers' Company, to which all printers and publishers had to belong, "ordered that no plays that his Majesty's players do play shall be printed without consent of some of them." But the players were not able to stop the separate plays of the collection, bearing title pages that made them seem like old stock, from being sold. So the version of *King Lear* (a reprint of Q1) was given the date 1608 and Nathaniel Butter was again named, falsely this time, as its publisher. Account has to be taken of all of these editions in establishing the text of *King Lear*. Their complicated relationships are discussed in Appendix E.

The folio of 1623 was reprinted in 1632 (F2) and again in 1664 (F3). There were few alterations in the text, all of them minor and, of course, none of them authoritative. The plays were still full of difficulties due to their method of transmission. The author's own manuscript might have been copied and corrected for use as prompt book, and this in turn copied again, before a printer got to work on it; the printer may well have made errors of his own, only the most obvious of which would be picked up by the proofreading of the time. For the benefit of readers, the text seemed to need amending at many points. Nicholas Rowe, whose edition of Shakespeare's *Works* appeared in 1709, was the first to undertake these changes. Pope in 1725, Theobald (the best textual scholar among them) in 1733, Warburton in 1747, Johnson in 1765, and Capell in 1767–8 followed Rowe; each editor offered corrections of his own without trying to establish the ways in which the texts had been transmitted during and immediately after Shakespeare's lifetime. Careful study of the origins of the text does not begin until late in the eighteenth century with the work of Malone. It leads to the great Cambridge edition of 1863–6. In the present century, beginning in 1909 with Pollard's *Shakespeare Folios and Quartos*, many more of the facts about the transmission of the text have become available to editors. Some of the applications of these discoveries to the problem of the text of *King Lear* are set out in Appendix E.

The present edition does away with the scene locations which have been added in various forms by editors since Rowe. These can give only a spurious neatness to a play which is characterized, as Coleridge pointed out, by the vagueness of its indications of space and time. There is no sign that, as in the old play (Appendix B), Lear's court is at Troynovant, i.e., London; we are also left uncertain about where Lear's daughters live. We do know that travelers from the one place to the other will break their journey at Gloucester (I.v.1) and that it takes a day or so to reach Gloucester. The only other place named in the play is Dover, where Lear is taken so that the returned Cordelia may protect him. In this case Dover is not a town but a coastal district where Gloucester may believe he can fall from a cliff and where Cordelia's army from France may quickly encounter the British under Albany. The important point is the connection, throughout, of places with people.

Time is handled with similar freedom: it moves more quickly in events which are not presented on stage than in those which are. Greg (*M.L.R.*, XXXV [October, 1940], 431–446) gives the strict timetable that emerges from the direct indications in the foreground action and their implications for the background action. But in the theater we are not troubled by the possibility that, because news of the invasion reaches Kent by II.ii, it must have been planned before Cordelia could have known anything of her father's ill treatment. We are uncertain of the strict time taken even by the events on stage and we readily accept the swifter movement of those which are related or implied rather than shown.

The numbering of the scenes in this edition is that of the Folio. There are several exceptions: F runs II.ii–iv into one scene; it omits IV.iii, renumbering scenes iv to vi as iii to v, but resumes the series with vii as if nothing had been left out at all. The quarto is not divided into acts and scenes. In order to preserve something of the appearance of unbroken succession, their importance is not emphasized typographically in the present edition.

In dealing with the spelling and punctuation of the original texts, following the plan of this series, the principle has been to modernize for the convenience of the modern reader, yet keep such features as seem helpful. For instance, in *King Lear*, the punctuation of Q is casual and that of F rather heavy, yet each preserves the way in which at least one contemporary of Shakespeare's, the compositor, read the lines. Such punctuation tends to indicate the way in which a line or sentence was spoken rather than to mark its grammatical construction; the editor has preferred it in some cases to the grammatical pointing of today. Changes from the punctuation of the originals are mentioned in the notes only where they alter the sense. Two signs are used to assist the proper speaking of the lines: the grave accent to indicate a vowel pronounced in Shakespeare's English but not in ours (-èd) and an acute accent to show that the stress is different from ours (ovérture).

The stage directions are those of F unless square brackets or annotations indicate the contrary. The spelling of proper names follows F.

The source of a reading is the Folio, unless the contrary is stated. All references and quotations from other works of Shakespeare use the text and lineation of Peter Alexander's edition (London, 1951), even though this means that references to prose cannot be accurate to the line.

CHARACTERS[1]

LEAR *King of Britain*
GONERIL
REGAN   *his daughters*
CORDELIA
FOOL *his jester*
DUKE OF ALBANY *Goneril's husband*
OSWALD *Goneril's steward*
DUKE OF CORNWALL *Regan's husband*
KING OF FRANCE
                    Cordelia's suitors
DUKE OF BURGUNDY
EARL OF KENT
EARL OF GLOUCESTER
EDGAR *Gloucester's son*
EDMUND *Gloucester's bastard son*
AN OLD MAN *Gloucester's tenant*
CURAN *a Courtier*

A Doctor
A Herald
Knights, Officers, Gentlemen, Messengers, Soldiers, Attendants
and Servants

[1] A list of this kind was first added by Rowe in his edition of 1709.

M. William Shak-speare:

HIS
True Chronicle Historie of the life and
death of King LEAR and his three
Daughters.

With the vnfortunate life of Edgar, *sonne
and heire to the* Earle of Gloster, *and his
sullen and assumed humor of*
TOM of Bedlam:

*As it was played before the Kings Maiestie at Whitehall
vp. Stephans night in Christmas Hollidayes.*

By his Maiesties seruants playing vsually at the Gloabe
on the Bancke-side.

LONDON,
Printed for *Nathaniel Butter,* and are to be sold at his shop in *Paules*
Church-yard at the signe of the Pide Bull neere
S.t *Austins* Gate. 1608.

Facsimile of the Title Page of the Quarto of 1608.

The Tragedy of King Lear

Act I, Scene i: Enter KENT, GLOUCESTER, *and* EDMUND.

KENT

I thought the King had more affected the Duke of Albany than
Cornwall.

GLOUCESTER

It did always seem so to us; but now in the division of the
kingdom it appears not which of the dukes he values most, for
5   equalities are so weighed that curiosity in neither can make
choice of either's moiety.

Act I, scene i Lear's canopied chair of state is already placed upstage,
between the two entrance doors. In the quiet conversational exchange which
introduces both the plot and the subplot, Edmund stands upstage, perhaps
gazing at the throne and its surroundings to which he has recently returned
(line 27), until he is called into the conversation in line 20. In *King Leir*
(Appendix B) the court is in London.

1. *affected* liked, inclined towards.

5. *equalities* This, the Q reading, is rather more in line with the argument (which is already about equal shares for the two dukes) than F
"qualities"; the dukes' shares are so equally balanced that the most scrupulous care ("curiosity") on the part of either duke would not enable him to
choose between them. That Lear has no preference for one or other of the
dukes is meant to hint at his preference for Cordelia. He is to seek to disguise his favor in the ensuing love-test: she is to have the chance to outbid
her sisters in protestations of love (lines 80–1 below) and so appear to
deserve better treatment than they. The F reading "qualities" establishes a
point which is not in question, namely that the quality of each duke is nicely
balanced with that of the other. Therefore, scrupulous accuracy (compare
O.E.D., "curiosity", 2, 1630: "that curiosity that men use in weighing
Gold . . .") in determining either's quality could not lead to the choice of a
larger share than the other's ("moiety" is a share, not necessarily an equal
one; compare *I Henry IV*, III.i.96–7: ". . . my moiety . . . In quantity equals
not one of yours").

3

KENT

Is not this your son, my lord?

GLOUCESTER

His breeding sir, hath been at my charge. I have so often blushed to acknowledge him that now I am brazed to't.

KENT

10   I cannot conceive you.

GLOUCESTER

Sir, this young fellow's mother could; whereupon she grew round-wombed, and had indeed, sir, a son for her cradle ere she had a husband for her bed. Do you smell a fault?

KENT

I cannot wish the fault undone, the issue of it being so proper.

GLOUCESTER

15   But I have a son, sir, by order of law, some year elder than this, who yet is no dearer in my account. Though this knave came something saucily to the world before he was sent for, yet was his mother fair, there was good sport at his making, and the whoreson must be acknowledged.—Do you know this 20   noble gentleman, Edmund?

EDMUND [*coming forward*]

No, my lord.

GLOUCESTER

My Lord of Kent. Remember him hereafter as my honourable friend.

[handwritten: honorable friendship, indeed honor itself, is also an important concern]

[handwritten margin note: Natural vs. unnatural: S. strategy in opening play on 20 this theme]

---

9. *brazed* brazened.

10. *conceive* understand, with "you" as direct object; in the quibble which follows, on the other sense of "conceive", "you" is taken to be ethic dative = "for you". See Appendix C, p. 225.

14. *proper* good-looking; compare *Othello*, IV.iii.34–5: "a proper man . . . A very handsome man".

16–19. *knave . . . whoreson* boy . . . fellow, both used playfully without adverse connotation, as in *Love's Labour's Lost*, III.i.135: "My good knave Costard . . .", and *Romeo and Juliet*, IV.iv.20: ". . . well said; a merry whoreson, ha!"

EDMUND

My services to your lordship.

KENT

25   I must love you, and sue to know you better.

EDMUND

Sir, I shall study deserving.

GLOUCESTER

He hath been out nine years and away he shall again. [*Sennet.*]
The King is coming.
Enter one bearing a coronet; then LEAR, *then the* DUKES OF
ALBANY *and* CORNWALL, *next* GONERIL, REGAN, CORDELIA, *with
Followers.*

LEAR

Attend the Lords of France and Burgundy, Gloucester.

GLOUCESTER

30   I shall, my liege.   [*Exit* GLOUCESTER.]

---

26. *study*   take careful thought; compare line 271 below and *Two Gentlemen of Verona*, III.i.242: "And study help for that which thou lament'st".

27. *out*   abroad. See Appendix C, p. 222. *away he shall*   he must go;
compare V.iii.22 for "shall" = "will have to". *Sennet*   part of the following
S.D. in F and Q; a trumpet fanfare to announce the entrance or exit of a
procession. Kent, Gloucester, and Edmund must be well downstage so as not
to mask the ceremonial entry, stage-right.

28. S.D.   Q, adding to F the order of entry and *"one bearing a coronet"*.
The coronet is presumably for Cordelia (see line 134); it is given emphasis
by being brought on first, perhaps by a page who may stand with it beside
the throne. In the ceremonial entry which follows, Albany and Cornwall
may bow Lear to his throne and then move downstage right where they are
joined by their wives, after curtsies to the King. Cordelia may make her
obeisance in the center and move downstage left, past Kent: she will have
to be as near to the audience as possible for the asides in lines 57 and 71–3,
which separate her clearly from the others.

29–30. *attend . . . liege*   Gloucester accepts the command to wait upon
the guests as an attendant, as part of his allegiance (Q has "leige", F "Lord").
He goes off by the opposite door from that of the King's entry, i.e., stage-
left. Modern editors follow Capell in making Edmund go off with his father;
a producer may find reason for keeping him on to see a legitimate heir
deprived of her land (compare I.ii.16) and to observe, and perhaps even to
make a first impression upon, Goneril and Regan.

purpose and mood become darker as the action continues

LEAR

Meantime we shall express our <u>darker</u> purpose.
Give me the map there. Know that we have divided
In three our kingdom, and 'tis our fast intent
<u>To shake all cares and business from our age,</u>
35   Conferring them on younger strengths, while we
Unburdened crawl toward death. Our son of Cornwall,
And you our no less loving son of Albany,
We have this hour a constant will to publish
Our daughters' several dowers, that future strife
40   May be prevented now. The Princes, France and Burgundy,
Great rivals in our youngest daughter's love,
Long in our court have made their amorous sojourn
And here are to be answered. Tell me my daughters
(Since now we will divest us both of rule,
45   Interest of territory, cares of state)
Which of you shall we say doth love us most?
That we our largest bounty may extend
Where nature doth with merit challenge. Goneril,
Our eldest-born, speak first.

Lears decision will ironically have the opposite effect

GONERIL

50   Sir, I love you more than word can wield the matter,
Dearer than [eyesight] space, and liberty,

---

31. *darker purpose*   more recent intention (namely to stage a love-contest).

33. *fast*   firm; Q has "first".

34. *from our age*   Q has "of our state".

35. *conferring . . . strengths*   Q has "confirming . . . years" and omits the rest of this sentence and the next (lines 36–40).

40. *prevented*   met beforehand, forestalled, the Latin sense (see Appendix C, p. 223).

44–45. *(Since . . . state)*   not in Q.

45. *interest*   claim to possession.

48. *where . . . challenge*   where natural feeling (compare *Macbeth*, I.v.42: "compunctious visitings of nature"), together with merit, claims our bounty as its due (compare *Othello*, II.i.208–9: ". . . worthiness Does challenge much respect"); Q has "where merit doth most challenge it".

51. *space, and liberty*   The form of the statement and F punctuation (as

Beyond what can be valued, rich or rare,
No less than life, with grace, health, beauty, honour:
As much as child e'er loved, or father found.
55 A love that makes breath poor and speech unable,
Beyond all manner of so much I love you.

CORDELIA

[*Aside*] What shall Cordelia speak? Love, and be silent.

LEAR

Of all these bounds, even from this line, to this,
With shadowy forests and with champaigns riched,
60 With plenteous rivers and wide-skirted meads,
We make thee lady. To thine and Albany's issues
Be this perpetual.—What says our second daughter,
Our dearest Regan, wife of Cornwall? Speak.

REGAN

I am made of that self metal as my sister,
65 And prize me at her worth. In my true heart,
I find she names my very deed of love;

---

here) seem to require three terms, with "space" = "freedom from confinement" and "liberty" = "freedom of action," as Kittredge suggested. This
precludes taking the last two terms as a hendiadys = "spacious liberty".

54. *found* Q has "friend".

56. *all . . . much* all kinds of answer to the question "how much?"

57. *speak* Q has "doe".

59. *champaigns* open plains; compare *Twelfth Night*, II.v.142: "Daylight and champain discovers not more. This is open." Q omits "and with
champaigns . . . rivers".

60. *wide-skirted* with wide edges, extensive.

61. *issues* Q has "issue"; the plural usage was common (*O.E.D.*,
III,6,1614).

63. *Speak* Q; not in F.

64. *metal* mettle: either spelling is used in Shakespeare for both senses;
see Appendix C, p. 223. Q has "the selfe same mettall that".

65. *prize me* value or esteem myself. The common origin of "prize,"
"price," and "praise" in O.F. *preisier* affects their sense even in Shakespeare's
time (compare II.i.118).

66. *very deed* true action, actual performance.

Only she comes too short, that I profess
Myself an enemy to all other joys
Which the most precious square of sense possesses,
70 And find I am alone felicitate
In your dear Highness' love.

CORDELIA

[*Aside*] Then poor Cordelia!
And yet not so, since I am sure my love's
More ponderous than my tongue.

LEAR

To thee and thine, hereditary ever,
75 Remain this ample third of our fair kingdom,
No less in space, validity, and pleasure,
Than that conferred on Goneril.—Now, our joy,
Although our last and least; to whose young love
The vines of France and milk of Burgundy
80 Strive to be interested; what can you say to draw
A third more opulent than your sisters? Speak.

CORDELIA

Nothing my lord.

---

69. *most . . . sense*   choicest criterion or most delicate test of sensibility
(from the carpenter's square; compare *O.E.D., sb*, 2, 1604: "To govern the
body . . . by the square of prudence, and rule of reason"); or else the most
precious area of sense, i.e., the genitals.

70. *felicitate*   made happy.

71. *Highness' love*   love for your Highness.

73. *ponderous*   Q has "richer".

76. *validity*   worth, value (applied to a ring in *All's Well that Ends Well*,
V.iii.190).

77–80. *conferred . . . what*   Q has "confirm'd on *Gonorill*, but now our
ioy, Although the last, not least in our deere loue, What".

80. *to be interessed*   to have a right or share; a common expression,
justifying alteration of F "interest". (There were two forms of the verb,
one from the Latin infinitive *interesse*, the other from the Latin third person
singular *interest* = "it concerns".)   *draw*   gain (as in a lottery, III.iii.20);
Q has "win".

81. *a third more opulent*   "In default of sons, all the daughters of a

8

LEAR

Nothing?

CORDELIA

Nothing.

LEAR

85   Nothing will come of nothing. Speak again.

perhaps the principal theme of the play

CORDELIA

Unhappy that I am, I cannot heave
My heart into my mouth. I love your Majesty
According to my bond; no more nor less.

LEAR

How, how Cordelia? Mend your speech a little,
90   Lest you may mar your fortunes.

CORDELIA

                                        Good my lord,
You have begot me, bred me, loved me; I
Return those duties back as are right fit,
Obey you, love you, and most honour you.
Why have my sisters husbands, if they say

theme of proper allegience

95   They love you all? Haply, when I shall wed,
That lord whose hand must take my plight shall carry
Half my love with him, half my care and duty.
Sure I shall never marry like my sisters,

---

feudal lord succeeded to the estate in equal shares. Lear, therefore, only anticipates the division of his estate on his death. But, 'by the common law, freeholds of inheritance were not generally devisable by will; they were assignable only by formal delivery of the possession thereof in the tenant's lifetime.' If Lear wishes Cordelia's share to be a third more opulent than her sisters', he must assign it to her during his life, for on his death she will only inherit equally with Goneril and Regan." (P. A. McElwaine, *Notes and Queries*, 11th Series, IV [Nov. 25, 1911], 425.)

83–4. *Nothing? Nothing.*   not in Q.

88. *bond*   tie of duty. Compare I.ii.98; II.iv.172.

89. *How . . . Cordelia?*   Q has "Goe to, goe to,".

96. *plight*   pledge, plighting.

To love my father all.

LEAR

100   But goes thy heart with this?

CORDELIA

Ay my good lord.

LEAR

So young, and so untender?

CORDELIA

So young my lord, and true.

LEAR

Let it be so; thy truth then be thy dower.
For, by the sacred radiance of the sun,
105   The mysteries of Hécat and the night,
By all the operation of the orbs
From whom we do exist and cease to be,
Here I disclaim all my paternal care,
Propinquity and property of blood,
110   And as a stranger to my heart and me
Hold thee from this for ever. The barbarous Scythian,
Or he that makes his generation messes
To gorge his appetite, shall to my bosom

[handwritten marginal note: this disavowal of familial allegiance followed by the bestial allusion sets the pattern for the mood of animal imagery]

---

99. *To ... all.*   Q; not in F.

101–2. *So young ... and true.*   "She answers ... with pride to his pride ... To miss this likeness between the two is to miss Shakespeare's first important dramatic effect." (Granville-Barker, p. 303.)

105. *mysteries*   F has "miseries", Q "mistresse". *Hécat*   goddess of the infernal world, queen of night and witchcraft (pronounced so as almost to rhyme with "Beckett").

106. *operation of the orbs*   working or efficacy (compare *Antony and Cleopatra*, IV.xv.26) of the stars, in their influence upon human fate.

109. *propinquity*   closeness of relationship. *property*   (common) ownership, identity.

111. *from this*   from this time. *Scythian*   from the uncivilized regions north and northeast of the Black Sea; compare *Titus Andronicus*, I.i.131: "Was never Scythia half so barbarous!"

112. *generation*   offspring (Coverdale's translation, 1535, of Job 21:8 has

10

Be as well neighboured, pitied, and relieved,
115   As thou my sometime daughter.

KENT

Good my liege—

LEAR

Peace, Kent.
Come not between the [dragon] and his wrath.
I loved her most, and thought to set my rest
On her kind nursery. [*To Cordelia*] Hence and avoid my
        sight!—
120   So be my grave my peace as here I give
Her father's heart from her. Call France.—Who stirs?
Call Burgundy. Cornwall and Albany,
With my two daughters' dowers digest the third.
Let pride, which she calls plainness, marry her.
125   I do invest you jointly with my power,
Pre-eminence, and all the large effects
That troop with majesty. Ourself, by monthly course,
With reservation of an hundred knights
By you to be sustained, shall our abode
130   Make with you by due turn. Only we shall retain
[The name,] and all th' addition to a king: *soon only the name; later not even that*

"generation" where A.V. has "offspring"); also family, race, as in *Timon of
Athens*, I.i.203–4: "Thy mother's of my generation; what's she if I be a dog?"
messes   dishes of food.
    115. *liege*—   Rowe (as at line 137); Q and F have a full stop.
    117. *his wrath*   the object of his wrath.
    118. *set . . . rest*   to stake all (French *reste*, remainder, the stake kept in
reserve) here with a quibble on the English sense, repose (with "nursery" =
"nursing").
    119. *avoid*   depart from (not, as in Modern English, keep out of).
    123. *digest*   assimilate completely.
    124. *marry her*   give her, with a dowry, in marriage.
    126. *effects*   outward signs (compare II.iv.173).
    128. *reservation*   retention for myself (compare line 130).
    131. *addition*   what is added to a name as a mark of distinction, honor, or
precedence. Compare II.ii.20; V.iii.69.

11

The sway, revénue, execution of the rest,
Beloved sons be yours, which to confirm,
This coronet part between you.

KENT

Royal Lear,
135   Whom I have ever honoured as my King,
Loved as my father, as my master followed,
As my great patron thought on in my prayers—

LEAR

The bow is bent and drawn; make from the shaft.

KENT

Let it fall rather, though the fork invade
140   The region of my heart. Be Kent unmannerly
When Lear is mad. What wouldst thou do, old man?
Think'st thou that duty shall have dread to speak
When power to flattery bows? To plainness honour's bound
When majesty falls to folly. Reserve thy state,
145   And in thy best consideration check
This hideous rashness. Answer my life my judgment:
Thy youngest daughter does not love thee least,
Nor are those empty-hearted whose low sounds
Reverb no hollowness.

---

134. *This . . . you* Lear keeps the crown on his own head; but, to symbolize the fact that they share the executive office, he gives the coronet to Albany and Cornwall.

138. *make from* avoid.

139. *fall* strike. *fork* barbed head of the arrow.

140. *unmannerly* ill-bred, discourteous.

144. *falls* Q has "stoops". *Reserve thy state* keep your kingdom. Q has "Reuerse thy doome" (compare *King Leir*, Appendix B1, lines 505, 567).

145. *best consideration* mature reflection.

146. *Answer . . . judgment* Let my life answer for (take the consequences of) my opinion.

149. *reverb* re-echo (shortened from "reverberate," perhaps for a quibble on "verb" = "word"). *hollowness* insincerity (compare I.ii.102) as well as the literal sense which continues the metaphor.

LEAR

Kent, on thy life no more!

KENT

150 My life I never held but as a pawn
To wage against thine enemies; ne'er fear to lose it,
Thy safety being motive.

LEAR

Out of my sight!

KENT

[See better] Lear, and let me still remain
The true blank of thine eye.

Lear will see worse before he sees better

LEAR

155 Now by Apollo—

KENT

Now by Apollo, King,
Thou swearest thy gods in vain.

LEAR

O vassal! miscreant!
[*Laying his hand on his sword.*]

ALBANY and CORNWALL

Dear sir, forbear.

KENT

Kill thy physician, and thy fee bestow
Upon the foul disease. Revoke thy gift,
160 Or whilst I can vent clamour from my throat
I'll tell thee thou dost evil.

---

151. *wage*　to stake, venture. *ne'er*　Q has "nor".
152. *motive*　what moves me to action. Q has "the motive".
154. *blank*　the white center of the target, hence the true aim of your eyes, the man you will always "look to".
156. *miscreant*　misbeliever, villain.
157. not in Q.
159. *gift*　Q has "doome", echoing its version of line 144 above.

13

LEAR

Hear me, recreant,

On thine allegiance hear me.

That thou has sought to make us break our vows—

Which we durst never yet—and with strained pride

165 To come betwixt our sentence and our power—

Which nor our nature nor our place can bear—

Our potency made good, take thy reward.

Five days we do allot thee for provision

To shield thee from disasters of the world,

170 And on the sixth to turn thy hated back

Upon our kingdom; if on the tenth day following

Thy banished trunk be found in our dominions,

The moment is thy death. Away! By Jupiter,

This shall not be revoked.

KENT

175 Fare thee well, King. Sith thus thou wilt appear,

Freedom lives hence, and banishment is here.

[*To Cordelia*] The gods to their dear shelter take thee, maid,

That justly think'st, and hast most rightly said.

[*To Regan and Goneril*] And your large speeches, may your
deeds approve

180 That good effects may spring from words of love.

Thus Kent, O princes, bids you all adieu;

---

161. *recreant*   one who gives up his cause, deserter, traitor.

163. *That*   seeing that. See Appendix C, p. 225.

164. *strained*   forced, excessive; compare *2 Henry IV*, I.i.161: "This strained passion doth you wrong, my lord."

165. *sentence*   Q; F has "sentences"; see Hinman I, 305.

167. *made good*   (a) carried into effect, as in *Coriolanus*, I.vi.86: "Make good this ostentation"; (b) maintained, defended, as in *O.E.D.*, "good" 22d, 1617: "This Fort his Lordship . . . made good"; (c) repaired (after Kent's attacks upon it), compensated for, atoned for (*O.E.D.*, "good" 22f).

168. *provision*   preparation in advance.

169. *disasters*   misfortunes; Q has "diseases".

176. *Freedom*   Q has "Friendship".

177. *dear shelter*   Q has "protection".

179. *approve*   make proof of, confirm; compare II.ii.148; iv.177.

14

He'll shape his old course in a country new.   *Exit.*
    Flourish. [Re-]enter GLOUCESTER, *with* FRANCE *and*
        BURGUNDY, *Attendants.*

GLOUCESTER

Here's France and Burgundy, my noble lord.

LEAR

My Lord of Burgundy,
185 We first address toward you, who with this king
Hath rivalled for our daughter. What in the least
Will you require in present dower with her,
Or cease your quest of love?

BURGUNDY

               Most royal Majesty,
I crave no more than hath your Highness offered;
190 Nor will you tender less?

LEAR

             Right noble, Burgundy,
When she was dear to us, we did hold her so;
But now her price is fallen. Sir, there she stands:
If aught within that little seeming substance,
Or all of it, with our displeasure pieced,

---

182. *course* habit (of plain speaking); compare *Troilus and Cressida*,
I.iii.9: "... errant from his course of growth."

182. S.D. *GLOUCESTER* Q has "Glos", F "Cor"; compare I.v.1.

185. *this* "a" in Q; perhaps the indefinite article shows how the players
understood the line—as requiring emphasis on "king."

192. *price* esteem, estimation; see I.i.65 note.

193. *little seeming* (a) appearing to be little; (b) manifesting, showing
little (compare *Hamlet*, I.ii.83–5: "These indeed seem; . . . But I have that
within which passes show"); (c) small and specious (compare *The Merry
Wives of Windsor*, III.ii.35: "pluck the borrowed veil of modesty from the
so seeming Mistress Page"). The contrast with "substance" = "reality" (as
in *Titus Andronicus*, III.iii.80: "He takes false shadows for true substances")
makes plain the undercurrent of reference to her professions and to the
charges of insincerity against her sisters.

194. *pieced* added on; compare III.vi.1–2.

195 And nothing more, may fitly like your Grace,
She's there, and she is yours.

BURGUNDY

I know no answer.

LEAR

Will you, with those infirmities she owes,
Unfriended, new-adopted to our hate,
Dowered with our curse, and strangered with our oath,
200 Take her, or leave her?

BURGUNDY

Pardon me royal sir;
Election makes not up in such conditions.

LEAR

Then leave her sir, for by the power that made me,
I tell you all her wealth. [*To France*] For you great king,
I would not from your love make such a stray
205 To match you where I hate, therefore beseech you
T'avert your liking a more worthier way
Than on a wretch whom nature is ashamed
Almost t'acknowledge hers.

FRANCE

This is most strange,
That she whom even but now was your best object,

---

195. *fitly like* please (Appendix C, p. 225), fittingly, suitably, i.e. as suitable; or opportunely, at a fitting time, as in I.ii.151.

197. *owes* owns.

199. *strangered* make a stranger; compare line 110.

201. *Election . . . conditions* One does not make choice on such conditions, or in view of such characteristics or qualities (of Cordelia); compare IV.iii.33.

206. *T'avert . . . way* to turn your affection in a worthier direction, i.e. to someone worthier.

209. *best object* "best", found only in Q (which also mends the grammar with "that" for "whom"), is not strictly necessary, since "object" = "object of love", as in *Venus and Adonis*, 255: "Her object will away, And from her twining arms doth urge releasing."

16

210   The argument of your praise, balm of your age,
      The best, the dearest, should in this trice of time
      Commit a thing so monstrous to dismantle
      So many folds of favour. Sure her offence
      Must be of such[unnatural]degree
215   That monsters it, or your fore-vouched affection
      Fall into taint—which to believe of her
      Must be a faith that reason without miracle
      Should never plant in me.

                    CORDELIA
                            I yet beseech your Majesty—
      If for I want that glib and oily art
220   To speak and purpose not, since what I well intend
      I'll do 't before I speak—that you make known
      It is no vicious blot, murder, or foulness,
      No unchaste action or dishonoured step
      That hath deprived me of your grace and favour,
225   But even for want of that for which I am richer—
      A still-soliciting eye, and such a tongue
      That I am glad I have not, though not to have it
      Hath lost me in your liking.

---

210. *argument*   subject (the words are synonyms in Sonnet 38, 1–3).

211. *The . . . the*   perhaps a sophistication; but Q "most best, most dearest" no doubt anticipates lines 245–6, as Duthie suggests.

212. *dismantle*   to divest of a cloak, hence to remove.

215. *monsters it*   makes it a monster, something unnatural (compare I.ii.86).

216. *fall*   infinitive, after "must" (Q "falne", past participle after "be", is smoother but suspect): either what she has done must be monstrous or the affection you formerly professed must fall into discredit. To believe this of *her* is impossible for me.

219. *for*   because.

220. *well*   Q; F has "will".

221. *make known*   Q has "may know".

223–5. *unchaste . . . richer*   "uncleane . . . rich" in Q are weaker, not to mention the jingle with "for which" (= "for want of which").

226. *still-soliciting*   always asking for favors. The hyphen is Theobald's.

228. *lost*   ruined; compare "loss", III.vi.88. *liking*   favorable regard

LEAR

Better thou
Hadst not been born than not t' have pleased me better.

FRANCE

230   Is it but this? A tardiness in nature,
Which often leaves the history unspoke
That it intends?—My Lord of Burgundy,
What say you to the lady? Love's not love
When it is mingled with regards that stands
235   Aloof from th' entire point. Will you have her?
She is herself a dowry.

BURGUNDY

Royal King,
Give but that portion which yourself proposed,
And here I take Cordelia by the hand,
Duchess of Burgundy.

LEAR

240   Nothing; I have sworn; I am firm.

(O.E.D.); not always "a colder word than love" (Arden)—compare *As You Like It*, I.iii.26–7: "Is it possible, on a such sudden, you should fall into so strong a liking with old Sir Rowland's youngest son?"

230. *a tardiness in nature*   a natural hesitation.

232. *intends*   purposes to express; "to do", added by F and Q, spoils meter and sense (Walker, *Textual Problems of the First Folio*, 1953, p. 7).

233. *Love's*   Q has "Love is", recalling even more clearly *Sonnet* 116, 2–6.

234. *regards*   things considered—such as the dowry. Q "respects" anticipates line 243. *stands*   a frequent form to agree with a plural subject in Shakespeare; see Franz § 155, and Appendix C, p. 224.

235. *entire*   unmixed; compare *2 Henry IV*, II.iv.313: "pure fear and entire cowardice".

236. *a dowry*   "And dowre" in Q presumably means, "What you see comprises both Cordelia and her dowry." *Royal*   generous, munificent, as at IV.vi.193 (referring to the King's ransom).

240. *I am firm*   not in Q.

BURGUNDY

I am sorry, then, you have so lost a father
That you must lose a husband.

CORDELIA

                Peace be with Burgundy!
Since that respects of fortune are his love
I shall not be his wife.

FRANCE

245   Fairest Cordelia, that art most rich being poor,
Most choice forsaken, and most loved despised!
Thee and thy virtues here I seize upon;
Be it lawful I take up what's cast away.
Gods, gods! 'Tis strange that from their cold'st neglect
250   My love should kindle to inflamed respect.
Thy dowerless daughter, King, thrown to my chance,
Is queen of us, of ours, and our fair France.
Not all the dukes of waterish Burgundy
Can buy this unprized precious maid of me.
255   Bid them farewell Cordelia, though unkind;
Thou losest here, a better where to find.

[handwritten margin note: image suggests watered down wine; i.e. something not genuine, not to be relied on]

LEAR

Thou hast her, France; let her be thine, for we
Have no such daughter, nor shall ever see

---

243. *respects of fortune* Q, i.e. considerations of wealth. F reads "respect and Fortunes", but it is hard to believe that the same word "respect" would be used here to depreciate Burgundy's love and, in line 250, to recommend the love offered by the King of France. (In F this is sig. qq³, set by compositor E; see Appendix E, p. 231).

251. *my chance* my lot, (good) fortune; compare *Antony and Cleopatra*, II.iii.35–6: "my better cunning faints Under his chance"; Q has "thy chance".

255. *though unkind* though they have no natural affection; compare III.iv.62–63.

256. *here . . . where* used as nouns.

That face of hers again. [*To Cordelia*] Therefore be gone
260 Without our grace, our love, our benison.
Come noble Burgundy.
     Flourish. Exeunt [LEAR, BURGUNDY, CORNWALL, ALBANY,
              GLOUCESTER, EDMUND, *and Attendants*].

FRANCE

Bid farewell to your sisters.

CORDELIA

The jewels of our father, with washed eyes
Cordelia leaves you. I know you what you are,
265 And like a sister am most loath to call
Your faults as they are named. Love well our father.
To your professèd bosoms I commit him;
But yet alas, stood I within his grace,
I would prefer him to a better place.
270 So farewell to you both.

REGAN

Prescribe not us our duty.

GONERIL

Let your study
Be to content your lord, who hath received you
At Fortune's alms. You have obedience scanted,
And well are worth the want that you have wanted.

---

263. *jewels*   darlings; used, for instance, by Brabantio to Desdemona in
Othello, I.iii.195.

266. *Love*   Q has "use" (perhaps anticipating I.v.10). "She had yet no
ground for supposing they would use the old man ill" (Greg, *The Editorial
Problem in Shakespeare*, p. 93).

267. *professèd bosoms*   the love (compare V.iii.50) you have professed.

269. *prefer*   recommended for promotion, as in *Julius Caesar*, V.v.62: "If
Messala will prefer me to you. . . ."

271. *study*   careful endeavor; compare line 26 above.

273–4. *At Fortune's alms . . . wanted*   as a mere charitable gift from
good luck. You have stinted your submission to your father and (a) well deserve (compare II.iv.43) to lack the dowry you have had to go without, or

CORDELIA

275 Time shall unfold what plighted cunning hides,
Who covers faults, at last with shame derides.
Well may you prosper!

FRANCE

Come my fair Cordelia.

Exeunt FRANCE *and* CORDELIA.

GONERIL

Sister, it is not little I have to say of what most nearly apper-
tains to us both. I think our father will hence to-night.

REGAN

280 That's most certain, and with you; next month with us.

GONERIL

You see how full of changes his age is; the observation we have
made of it hath not been little. He always loved our sister
most, and with what poor judgment he hath now cast her off
appears too grossly.

REGAN

285 'Tis the infirmity of his age; yet he hath ever but slenderly
known himself.

GONERIL

The best and soundest of his time hath been but rash; then
must we look from his age to receive not alone the imperfec-

(b) you are indeed worth (compare IV.ii.29) no more than the absence of a
dowry. (Q "worth the worth that you have wanted" = "worth your lack
of value".)

275. *plighted* folded (collateral form of "plaited", by which it is now
superseded, and of which Q "pleated" is a by-form), complicated, devious.

276. *covers* "covert" in New Cambridge text. "Who" = "Time". With
the Q reading "shame them derides", "who" = "those who".

278ff. The scene ends as it began, with talk, knowing and confident, in
prose.

282. *not* Q; F omits.

284. *grossly* flagrantly; Q has "grosse".

287. *The best . . . rash* In his prime he was ever headstrong.

tions of long-engraffed condition, but therewithal the unruly
290   waywardness that infirm and choleric years bring with them.

REGAN

Such unconstant starts are we like to have from him as this of
Kent's banishment.

GONERIL

There is further compliment of leave-taking between France
and him. Pray you, let us hit together; if our father carry
295   authority with such disposition as he bears, this last surrender
of his will but offend us.

REGAN

We shall further think of it.

GONERIL

We must do something, and i' th' heat.   *Exeunt.*

Scene ii: Enter EDMUND.

EDMUND

Thou ⌜Nature⌝ art my goddess; to thy law
My services are bound. Wherefore should I

---

289. *long-engraffed condition*   long and firmly implanted character; F
has "long ingraffed", Q "long ingrafted".

290. *choleric*   having a preponderance of bile, which, as one of the four
humors, was supposed to cause irascibility.

291. *unconstant starts*   uncertain or abrupt impulses; compare *I Henry
IV*, III.ii.125: "the start of spleen".

293. *further compliment of leave-taking*   ironical after 257ff; compare
I.ii.23.

294. *hit*   Q; F has "sit", probably a sophistication (= "take counsel") as
"hit" = "agree" is not found before Shakespeare.

294–6. *if . . . offend us*   If Lear continues to wield authority with the sort
of mood or humor he still shows, his recent abdication will merely do us
harm. (Q has "dispositions".) The removal from the stage of the chair of
state will underline the abdication.

Scene ii   At the Earl of Gloucester's, next day (line 24).

Stand in the plague of custom, and permit
The curiosity of nations to deprive me,
5   For that I am some twelve or fourteen moonshines
Lag of a brother? Why bastard? Wherefore base?
When my dimensions are as well compact,
My mind as generous, and my shape as true,
As honest madam's issue? Why brand they us
10   With base? with baseness? bastardy? base, base?
Who, in the lusty stealth of nature, take
More composition and fierce quality
Than doth within a dull stale tired bed
Go to th' creating a whole tribe of fops
15   Got 'tween asleep and wake? Well then,
Legitimate Edgar, I must have your land.   sub plot
Our father's love is to the bastard Edmund
As to th' legitimate. Fine word "legitimate"!
Well, my legitimate, if this letter speed,
20   And my invention thrive, Edmund the base
Shall top th' legitimate. I grow; I prosper.

---

3. *stand in the plague of custom*   be dependent on (compare "stand on" IV.vi.206; V.i.69) that nuisance custom, be subject to the scourge of convention. But see Psalm 38:17 for the stronger sense of "plague": (Prayer Book) "And truly I am set in the plague."

4. *curiosity*   fastidiousness; compare I.iv.59. *deprived*   debar (from inheriting; though, since he is younger, he would not inherit anyway).

6. *lag of*   (lagging) behind. *base*   illegitimate, inferior.

7. *my dimensions . . . compact*   my bodily proportions (compare *Merchant of Venice*, III.i.53: "Hath not a Jew hands, organs, dimensions . . . ?") are as well put together (from the Latin *compingere*, to fasten together).

8. *generous*   of noble lineage, as in *Othello*, III.iii.284, hence magnanimous. *shape . . . true*   well-proportioned as in Sonnet 62, 5–6: "Methinks no face so gracious is as mine, No shape so true . . ."

10. *With . . . base?*   Q has "with base, base bastardie?"

12. *composition*   proper combination or congruity of parts (compare *King John*, I.i.88–90).

19. *speed*   succeed in its purpose; compare IV.vi.200 and Appendix C, p. 222.

21. *top*   surpass; Capell's emendation of "to" F, Q; with "shall", F "to"

Now gods, stand up for bastards.

Enter GLOUCESTER.

GLOUCESTER

Kent banished thus? and France in choler parted?
And the King gone to-night? Prescribed his power?
25 Confined to exhibition? All this done
Upon the gad? Edmund, how now? What news?

EDMUND

So please your lordship, none.

GLOUCESTER

Why so earnestly seek you to put up that letter?

EDMUND

I know no news my lord.

GLOUCESTER

30 What paper were you reading?

EDMUND

⌈Nothing⌉ my lord.

GLOUCESTER

No? What needed then that terrible dispatch of it into your

("to'th'"; Q "tooth'") means "move against" but it a weak climax to
the speech since Edmund is doing this with the letter anyway. On the other
hand, "top" contrasts well with "base" and fits in with "grow".

23. *choler*   Compare I.i.293.

24. *tonight*   last night, as in *Merchant of Venice*, II.v.18: "I did dream of
money bags tonight." *prescribed*   restricted. Q "subscribd" (= "yielded",
compare "subscription" III.ii.17) perhaps anticipates III.vii.62 (Q).

25. *exhibition*   regular word for an allowance for sustenance, as in *Two
Gentlemen of Verona*, I.iii.68–9: "What maintenance he . . . receives, Like
exhibition thou shalt have."

26. *Upon the gad*   suddenly (as if stirred by a gad or spike).

31. *Nothing*   echoing I.i.82ff., as Edmund's "I dare pawn down my life"
(lines 78–9) recalls I.i.150. Compare too, "bond" line 98 and I.i.88, "disasters"
line 101 and I.i.169.

32. *terrible*   fearful. But from *O.E.D.* (1596: "a terrible feir"), it looks
as if the word may be merely intensive, so that the phrase merely = "great
haste".

pocket? The quality of ⌐nothing⌐ hath not such need to hide
itself. Let's see. Come, if it be nothing, I shall not need
35   spectacles.

EDMUND

I beseech you sir, pardon me. It is a letter from my brother
that I have not all o'er-read; and for so much as I have perused,
I find it not fit for your o'erlooking.

GLOUCESTER

Give me the letter sir.

EDMUND

40   I shall offend either to detain or give it. The contents, as in
part I understand them, are too blame.

GLOUCESTER

Let's see, let's see.

EDMUND

I hope, for my brother's justification, he wrote this but as an
essay or taste of my virtue.

GLOUCESTER [reads]

45   "This policy and reverence of age makes the world bitter to
the best of our times; keeps our fortunes from us till our old-
ness cannot relish them. I begin to find an idle and fond bond-

---

38. *o'erlooking*   perusal; Q has "liking".

41. *too blame*   F; the infinitive was understood in the sixteenth and seventeenth centuries as "too" + adjective = "blameworthy," which the sense
requires here. See II.ii.147 and Franz § 455 note.

44. *essay or taste*   synonyms = "trial," "test"—the first a doublet of
"assay," the second from Old French *tast* "touch" (compare modern
tâter; "touch" itself = "test" in *Richard III*, IV.ii.8 and *Timon of Athens*,
IV.iii.387).

45. *policy*   course of action, or even crafty contrivance (opposed to
"honour" in *Coriolanus*, III.ii.42). *This . . . age*   both this habit of revering
the old and this craftiness of the old and revered. Q omits "and reverence".

46. *best of our times*   best part of our lives, as in I.i.287.

47. *idle and fond*   useless (compare IV.iv.5, vi.21) and silly (compare
I.iv.277, IV.vii.60).

age in the oppression of aged tyranny, who sways not as it
hath power, but as it is suffered. Come to me, that of this I
50   may speak more. If our father would sleep till I waked him,
you should enjoy half his revenue for ever, and live the beloved of your brother. Edgar."
Hum? Conspiracy? "Sleep till I wake him, you should enjoy
half his revenue"—my son Edgar, had he a hand to write this?
55   a heart and brain to breed it in? When came you to this? Who
brought it?

EDMUND

It was not brought me, my lord; there's the cunning of it. I
found it thrown in at the casement of my closet.

GLOUCESTER

You know the character to be your brother's?

EDMUND

60   If the matter were good, my lord, I durst swear it were his;
but in respect of that, I would fain think it were not.

GLOUCESTER

It is his.

EDMUND

It is his hand, my lord; but I hope his heart is not in the
contents.

GLOUCESTER

65   Has he never before sounded you in this business?

EDMUND

Never my lord; but I have heard him oft maintain it to be fit
that, sons at perfect age and fathers declined, the father should
be as ward to the son, and the son manage his revenue.

GLOUCESTER

O villain, villain! His very opinion in the letter. Abhorred

---

50. *waked*   Q; F has "wake".
59. *character*   handwriting, as in *Hamlet*, IV.vii.51.

70   villain! Unnatural, detested, brutish villain! Worse than brutish! Go sirrah, seek him; I'll apprehend him. Abominable villain! Where is he?

EDMUND

I do not well know, my lord. If it shall please you to suspend
your indignation against my brother till you can derive from
75   him better testimony of his intent, you should run a certain
course; where, if you violently proceed against him, mistaking
his purpose, it would make a great gap in your own honour,
and shake in pieces the heart of his obedience. I dare pawn
down my life for him that he hath writ this to feel my affection
80   to your honour, and to no other pretence of danger.

GLOUCESTER

Think you so?

EDMUND

If your honour judge it meet, I will place you where you shall
hear us confer of this, and by an auricular assurance have your
satisfaction, and that without any further delay than this very
85   evening.

GLOUCESTER

He cannot be such a monster.

EDMUND

Nor is not, sure.

---

70. *detested*   detestable, as in *Richard II*, II.iii.109: "In gross rebellion
and detested treason".

75. *certain*   reliable. *where*   whereas.

80. *pretense*   purpose; compare I.iv.59 and *Macbeth*, II.iii.130–1: "the
undivulg'd pretence . . . Of treasonous malice."

82–5. *I will . . . evening*   Edmund does not fulfill his promise, but pre-
tends that Edgar has fled after a fight immediately before his father arrives
(II.i.36ff).

83. *auricular*   addressed privately to your ear; Q has "aurigular".

86. *monster*   Compare I.i.215.

87–9. *Nor . . . earth!*   Q; not in F.

GLOUCESTER

To his father, that so tenderly and entirely loves him. Heaven
and earth! Edmund, seek him out; wind me into him, I pray
90   you. Frame the business after your own wisdom. I would unstate myself to be in a due resolution.

EDMUND

I will seek him sir presently, convey the business as I shall
find means, and acquaint you withal.

GLOUCESTER

These late eclipses in the sun and moon portend no good to
95   us. Though the wisdom of [nature] can reason it thus and thus,
yet [nature] finds itself scourged by the sequent effects: love
cools, friendship falls off, brothers divide; in cities, mutinies;
in countries, discord; in palaces, treason; and the bond cracked,
'twixt son and father. This villain of mine comes under the
100   prediction; there's son against father. The King falls from bias
of [nature] there's father against child. We have seen the best
of our time: machinations, hollowness, treachery, and all
ruinous disorders follow us disquietly to our graves. Find out
this villain, Edmund; it shall lose thee nothing; do it carefully.
105   And the noble and true-hearted Kent banished; his offence,
honesty. 'Tis strange.   *Exit.*

---

89. *wind . . . him*   get into his confidence for me (Appendix C, p. 225).

90–1. *unstate . . . resolution*   lose my rank (as Lear has) to be properly
resolved, i.e., convinced.

92. *convey*   manage with secrecy or craft (*O.E.D.*).

95. *the wisdom of nature*   natural science.

97. *falls off*   revolts, as in *I Henry IV*, I.iii.93–4: "Revolted Mortimer!
He never did fall off. . . ." *mutinies*   contentions, discord, as in *I Henry VI*,
IV.i.131: "To raise a mutiny betwixt yourselves".

98. *discord . . . treason*   Q has "discords, Pallaces treason".

99–103. *This . . . graves.*   not in Q.

100. *bias*   tendency, bent; compare *Twelfth Night*, V.i.252: ". . . nature
to her bias drew in that." The metaphor (from the game of bowls) is ex-
panded in *King John*, II.i.574ff.

105–6. *offence . . . strange.*   Q has "offence honest, strange strange!"

EDMUND

This is the excellent foppery of the world, that when we are
sick in fortune, often the surfeits of our own behaviour, we
make guilty of our disasters the sun, the moon, and stars; as if
110   we were villains on necessity, fools by heavenly compulsion,
knaves, thieves, and treachers by spherical dominance, drunk-
ards, liars, and adulterers by an enforced obedience of planetary influence, and all that we are evil in by a divine thrusting
on. An admirable evasion of whoremaster man, to lay his
115   goatish disposition on the charge of a star! My father com-
pounded with my mother under the Dragon's tail, and my na-
tivity was under Ursa Major, so that it follows I am rough and
lecherous. Fut, I should have been that I am, had the maiden-
liest star in the firmament twinkled on my bastardizing.
120   Edgar—

Enter EDGAR.

Pat! He comes like the catastrophe of the old comedy. My cue
is villainous melancholy, with a sigh like Tom o' Bedlam.—O
these eclipses do portend these divisions. Fa, sol, la, mi.

---

107. *excellent foppery*   extreme folly; compare *Richard III*, IV.iv.52:
"That excellent grand tyrant"; *Measure for Measure*, I.ii.126–8: "I had as
lief have the foppery of freedom as the morality of imprisonment."

108. *surfeits of*   sicknesses caused by (compare *O.E.D., sb.,* 5, 1606: "He
caught a surfeit by the heat of the sun.")

111. *treachers* deceivers, traitors. *spherical* planetary (referring to the
position of a planet at the time of a person's birth); Q has "spiritual".

115. *goatish* lascivious, as goats were considered (compare *Cymbeline*,
IV.iv.37: ". . . hot goats").

118. *Fut,* Q; purged from F presumably because it is a profane abbreviation of the oath "by Christ's foot".

120. *Edgar—* not in F; Q has *"Edgar;"*.

121. *catastrophe* dénouement (coming, by obvious contrivance, just at
the right moment); compare *Love's Labour's Lost*, IV.i.72: "The catastrophe
is a nuptial."

122. *Tom o' Bedlam* a beggar pretending to have come from Bedlam,
i.e., the hospital of St. Mary of Bethlehem for the insane; compare II.iii.14.
Q has "them of Bedlam".

EDGAR

125   How now brother Edmund, what serious contemplation are you in?

EDMUND

I am thinking, brother, of a prediction I read this other day, what should follow these eclipses.

EDGAR

Do you busy yourself with that?

EDMUND

I promise you, the effects he writes of succeed unhappily; as of
130   [unnaturalness] between the child and the parent; death, dearth, dissolutions of ancient amities; divisions in state; menaces and maledictions against king and nobles; needless diffidences, banishment of friends, dissipation of cohorts, nuptial breaches, and I know not what.

EDGAR

135   How long have you been a sectary astronomical?

EDMUND

Come, come! When saw you my father last?

EDGAR

The night gone by.

EDMUND

Spake you with him?

EDGAR

Ay, two hours together.

---

129. *succeed*   follow, happen.

129–36. *as . . . come!*   Q; not in F.

132. *diffidences*   suspicions, doubts; compare *King John*, I.i.64–5: "Thou dost shame thy mother, And wound her honour with this diffidence."

133. *dissipation*   dispersing (because of disease or desertion).

135. *sectary astronomical*   an adherent of the sect or party of astrologers.

EDMUND

140   Parted you in good terms? Found you no displeasure in him by
word nor countenance?

EDGAR

None at all.

EDMUND

Bethink yourself wherein you may have offended him; and at
my entreaty forbear his presence, until some little time hath
145   qualified the heat of his displeasure, which at this instant so
rageth in him that with the mischief of your person it would
scarcely allay.

EDGAR

Some villain hath done me wrong.

EDMUND

That's my fear. I pray you have a continent forbearance till
150   the speed of his rage goes slower; and as I say, retire with me
to my lodging, from whence I will fitly bring you to hear my
lord speak. Pray ye go; there's my key. If you do stir abroad,
go armed.

EDGAR

Armed, brother?

EDMUND

155   Brother, I advise you to the best. I am no honest man if there
be any good meaning toward you. I have told you what I have

---

145. *qualified*   moderated; compare *Measure for Measure*, I.i.66: "[ei-
ther] to enforce or qualify the laws."

146. *with . . . person*   even through an injury to your person.

149–54. *I . . . brother?*   not in Q.

149. *have . . . forbearance*   make a temperate withdrawal. (Compare line
144: even without "presence", "forbear" would mean avoid, leave alone, as
in *Antony and Cleopatra*, II.vii.38: "Forbear me till anon.")

151. *fitly*   at a fitting time.

155. *best*   Q adds "goe arm'd", taken over from the omitted passage,
line 153.

seen and heard—but faintly, nothing like the image and horror
of it. Pray you away.

EDGAR

Shall I hear from you anon?

EDMUND

160 I do serve you in this business.   *Exit* EDGAR.
A credulous father, and a brother noble
Whose [nature] is so far from doing harms
That he suspects none, on whose foolish honesty
My practices ride easy—I see the business.
165 Let me, if not by birth, have lands by wit;
All with me's meet that I can fashion fit.   *Exit.*

Scene iii: Enter GONERIL *and [*OSWALD, *her] steward.*

GONERIL

Did my father strike my gentleman for chiding of his Fool?

OSWALD

Ay madam.

GONERIL

By day and night he wrongs me; every hour
He flashes into one gross crime or other
5 That sets us all at odds. I'll not endure it.

---

160. S.D. as in Q. F has "*Exit*" after 159.

164. *practices* schemes; compare II.i.71, iv. 110 and *Measure for Measure*, V.i.106–7 "... thou art suborn'd against his honour In hateful practice."

165. *wit* contrivance, stratagem; compare *The Merry Wives of Windsor*, IV.v.110ff.: Falstaff's "excellent dexterity of wit" in "counterfeiting the action of an old woman".

166. *All . . . fit* Everything suits me which I can make fitting, adapt [to my ends].

Scene iii S.D. *steward* Oswald is not named in F or Q until Goneril calls him (I.iv.290). This and the following scene are clearly at Goneril's, i.e., the Duke of Albany's, residence.

4. *crime* injurious act (less strong than the modern sense: compare *O.E.D.*, 2, 1526: "crimes of the tongue, as slanders ... and ... backbitings").

His knights grow riotous, and himself upbraids us
On every trifle. When he returns from hunting
I will not speak with him; say I am sick.
If you come slack of former services
10   You shall do well; the fault of it I'll answer.

OSWALD

He's coming madam; I hear him.

GONERIL

Put on what weary negligence you please,
You and your fellows; I'd have it come to question.
If he distaste it, let him to my sister,
15   Whose mind and mine, I know, in that are one,
Not to be overruled. Idle old man,
That still would manage those authorities
That he hath given away! Now, by my life,
Old fools are babes again, and must be used
20   With checks as flatteries, when they are seen abused.
Remember what I have said.

OSWALD

        Well, madam.

GONERIL

And let his knights have colder looks among you;
What grows of it, no matter. Advise your fellows so.
I would breed from hence occasions, and I shall,
25   That I may speak. I'll write straight to my sister
To hold my very course. Prepare for dinner.   *Exeunt.*

---

9. *come slack of* fall short of.
10. *answer* answer for, take responsibility for.
14. *distaste* Q has "dislike", the commoner equivalent.
16–20. *Not to be over-ruled . . . abused* Q (as prose); not in F. The last
line is possibly corrupt, but it can be read as meaning "with rebukes for
flatteries when these latter are seen to be misused [by the old fools]" or
"with rebukes as [well as] with flatteries when old men are seen to be deceived [by their followers]"; compare II.iv.301; IV.i.22.
24–5. *I would . . . speak* Q; not in F. I would make grow from it opportunities . . . to speak out.
26. *very* Q; not in F. *Prepare* Q has "goe prepare".

Scene iv: Enter KENT *[disguised].*

If but as well I other accents borrow
That can my speech defuse, my good intent
May carry through itself to that full issue
For which I razed my likeness. Now, banished Kent,
5   If thou canst serve where thou dost stand condemned,
So it may come, thy master whom thou lov'st
Shall find thee full of labours.
Horns within. Enter LEAR, *[Knights,] and Attendants.*

LEAR

Let me not stay a jot for dinner; go get it ready. How now,
what art thou?

KENT

10   A man sir.

LEAR

What dost thou profess? What wouldst thou with us?

KENT

I do profess to be no less than I seem, to serve him truly that

---

Scene iv 1. *as well* Q, meaning "as well as I have disguised my appearance". F "as will" leaves the sentence incomplete, with "if" introducing the
second verb "may carry".

2. *defuse* obscure, confuse.

2–4. *my good ... likeness* my good purpose may be carried through to
the complete end for which I erased [by taking a razor to my beard?] my
usual appearance.

7. *full of labours* most serviceable, balancing "canst serve" in the first
clause, as "thy master ... lov'st" balances "thou ... condemned"; Q has
"labour."

8. Notice the contrast with the "formal and self-contained" Lear of
Scene i; from this point to III.vi.78 is "the master-movement of the play ...
and in the acting ... there should be no break allowed" (Granville-Barker,
p. 272).

11. *profess* make your occupation. Kent replies as if the sense "claim,
avow" (as in I.i.67) were intended.

12. *no less than I seem* compare I.i.193 and II.ii.85ff.

will put me in trust, to love him that is honest, to converse
with him that is wise and says little, to fear judgment, to fight
15 when I cannot choose, and to eat no fish.

                              LEAR

What art thou?

                              KENT

A very honest-hearted fellow, and as poor as the King.

                              LEAR

If thou be'st as poor for a subject as he's for a king, thou art
poor enough. What wouldst thou?

                              KENT

20 Service.

                              LEAR

Who wouldst thou serve?

                              KENT

You.

                              LEAR

Dost thou know me, fellow?

                              KENT

No sir; but you have that in your countenance which I would
25 fain call master.

                              LEAR

What's that?

                              KENT

Authority.

---

13. *converse* associate.
14. *fear judgment* fear God; compare Psalm 1:6: "Therefore the un-
godly shall not be able to stand in the judgment" (Book of Common Prayer).
15. *fish* sign of either frugality or popery.
24. *countenance* demeanor, as in *I Henry IV*, V.i.69: "By unkind usage,
dangerous countenance".

LEAR

What services canst thou do?

KENT

30 I can keep honest counsel, ride, run, mar a curious tale in telling it, and deliver a plain message bluntly. That which ordinary
men are fit for, I am qualified in; and the best of me, is
diligence.

LEAR

How old art thou?

KENT

35 Not so young, sir, to love a woman for singing, nor so old to
dote on her for anything: I have years on my back forty-eight.

LEAR

Follow me; thou shalt serve me. If I like thee no worse after
dinner, I will not part from thee yet. Dinner ho, dinner!
Where's my knave? my Fool?—Go you and call my Fool
hither.　　　　　　　　　　　　　　　　　[*Exit an Attendant.*]

Enter OSWALD.

40 You you sirrah, where's my daughter?

OSWALD

So please you—　　　　　　　　　　　　　　　　　*Exit.*

LEAR

What says the fellow there? Call the clotpoll back. [*Exit a
Knight.*] Where's my Fool, ho? I think the world's asleep.
　　　　　　　　　　　[*Re-enter Knight.*]
How now! Where's that mongrel?

---

29. *keep . . . counsel*　keep a secret or confidence when it is honorable.
curious　skillfully made, subtle, complicated.
36. *me. If*　Both Q and F have "me, if".
38. *knave*　Compare I.i.16.
39. S.D.　Q and F have "*Enter Steward*", after the next line.
41. *So please you*　Excuse me; spoken with "weary negligence" (I.iii.12).
42. *clotpoll*　thick-head.

KNIGHT

45   He says, my lord, your daughter is not well.

LEAR

Why came not the slave back to me when I called him?

KNIGHT

Sir, he answered me in the roundest manner, he would not.

LEAR

He would not!

KNIGHT

My lord, I know not what the matter is; but, to my judgment,
50   your Highness is not entertained with that ceremonious affection as you were wont; there's a great abatement of kindness
appears as well in the general dependants as in the duke himself also, and your daughter.

LEAR

Ha! say'st thou so?

KNIGHT

55   I beseech you pardon me my lord, if I be mistaken, for my duty
cannot be silent when I think your Highness wronged.

LEAR

Thou but rememb'rest me of mine own conception. I have perceived a most faint neglect of late, which I have rather blamed
as mine own jealous curiosity than as a very pretence and pur-
60   pose of unkindness. I will look further into't. But where's my
Fool? I have not seen him this two days.

KNIGHT

Since my young lady's going into France sir, the Fool hath
much pined away.

---

45. *daughter*   Q; F has "Daughters".
47. *roundest*   bluntest; compare *Henry V*, IV.i.201: "*King.* Your reproof
is something too round; I should be angry with you . . ."
57. *conception*   notion.
59. *jealous curiosity*   suspicious (compare V.i.56 ff.) over-particularity
(compare I.i.5; I.ii.4). *Pretence*   intention; see I.ii.80 and n.

LEAR

No more of that; I have noted it well. Go you and tell my
65 daughter I would speak with her. [*Exit an Attendant.*] Go you
call hither my Fool.   [*Exit another Attendant.*]
[*Re-enter* OSWALD.]

O, you sir, you! Come you hither, sir. Who am I, sir?

OSWALD

My lady's father.

LEAR

My lady's father? my lord's knave; you whoreson dog, you
70 slave, you cur.

OSWALD

I am none of these my lord; I beseech your pardon.

LEAR

Do you bandy looks with me, you rascal?   [*Strikes him.*]

OSWALD

I'll not be strucken, my lord.

KENT

Nor tripped neither, you base football player.
[*Trips up his heels.*]

LEAR

75 I thank thee fellow; thou serv'st me and I'll love thee.

KENT

Come sir, arise, away! I'll teach you differences. Away, away!
If you will measure your lubber's length again, tarry; but
away, go to! Have you wisdom? So.   [*Pushes him out.*]

---

74. *base . . . player* New Cambridge ed. quotes Elyot *Governour*, 1531:
"Foot balle . . . to be utterly abiected of al noble men . . . wherein is nothing
but beastly furie and extreme violence."

76. *differences* distinctions (of rank) referring to lines 67–73.

78. *Go to!* Enough! *Have you wisdom? So.* Theobald; F reads "have
you wisedome, so." (= "be sensible"); Q reads "you have wisedome."

LEAR

Now my friendly knave I thank thee; there's earnest of thy
80   service.

Enter FOOL.

FOOL

[*To Kent*] Let me hire him too; here's my coxcomb.

[*Offers Kent his cap.*]

LEAR

How now my pretty knave, how dost thou?

FOOL

Sirrah, you were best take my coxcomb.

KENT

Why, Fool?

*the exchange
with the Fool
points up Lear's
foolishness*

FOOL

85   Why? For taking one's part that's out of favour. Nay, and thou
canst not smile as the wind sits, thou'lt catch cold shortly.
There, take my coxcomb. Why, this fellow has banished two
on's daughters and did the third a blessing against his will; if
thou follow him, thou must needs wear my coxcomb. How now
90   nuncle? Would I had two coxcombs and two daughters!

LEAR

Why, my boy?

FOOL

If I gave them all my living, I'd keep my coxcombs myself.
There's mine; beg another of thy daughters.

---

79. *earnest*   payment as an instalment (to confirm your service).

81. *coxcomb*   traditional fool's cap with the comb of a cock on its
crest.

83. *you were best.*   See Appendix C, p. 224–5.

84. *KENT Why, Fool?*   Q; F has "*Lear. Why my Boy?*".

88. *on's*   of his.

92. *If . . . coxcombs myself*   New Cambridge ed. quotes Tilley, A 187:
"He that gives all before he dies is a fool" (reference to which is lost by
Q "any" for "all my"); "living" = "property," especially land (*O.E.D.* cites
Bacon: "Men whose living lieth together in one shire").

LEAR

Take heed sirrah—the whip.

FOOL

95   Truth's a dog must to kennel; he must be whipp'd out, when
the Lady Brach may stand by th' fire and stink.

LEAR

A pestilent gall to me!

FOOL

Sirrah, I'll teach thee a speech.

LEAR

Do.

FOOL

100   Mark it, nuncle:

Have more than thou showest,
Speak less than thou knowest,
Lend less than thou owest,
Ride more than thou goest,

---

96. *the Lady Brach*   Q has "Ladie oth'e brach". A brach is a hound
bitch. Steevens, "Lady the brach", makes "Lady" a proper name (as in
1 Henry IV, III.i.237: "Lady, my brach"); this reading weakens the contrast
between outcast and aristocrat, with its glance at Cordelia expelled and disinherited for telling truth while her sisters were welcomed in. Attempts to
improve the invective, by sharpening the contrast not between truth and
flattery but between truth and lying (compare lines 160–1), include Duthie's
conjecture "Liar the brach" and Walker's "the lie o' the brach" (with quibble
on "lye" = a detergent which may be made from urine), misread by Q as
abbreviation for "lady" and sophisticated by F. New Cambridge prints "the
Lady's brach" = Oswald, contrasted with the Fool himself. This is much
less apposite—if indeed "brach" can be used abusively of a male at this date
—for Oswald has just been driven out by Kent.
    97. *gall*   secretion of the liver, used as the very type of bitterness (com-
pare line 117) or a sore produced by chafing, hence an irritation; Q has
"gull".
    101–10. *Have . . . score*   Possess more than you parade, be reticent, lend
less than you own, ride more than you walk, learn more than you believe,
stake less than the number you throw at dice . . . , i.e., be canny, and you'll
turn a score into more than two tens.

105   Learn more than thou trowest,
                       Set less than thou throwest;
                       Leave thy drink and thy whore,
                       And keep in-a-door,
                       And thou shalt have more
110   Than two tens to a score.

KENT

This is nothing, Fool.

FOOL

Then 'tis like the breath of an unfee'd lawyer—you gave me
nothing for't. Can you make no use of nothing, nuncle?

LEAR

Why no boy; nothing can be made of nothing.

FOOL

115   [*To Kent*] Prithee tell him, so much the rent of his land comes
to; he will not believe a fool.

LEAR

A bitter fool!

FOOL

Dost thou know the difference my boy, between a bitter fool
and a sweet one?

LEAR

120   No, lad; teach me.

FOOL

                       That lord that counselled thee
                       To give away thy land,
                       Come place him here by me—

---

111. *KENT*   Q has "*Lear.*"
112. *breath*   speech, as in *Midsummer Night's Dream*, III.ii.43–4: "O,
why rebuke you him that loves you so? Lay breath so bitter on your bitter
foe."
113. *use*   usury, interest, referring back to lines 109–10.
121–36. *That . . . snatching*   Q; not in F.

                    Do thou for him stand.
125   The sweet and bitter fool
                      Will presently appear;
                      The one in motley here,
                      The other found out there.

LEAR

Dost thou call me fool, boy?

FOOL

130 All thy other titles thou hast given away; that thou wast born
     with.

KENT

This is not altogether fool, my lord.

FOOL

No, faith, lords and great men will not let me; if I had a
monopoly out, they would have part on't. And ladies too—
135 they will not let me have all the fool to myself; they'll be
snatching. Nuncle, give me an egg, and I'll give thee two
crowns.

LEAR

What two crowns shall they be?

FOOL

Why, after I have cut the egg i' th' middle and eat up the meat,
140 the two crowns of the egg. When thou clovest thy crown i' th'
middle, and gav'st away both parts, thou borest thine ass on
thy back o'er the dirt. Thou hadst little wit in thy bald crown

---

132. *altogether fool* (a) entirely foolish (b) everything foolish: compare
Tindale's translation of I Corinthians, 7:19: "Circumcision is nothing . . .
but the keeping of the commandments of God is altogether." The Fool as-
sumes (b) is meant.

140. *crown* Q; F has "crowns".

141–2. *borest . . . dirt* Like the man in Aesop's fable, you subverted the
order of things.

when thou gav'st thy golden one away. If I speak like myself
in this, let him be whipped that first finds it so.

145   Fools had ne'er less grace in a year;
           For wise men are grown foppish
       And know not how their wits to wear,
           Their manners are so apish.

LEAR

When were you wont to be so full of songs sirrah?

FOOL

150 I have used it nuncle, e'er since thou mad'st thy daughters thy
mothers; for when thou gav'st them the rod, and put'st down
thine own breeches,

       Then they for sudden joy did weep,
           And I for sorrow sung,
155   That such a king should play bo-peep
           And go the fools among.

Prithee nuncle, keep a schoolmaster that can teach thy Fool to
lie. I would fain learn to lie.

LEAR

And you lie sirrah, we'll have you whipped.

FOOL

160 I marvel what kin thou and thy daughters are. They'll have me

---

143–4. *If . . . so*   If I speak like a fool in saying this, let the man who
will first find it is true [Lear] have the whipping which truth is due to get
(line 95).

145. *grace*   favor (Q has "wit", recalling the proverb, Tilley F 535: "Fools
had never less wit in a year"). Fools are out of favor because wise men become fools ("foppish") and take their place.

150. *e'er*   F has "ere"; Q "euer".

151. *mothers*   Q has "mother".

153–6. *Then . . . among*   Adapting the ballad of John Careless, a prot-
estant martyr, printed in Coverdale, *Certain most godly . . . letters of . . .
Martyrs . . . 1564*, and separately licensed 1 August 1586.

155. *play bo-peep*   play hide-and-seek; hide (having renounced the
kingdom).

whipped for speaking true: thou'lt have me whipped for lying;
and sometimes I am whipped for holding my peace. I had
rather be any kind o' thing than a fool, and yet I would not
be thee, nuncle: thou hast pared thy wit o' both sides, and left
165 nothing i' th' middle. Here comes one o' th' parings.

Enter GONERIL.

LEAR

How now daughter? What makes that frontlet on? You are
too much of late i' th' frown.

FOOL

Thou wast a pretty fellow when thou hadst no need to care for
her frowning; now thou art an O without a figure. I am better
170 than thou art now: I am a fool, thou art nothing. [*To Goneril*]
Yes forsooth, I will hold my tongue; so your face bids me,
though you say nothing.

　　　　Mum, mum!
　　　　He that keeps nor crust nor crumb,
175 　　　　Weary of all, shall want some.
[*Pointing to Lear*] That's a shelled peascod.

GONERIL

Not only sir, this your all-licensed Fool,
But other of your insolent retinue
Do hourly carp and quarrel, breaking forth
180 In rank and not-to-be-endured riots. Sir,
I had thought by making this well known unto you
To have found a safe redress, but now grow fearful,
By what yourself too late have spoke and done,

---

164. *wit* understanding, intelligence; compare I.ii.165.
166. *frontlet* band for the forehead, hence frown.
169. *O ... figure* zero with no number before it, i.e., nothing.
174. *nor* Q; F has "not".
176. *a shelled peascod* the pod of a shelled pea, i.e., an empty pod.
180. *rank* excessive, swollen, as in 2 *Henry IV*, IV.i.63–4: "... like fearful war To diet rank minds sick of happiness". *and ... riots, Sir* F has "and (not to be endur'd) riots Sir."; Q has "& (not to be indured riots,) Sir."
182 *safe* sure, trustworthy; compare IV.vi.81.
183. *too late* only too recently, well after the proper time.

That you protect this course, and put it on
185   By your allowance, which if you should, the fault
Would not 'scape censure nor the redresses sleep,
Which in the tender of a wholesome weal
Might in their working do you that offence
Which else were shame, that then necessity
190   Will call discreet proceeding.

FOOL

For you know, nuncle,
The hedge-sparrow fed the cuckoo so long
That it's had it head bit off by it young.
So out went the candle, and we were left darkling.

LEAR

195   Are you our daughter?

GONERIL

I would you would make use of your good wisdom
(Whereof I know you are fraught) and put away
These dispositions which of late transport you
From what you rightly are.

FOOL

200   May not an ass know when the cart draws the horse? Whoop,
Jug! I love thee.

184–5. *put . . . allowance* encourage, promote (compare II.i.97) it by
your approbation (compare II.ii.96). Q omits "it".

187–90. *in the tender . . . proceeding* In my tender care for an orderly
community, my remedies for the disorder may do you harm; this action in
any other circumstances would be shameful but it will then, because it is
necessary, be called circumspect and judicious.

191. *know* Q has "trow".

193. *it* its (see Appendix C, p. 224).

194. *darkling* in the dark (adverb). Compare Appendix B, p. 218, xxx.

198. *dispositions* inclinations, hence moods; compare *Coriolanus*,
III.ii.20–22: "lesser had been The thwartings of your dispositions if You
had not show'd them how ye were dispos'd." *transport* carry away with
emotion; Q has "transforme".

200. *May not . . . horse?* May not a Fool see how order is upset (compare lines 141–2, 150–1, 210) when a daughter takes her father to task?

201. *Jug* pet name for Joan, a plain homely woman, servant, or even

LEAR

Does any here know me? This is not Lear.
Does Lear walk thus? speak thus? Where are his eyes?
Either his notion weakens, or his discernings
205   Are lethargied.—Ha! waking? 'Tis not so?
Who is it that can tell me who I am?

FOOL

Lear's shadow.

LEAR

I would learn that; for by the marks of sovereignty, knowledge
and reason I should be false persuaded I had daughters.

FOOL

210   Which they will make an obedient father.

LEAR

Your name, fair gentlewoman?

GONERIL

This admiration sir, is much o' th' savour
Of other your new pranks. I do beseech you
To understand my purposes aright,

---

whore. (Compare *King John* I.i.184: "Well, now can I make any Joan a
lady.") There is a glance back at line 96.

   204–5. *Either . . . lethargied*   Either his understanding weakens or his
senses are dulled.

   204–7. *Either . . . shadow.*   F has "Either his Notion weakens, his Discernings . . . shadow." Q has "either his notion, weaknes, or his discernings
are lethergie, sleeping or wakeing; ha! sure tis not so, who is it that can
tell me who I am? *Lears* shadow?"

   208–10. *I . . . father*   Q (as prose; omitted from F, possibly by accident,
since an obvious gap is left unless the actor could, by emphasizing "*Your*
name . . .", imply the connection: "If I am not Lear who are you?") I want
to learn who I am, for if I try to judge by the usual signs of authority—
namely deference from others—and of consciousness (compare IV.vi.273)
and reason in myself, it would seem that I was wrong to think I had
daughters.

   212. *admiration*   wondering, astonishment.

215   As you are old and reverend, should be wise.
Here do you keep a hundred knights and squires,
Men so disordered, so deboshed and bold,
That this our court, infected with their manners,
Shows like a riotous inn. Epicurism and lust
220   Makes it more like a tavern or a brothel
Than a graced palace. The shame itself doth speak
For instant remedy. Be then desired
By her that else will take the thing she begs
A little to disquantity your train;
225   And the remainders that shall still depend,
To be such men as may besort your age,
Which know themselves, and you.

LEAR

     Darkness and devils!
Saddle my horses; call my train together.
Degenerate bastard, I'll not trouble thee;
230   Yet have I left a daughter.

GONERIL

You strike my people; and your disordered rabble
Make servants of their betters.

Enter ALBANY.

LEAR

Woe that too late repents!—O sir, are you come?
Is it your will? Speak sir.—Prepare my horses.

---

217. *deboshed* depraved (a variant closer to the pronunciation of French *debauché*); Q has "deboyst".

219. *Epicurism* living for pleasure; gluttony.

221. *graced* made honorable, dignified (by the presence of the King); Q has "great".

222. *desired* requested (as a favor), invited.

224–6. *A little . . . age* to reduce a little the number of your followers; and [allow] the rest who shall still be dependent upon you to be such men as suit your years.

233. *Woe that . . . repents* Woe to him who . . . ; Q has "We that . . . repent's". *O . . . come?* Q; not in F.

234. *will? . . . my* Q has "will that wee prepare any".

235 Ingratitude, thou marble-hearted fiend,
    More hideous when thou show'st thee in a child
    Than the sea-monster!

ALBANY

Pray sir be patient.

LEAR

[*To Goneril*] Detested kite, thou liest:
My train are men of choice and rarest parts
240 That all particulars of duty know
    And in the most exact regard support
    The worships of their name.—O most small fault,
    How ugly didst thou in Cordelia show!
    Which like an engine wrench'd my frame of nature
245 From the fixed place, drew from my heart all love
    And added to the gall. O Lear, Lear, Lear!
    Beat at this gate that let thy folly in   [*Strikes his head.*]
    And thy dear judgment out! Go, go, my people.

                              [*Exeunt* KENT *and Knights.*]

ALBANY

My lord, I am guiltless, as I am ignorant
250 Of what hath moved you.

LEAR

                    It may be so, my lord.
—Hear Nature, hear dear goddess, hear:
Suspend thy purpose if thou didst intend

[handwritten margin note: Lear recognizes his folly, but although it can be remedied his thinking the event he has set in motion cannot be reversed]

---

237. *ALBANY ... patient.*   not in Q.

241–2. *And in . . . name*   and with the most scrupulous attention, keep up the honor of their respective reputations (compare *I Henry IV*, V.iv.70: "Thy name in arms").

244. *engine*   implement, lever. *nature*   natural, i.e., filial, feeling (compare I.i.48).

245. *fixed place*   center, fixed like that of the earth in the (Ptolemaic) universe (compare *Romeo and Juliet*, II.i.1–2: "Can I go forward when my heart is here? Turn back, dull earth, and find thy centre out").

250. *Of . . . you*   not in Q.

To make this creature fruitful.
Into her womb convey sterility;
255 Dry up in her the organs of increase;
And from her derogate body never spring
A babe to honour her. If she must teem,
Create her child of spleen, that it may live
And be a thwart disnatured torment to her.
260 Let it stamp wrinkles in her brow of youth,
With cadent tears fret channels in her cheeks,
Turn all her mother's pains and benefits
To laughter and contempt, that she may feel
How sharper than a serpent's tooth it is
265 To have a thankless child. Away, away!   *Exit.*

ALBANY

Now gods that we adore, whereof comes this?

GONERIL

Never afflict yourself to know more of it;
But let his disposition have that scope
As dotage gives it.

[Re-]enter LEAR.

LEAR

270 What, fifty of my followers at a clap?
Within a fortnight?

ALBANY

What's the matter, sir?

---

256. *derogate*   disparaged (because of sterility), degenerate, debased.
257. *teem*   bear offspring.
258. *spleen*   violent ill-nature (from the abdominal organ considered as the seat of strong emotion).
259. *thwart, disnatured*   perverse, unnatural (i.e., without natural affection; compare line 244).
261. *cadent*   falling; Q has "accent".
262. *pains*   anxieties, exertions (compare III.i.53); birth-pangs.
268. *disposition*   See line 198, n.
269. *As*   = Q "that"; compare I.i.92 and Franz § 340 (c).

LEAR

I'll tell thee. [*To Goneril*] Life and death! I am asham'd
That thou hast power to shake my manhood thus,
That these hot tears which break from me perforce
275   Should make thee worth them. Blasts and fogs upon thee!
Th' untented woundings of a father's curse
Pierce every sense about thee!—Old fond eyes,
Beweep this cause again, I'll pluck ye out,
And cast you with the waters that you loose
280   To temper clay. Ha! Is't come to this?—
Let it be so. I have another daughter,
Who, I am sure, is kind and comfortable.
When she shall hear this of thee, with her nails
She'll flay thy wolfish visage. Thou shalt find
285   That I'll resume the shape which thou dost think
I have cast off for ever.   *Exit.*

GONERIL

Do you mark that?

ALBANY

I cannot be so partial, Goneril,
To the great love I bear you—

275-6. *thee worth . . . untented*   Q has "the worst blasts and fogs upon the untented".

275. *blasts*   gusts of wind bringing infection (compare *Tempest*, I.ii.323-4: "A southwest [plague-bearing] blow on ye And blister you all o'er!"). *fogs*   thought to bear the plague.

276. *untented woundings*   wounds too deep to be probed with a roll of lint (tent).

277. *fond*   foolish (the commonest sense in Shakespeare, although the word is found by this time also in the more favorable modern sense "having strong affection", as in *Winter's Tale*, I.ii.164, or *Othello*, V.ii.160).

279. *loose*   give forth (compare *As You Like It*, III.v.102-3: "loose now and then A scatter'd smile, and that I'll live upon"). Q has "make".

280. *temper*   moisten (and so soften); compare *2 Henry VI*, III.i.310-11: "Th'uncivil kerns of Ireland are in arms And temper clay with blood of Englishmen . . ." *Is't come to this?*   Q; not in F.

282. *comfortable*   comforting, sustaining; compare Jonson, *Bartholomew Fair*, II.v.9: "comfortable bread".

286. *ever.*   Q has "ever, thou shalt I warrant thee."

GONERIL

290   Pray you content.—What, Oswald, ho!

     [*To the Fool*] You sir, more knave than Fool, after your master.

FOOL

Nuncle Lear, nuncle Lear, tarry; take the Fool with thee.

              A fox, when one has caught her,

              And such a daughter,

295   Should sure to the slaughter,

              If my cap would buy a halter.

              So the Fool follows after.   *Exit.*

GONERIL

This man hath had good counsel! A hundred knights?

'Tis politic and safe to let him keep

300   At point a hundred knights; yes, that on every dream,

Each buzz, each fancy, each complaint, dislike,

He may enguard his dotage with their powers

And hold our lives in mercy. Oswald, I say!

ALBANY

Well, you may fear too far.

GONERIL

305   Safer than trust too far.

Let me still take away the harms I fear,

---

290. *Pray . . . ho!*   Q has "Come sir no more", anticipating II.iv.151.

292. *take . . . thee*   Kittredge compares *1 Henry IV*, V.iii.22: "A fool go with thy soul whither it goes" for the quibbling sense "Take the epithet 'fool' with you—fool as you are."

296–7. *halter . . . after*   true ("au") rhymes with "slaughter"; see Dobson § 423.

298–309. *This man . . . th'unfitness*   not in Q.

298. *hath had . . . counsel*   ironic = "has been incited to insolence".

300. *At point*   prepared; compare III.i.33 and *O.E.D., sb.*[1], D.1.b, 1611: "to be in readiness, to be at a point".

301. *buzz*   rumor; compare *Hamlet*, IV.v.87–8: "[Laertes] wants not buzzers to infect his ear With pestilent speeches of his father's death."

303. *in mercy*   at discretion, in his power; compare *Merchant of Venice*, IV.i.350–51: "th'offender's life lies in the mercy Of the Duke only."

Not fear still to be taken. I know his heart;
What he hath uttered I have writ my sister.
If she sustain him and his hundred knights,
310   When I have showed th'unfitness—
>   [*Re-*]*enter* OSWALD.
>   How now Oswald?
What, have you writ that letter to my sister?

OSWALD

Ay madam.

GONERIL

Take you some company and away to horse,
Inform her full of my particular fear
315   And thereto add such reasons of your own
As may compact it more. Get you gone,
And hasten your return. [*Exit* OSWALD.] No, no, my lord,
This milky gentleness and course of yours
Though I condemn not, yet, under pardon,
320   You are much more attaxed for want of wisdom
Than praised for harmful mildness.

ALBANY

How far your eyes may pierce I cannot tell;
Striving to better, oft we mar what's well.

---

307. *taken*   stricken, attacked [by harm].

309. *sustain*   keep, provide for; compare Modern English "sustenance."

310. *How now Oswald?*   Because of the previous cut, Q has "What Oswald, ho. *Oswald.* Here Madam."

314. *particular*   personal, private; compare V.i.30.

316. *compact*   confirm; Arden quotes Cotgrave: "*Affermir*, to strengthen, . . . confirm, . . . compact."

317. *No . . . my*   F has "no . . . thy"; Q "now my".

320. *attaxed*   Greg; F has "at task"; Q uncorr. "alapt"; Q corr. "attaskt". Greg argues that Q uncorr. "alapt", wrongly emended by corrector and by F, was a misreading of "ataxt". For the sense "taxed, blamed", as well as for the Q emendation, compare III.ii.15 and note.

323. *better, oft*   Q has "better ought,". For the pronunciation of "ought" like "oft", see Dobson § 34 (1).

GONERIL

Nay then—

ALBANY

325   Well, well; th'event.   *Exeunt.*

Scene v: Enter LEAR, KENT, *and* FOOL.

LEAR

Go you before to Gloucester with these letters. Acquaint my daughter no further with anything you know than comes from her demand out of the letter. If your diligence be not speedy, I shall be there afore you.

KENT

5   I will not sleep my lord, till I have delivered your letter.   *Exit.*

FOOL

If a man's brains were in's heels, were't not in danger of kibes?

LEAR

Ay boy.

FOOL

Then I prithee be merry; thy wit shall not go slip-shod.

LEAR

Ha, ha, ha!

---

325. *th'event*   the outcome; i.e., wait and see what happens.

Scene V   1. *Gloucester*   apparently the central place where it is usual to break a journey from Albany to Cornwall. The letters are for Regan and perhaps Cornwall, and are delivered to them "at their home" (II.iv.26). It is not necessary to follow Greg (*MLR*, XXXV [1940], 434, note) and Granville-Barker (p. 333), who suggest we read "Cornwall" (where Regan's home might be). See Introduction, p. xxvii.

3. *out of*   arising from.

6. *were't*   Q; F has "wert"; "it" = "brains", taken as a singular. *kibes*   chaps, chilblains.

8. *slip-shod*   wearing slippers (because of chilblains); the implication is that Lear has no brains in his heels, running off like this after Regan.

FOOL

ee thy other daughter will use thee kindly; for though
s like this as a crab's like an apple, yet I can tell what I
can tell.

LEAR

What canst tell, boy?

FOOL

She will taste as like this as a crab does to a crab. Thou canst
15   tell why one's nose stands i' th' middle on's face?

LEAR

No.

FOOL

Why, to keep one's eyes of either side's nose, that what a man
cannot smell out, he may spy into.

LEAR

I did her wrong.

FOOL

20   Canst tell how an oyster makes his shell?

LEAR

No.

FOOL

Nor I neither; but I can tell why a snail has a house.

LEAR

Why?

---

10. *kindly*   (a) in accordance with nature ("kind") hence with natural
affection, or (b) according to her nature; compare line 26 below.
11, 14. *she ... this*   Regan ... Goneril.
15. *on's*   of his.
17. *of ... nose*   on either side of his nose.
19. *her*   Cordelia.

FOOL

Why, to put's head in, not to give it away to his daughters and
25   leave his horns without a case.

LEAR

I will forget my [nature] So kind a father! Be my horses ready?

FOOL

Thy asses are gone about 'em. The reason why the seven stars
are no moe than seven is a pretty reason.

LEAR

Because they are not eight.

FOOL

30   Yes indeed; thou would'st make a good Fool.

LEAR

To take't again perforce! Monster Ingratitude!

FOOL

If thou wert my Fool nuncle, I'd have thee beaten for being old
before thy time.

LEAR

How's that?

FOOL

35   Thou should'st not have been old till thou hadst been wise.

LEAR

O, let me not be mad, not mad, sweet heaven!
Keep me in temper; I would not be mad.

---

25. *horns*   usually the marks of cuckoldry; to the Fool, of married men
in general.

27. *asses*   Compare I.iv.141.

27–28. *the seven stars are no moe*   the Pleiades are no greater in number
(O.E. *mā*; Shakespeare keeps this sense separate from that of "more," O.E.
māra, greater in degree. See Appendix C, p. 223).

31. *To . . . perforce*   "He is meditating on the resumption of his royalty"
(Johnson) by force (compare I.iv.284–6; II.i.9).

[*Enter* Gentleman.]

How now! Are the horses ready?

GENTLEMAN

Ready my lord.

LEAR

40   Come boy.

FOOL

She that's a maid now, and laughs at my departure,
Shall not be a maid long, unless things be cut shorter.

Exeunt.

Act II, Scene i: Enter EDMUND *and* CURAN, *severally.*

EDMUND

Save thee, Curan.

CURAN

And you sir. I have been with your father, and given him
notice that the Duke of Cornwall and Regan his Duchess will
be here with him this night.

EDMUND

5   How comes that?

CURAN

Nay I know not; you have heard the news abroad, I mean the
whispered ones, for they are yet but ear-bussing arguments?

---

42. *Shall . . . shorter*   has not wit enough to preserve her virginity (if she
is silly enough to think this "departure" funny). The rhyme would be on the
"a" vowel; compare spellings such as *hars* "horse," *marrow* "morrow"—cited
from the sixteenth century by Wyld, p. 240, and Dobson, § 87.

Act II, Scene i   4. *here*   the Earl of Gloucester's castle, as in I.ii.
7. *ear-bussing*   Q; F "ear-kissing" is commonly taken to be a sophistication. Q has the same meaning, but has a quibble on "buzzing" (whispering;
compare I.iv.301). *arguments*   topics; compare I.i.210.

EDMUND

Not I: pray you what are they?

CURAN

Have you heard of no likely wars toward 'twixt the Dukes of
10   Cornwall and Albany?

EDMUND

Not a word.

CURAN

You may do then in time. Fare you well sir.   *Exit.*

EDMUND

The duke be here tonight? The better! best!
This weaves itself perforce into my business.
15   My father hath set guard to take my brother;
And I have one thing, of a queasy question,
Which I must act. Briefness and fortune, work!
                    Enter EDGAR [*above.*]
Brother, a word; descend; brother I say.   [EDGAR *comes down.*]
My father watches; O sir, fly this place!
20   Intelligence is given where you are hid;
You have now the good advantage of the night.
Have you not spoken 'gainst the Duke of Cornwall?
He's coming hither, now i'th'night, i'th'haste,

---

13. *The . . . best!*   Q does not change to verse until line 88.

16. *of a queasy question*   delicate, risky (compare *O.E.D.*, "queasy", 1, b, 1589: "a queisie and dangerous matter") if it is examined or put to trial.

17. *Which . . . work!*   Q has "which must aske breefnes and fortune helpe" (the verb influenced by "question" and the rest altered to fit it).

18. *say.*   F and Q have "say,". S.D.   Edgar's entry is here as in F, but the word *Edgar* appears in the margin even earlier in Q, after "weaves", line 14. He may appear first on an upper level (see Introduction, p. xxiii). He has apparently been hiding from the guard and would first show himself rather gingerly. Edmund has been soliloquizing downstage; while Edgar is descending the stairs backstage, Edmund goes to one of the tiring-house doors and they converse beside it.

19. *watches*   keeps vigil, i.e., is looking for you.

And Regan with him. Have you nothing said
25   Upon his party 'gainst the Duke of Albany?
Advise yourself.

EDGAR

I am sure on't, not a word.

EDMUND

I hear my father coming. Pardon me,
In cunning I must draw my sword upon you.
Draw, seem to defend yourself; now quit you well.—
30   Yield! Come before my father. Light ho here!—
Fly brother.—Torches, torches!—So farewell.   *Exit* EDGAR.
Some blood drawn on me would beget opinion
Of my more fierce endeavour. [*Wounds his arm.*] I have seen
        drunkards
Do more than this in sport—Father, father!
35   Stop, stop! No help?
            Enter GLOUCESTER, *and Servants with torches.*

GLOUCESTER

Now Edmund, where's the villain?

EDMUND

Here stood he in the dark, his sharp sword out,
Mumbling of wicked charms, conjuring the moon
To stand auspicious mistress.

---

25. *Upon his party*   on his side (compare *King John*, I.i.33–4: "Till she had kindled France and all the world Upon the right and party of her son"). Yet it is not impossible that it means "concerning the party formed by him [i.e., Cornwall] against Albany," mentioned as recently as line 10.

26. *Advise yourself*   take thought; compare *Henry V*, III.vi.154: "Go bid thy master well advise himself."

28. *In cunning*   by way of craft or stratagem "to avoid the appearance of collusion" (Arden). Q has "in craving".

29. *quit you*   behave, bear yourself, i.e., fight.

32–3. *opinion . . . endeavour*   belief that I have fought even more fiercely [than I seem to have].

37. *Mumbling*   Q has "warbling".

38. *stand*   act as (Gloucester, as we know from I.ii.94, would be ready to believe this); Q has "stand's", ie., stand his.

GLOUCESTER

But where is he?

EDMUND

Look sir, I bleed.

GLOUCESTER

Where is the villain, Edmund?

EDMUND

40　Fled this way sir, when by no means he could—

GLOUCESTER

Pursue him, ho! Go after. [*Exeunt Servants.*]—By no means
　　what?

EDMUND

Persuade me to the murder of your lordship;
But that I told him the revenging gods
'Gainst parricides did all the thunder bend,
45　Spoke with how manifold and strong a bond
The child was bound to th'father—sir, in fine,
Seeing how loathly opposite I stood
To his unnatural purpose, in fell motion
With his preparèd sword he charges home
50　My unprovided body, latched mine arm;
And when he saw my best alarumed spirits,

---

40. *could*—　Q; F has "could."

43. *that*　when; see Franz § 548, and Appendix C, p. 225.

44. *the thunder*　Q has "their thunders". *bend*　direct, bring to bear;
compare *King John*, II.i.37–8: "Our cannon shall be bent Against the brows
of this resisting town."

47. *loathly opposite*　opposed with abhorrence.

49. *preparèd*　ready unsheathed. *home*　so as to go right in at the point
he aimed for.

50. *unprovided*　unprepared; compare *Hamlet*, III.iii.2–7: "Therefore
prepare you; . . . We will ourselves provide." *latched*　caught—which gives
a more plausible tale than Q "lancht", pierced.

51. *my best alarumed spirits*　my best powers aroused to arms, to action
(Italian *all'arme!* to arms!); compare *Macbeth*, II.i.52–3: "murder, Alarum'd
by his sentinel, the wolf".

Bold in the quarrel's right, roused to th'encounter,
Or whether gasted by the noise I made,
Full suddenly he fled.

GLOUCESTER

Let him fly far;

55   Not in this land shall he remain uncaught;
And found—dispatch. The noble duke my master,
My worthy arch and patron, comes tonight;
By his authority I will proclaim it
That he which finds him shall deserve our thanks,

60   Bringing the murderous coward to the stake,
He that conceals him, death.

EDMUND

When I dissuaded him from his intent
And found him pight to do it, with curst speech
I threatened to discover him. He replied,

65   "Thou unpossessing bastard, dost thou think,
If I would stand against thee, would the reposal
Of any trust, virtue, or worth in thee
Make thy words faithed? No. What I should deny
(As this I would—ay, though thou didst produce

70   My very character) I'd turn it all

---

53. *gasted*   scared; compare *O.E.C. v.*^{1}, 1592: "men . . . so ghasted with feare . . . that they looked rather like to ghosts than men".

54–5. *Let . . . uncaught*   Let him fly ever so far, he shall be caught. See Appendix C, p. 224.

56. *And found—dispatch.*   and when found—death [to him] (compare line 61). F has "vncaught And found; dispatch," while Q has "uncaught and found, dispatch," (as prose).

57. *arch*   chief, compare *O.E.D., a.,* B, 1605: "Poole, that Arch, for truth and honesty".

60. *the stake*   execution.

63. *pight*   resolved (past participle of "pitch," to decide). *curst*   sharp; compare *2 Henry VI,* III.ii.311–12: "terms, As curst, as harsh, and horrible to hear".

66. *would the reposal*   Q has "could the reposure".

68. *I should*   Q; F has "should I".

69. *would—ay, though*   Q has "would, I, though", F "would, though".

70. *character*   handwriting.

To thy suggestion, plot, and damned practice;
And thou must make a dullard of the world,
If they not thought the profits of my death
Were very pregnant and potential spurs
75 To make thee seek it."

GLOUCESTER

O strange and fastened villain,
Would he deny his letter, said he? I never got him.

Tucket within.

Hark, the duke's trumpets! I know not where he comes;
All ports I'll bar; the villain shall not 'scape;
The duke must grant me that. Besides, his picture
80 I will send far and near, that all the kingdom

---

71. *suggestion* (a) false charge, compare Kyd, *The Spanish Tragedy*, III.i.45–6: "as heavens have known my secret thoughts, So am I free from this suggestion"; (b) temptation, compare *King John*, III.i.291–2: ". . . arm thy constant and thy nobler parts Against these giddy loose suggestions." See Appendix C, p. 224. *practice* stratagem; compare II.iv.110, V.iii.148. Q has "pretence".

72. *make . . . world* take everyone for dullards; compare *Cymbeline*, V.v.265: "What, mak'st thou me a dullard in this act?" (where the whole passage, to line 269, is reminiscent of *King Lear*).

74. *pregnant* (a) pressing (O.F. *preindre*), cogent, obvious (*O.E.D.*, *a*¹, 1601: "Because my proofs are not pregnant . . . I will pass him over in silence") perhaps fits the Q reading "spurres"; (b) resourceful, inventive (Latin *praegnans*) goes rather with F "spirits"; (c) full of meaning, suggestive (from the fifteenth century onwards in *O.E.D.*) would fit either. *potential* potent (with (a) and (b) above; compare *Othello*, I.ii.13–14: " a voice potential As double as the Duke's"); possible as opposed to actual, latent (with (c) above; compare *O.E.D.*, A.2,1626: "an actual or potential fall from grace"). *spurs* Q; F has "spirits".

75. *strange* abnormal, unnatural; not of my family or kin (an earlier sixteenth-century use but still found in A.V., *Proverbs*, 2:16, in the phrase "the strange woman," i.e., not one's own wife, harlot); Q has "strong". *fastened* confirmed, hardened.

76. *said he?* not in Q. *I . . . him* Q, not in F. *got* begot. S.D. after "seek it" in previous line, in F.

77–79. *where . . . that* Whichever gate (port) he will need, I must bar them all; . . . my guest must concede that to me as a favor. But if the meaning is that the duke, as lord of this part of England, must concede that closing of all sea-ports (compare II.iii.3), then F "wher" is less apposite; but Q "why" is no more relevant and anticipates line 116 (see Appendix E, p. 230).

May have due note of him; and of my land,
Loyal and natural boy, I'll work the means
To make thee capable.

　　　　　Enter CORNWALL, REGAN, *and Attendants.*

CORNWALL

How now my noble friend? Since I came hither
85　(Which I can call but now) I have heard strange news.

REGAN

If it be true, all vengeance comes too short
Which can pursue th'offender. How dost my lord?

GLOUCESTER

O madam, my old heart is cracked, it's cracked.

REGAN

What, did my father's godson seek your life?
90　He whom my father named, your Edgar?

GLOUCESTER

O lady, lady, shame would have it hid.

REGAN

Was he not companion with the riotous knights
That tended upon my father?

GLOUCESTER

I know not, madam. 'Tis too bad, too bad.

EDMUND

95　Yes madam, he was of that consórt.

---

81. *note*　See Appendix C, p. 224; compare *Rape of Lucrece*, 208: "my posterity, sham'd with the note".

83. *capable*　qualified to hold or possess, a legal sense first recorded in Shakespeare; compare *O.E.D.*, 7, 1610: "Bastards are not capable of their father's patrimony."

85. *strange news*　Q; F has "strangenesse".

93. *tended*　Q has "tends", but elision of "-ed" after "d" makes the metre regular (Abbott, § 472).

95. *consórt*　company.

REGAN

No marvel then though he were ill affected.
'Tis they have put him on the old man's death
To have th'expense and waste of his revénues.
I have this present evening from my sister

100   Been well informed of them, and with such cautions
That if they come to sojourn at my house
I'll not be there.

CORNWALL

Nor I, assure thee Regan.
Edmund, I hear that you have shown your father
A child-like office.

EDMUND

It was my duty sir.

GLOUCESTER

105   He did bewray his practice, and received
This hurt you see, striving to apprehend him.

CORNWALL

Is he pursued?

GLOUCESTER

Ay my good lord.

CORNWALL

If he be taken, he shall never more

---

96. *affected*   disposed, inclined; compare A.V. Acts, 14:2: "evil affected against the brethren".

97. *put . . . on*   incited him to.

98. *th' expense and waste*   Q has "the waste and spoyle", miscorrected from "these—and wast"; this reading may possibly conceal the correct reading, "the spence", which F sophisticates (Greg, pp. 155–6).

104. *child-like office*   filial duty, service; compare *Merry Wives of Windsor*, I.i.89: "I would I could do a good office between you."

105. *bewray*   reveal, expose; compare *3 Henry VI*, I.i.211: "Here comes the Queen, whose looks bewray her anger"; used in a good sense, unlike Q "betray". *practice*   Compare line 71.

Be feared of doing harm. Make your own purpose,
110   How in my strength you please. For you Edmund,
Whose virtue and obedience doth this instant
So much commend itself, you shall be ours.
Natures of such deep trust we shall much need;
You we first seize on.

EDMUND

I shall serve you sir

115   Truly, however else.

GLOUCESTER

For him I thank your Grace.

CORNWALL

You know not why we came to visit you?

REGAN

Thus out of season threading dark-eyed night:
Occasions, noble Gloucester, of some prize
Wherein we must have use of your advice.
120   Our father he hath writ, so hath our sister,
Of differences which I best thought it fit
To answer from our home. The several messengers
From hence attend dispatch. Our good old friend,

---

109. *of*   with regard to; see Franz, § 517.

109–10. *Make . . . please . . .*   Achieve your aims however you please, with my authority; compare *Sonnets*, 49, 13–14: "To leave poor me thou hast the strength of laws, Since why to love I can allege no cause."

117. *threading*   making way through (with difficulty); compare *O.E.D.*, *v.*4,1619: "See where he threads the thickets." The expression is so common in the seventeenth century that the quibble upon threading a needle's eye which some editors find in "dark-eyed" seems unlikely; Q has "threatning".

118. *prize*   Q has "poyse" (= "weight"), miscorrected from "prise" (= "worth"); compare I.i.65, n.

121. *differences*   disputes, compare II.ii.43. *thought*   Q; F has "though".

121–2. *best . . . from*   Q miscorrects "best" to "lest" (least) but, stressed, "from" means "away from" in opposition to "at home"; compare II.ii.157; II.iv.199.

122–3. *several . . . dispatch*   the separate messengers (Kent and Oswald) have come with us and wait to be sent from here (see II.ii.1, n.).

Lay comforts to your bosom and bestow
125 Your needful counsel to our businesses
Which craves the instant use.

GLOUCESTER
                    I serve you madam;
Your graces are right welcome.   *Flourish. Exeunt.*

Scene ii: Enter KENT *and* OSWALD, *severally.*

OSWALD
Good dawning to thee friend. Art of this house?

KENT
Ay.

OSWALD
Where may we set our horses?

KENT
                    I'th'mire.

OSWALD
Prithee, if thou lov'st me, tell me.

KENT
5 I love thee not.

OSWALD
Why then, I care not for thee.

---

126. *craves . . . use* demand immediate action. See Appendix C, p. 224.

Scene ii S.D. *severally* separately, by different doors. Compare
III.i.S.D., n.
1. *dawning* Q "even" and the uncorrected "deven" give the wrong time
of day (see lines 122–3 below), although it is still dark and the sun has not
risen by the end of the scene. *this house* Gloucester's. Both speakers are
messengers sent to Cornwall and Regan, and brought with them to Gloucester's castle; but Oswald apparently arrives after the main party.

KENT

If I had thee in Lipsbury Pinfold I would make thee care for
me.

OSWALD

Why dost thou use me thus? I know thee not.

KENT

10   Fellow I know thee.

OSWALD

What dost thou know me for?

KENT

A knave, a rascal, an eater of broken meats; a base, proud,
shallow, beggarly, three-suited, hundred-pound, filthy worsted-
stocking knave; a lily-livered, action-taking, whoreson, glass-
15   gazing, super-serviceable, finical rogue; one-trunk-inheriting
slave; one that wouldst be a bawd in way of good service, and
art nothing but the composition of a knave, beggar, coward,

---

7. *Lipsbury Pinfold*   In the sixteenth and seventeenth centuries "bury,"
in origin a form of "borough," is still found as an independent word = a
court, or a manor-house; compare *O.E.D.*, *sb.*, 1598: "The name of Alder-
man's bury (which is to say a Court) there kept in their Bury or Court-hall."
Therefore the first part of the name "Lipsbury" would stand out and the
whole be more readily interpreted as "the prison or trap belonging to the
court of my lips or teeth." *care for*   pay attention to, with a quibble on the
sense "like" from line 6.

12. *broken meats*   leftover food.

13. *three-suited, hundred-pound*   all hyphenated together in F. Three
suits a year were part of the allowance of a servant (compare III.iv.120).
"Hundred-pound" is commonly taken as an allusion to "a minimum
property-qualification for knights" (Onions), but even the charge of being a
pretender to gentility does not seem insulting enough here.

14. *lily-livered*   without the blood in the liver which a brave man has
(compare *2 Henry IV*, IV.iii.113: "the liver white and pale, which is the
badge of pusillanimity and cowardice"). *action-taking*   taking legal action
rather than fighting. *glass-gazing*   always looking at yourself in a mirror.

15. *super-serviceable*   offering more service than is needed (see line 16),
obsequious; compare IV.vi.242–4. *one-trunk-inheriting*   possessing (compare IV.vi.122) one trunk (of effects); the first hyphen is missing from F
and both are missing from Q.

pandar, and the son and heir of a mongrel bitch; one whom I
will beat into clamorous whining if thou deni'st the least syl-
20 lable of thy addition.

OSWALD

Why, what a monstrous fellow art thou thus to rail on one
that is neither known of thee nor knows thee!

KENT

What a brazen-faced varlet art thou to deny thou knowest me!
Is it two days since I tripped up thy heels and beat thee before
25 the King? Draw, you rogue; for though it be night yet the
moon shines. I'll make a sop o'th'moonshine of you, you
whoreson cullionly barber-monger. Draw!

OSWALD

Away! I have nothing to do with thee.

KENT

Draw, you rascal! You come with letters against the King and
30 take Vanity the puppet's part against the royalty of her father.
Draw, you rogue, or I'll so carbonado your shanks—draw, you
rascal; come your ways!

---

19. *clamorous*   Q; F has "clamours".
20. *addition*   see I.i.136, n.
26. *sop o'th'moonshine*   A sop is something steeped in liquid, here
perhaps in a puddle reflecting the moon (Arden). Moonshine was also a name
for a dish made from eggs, so that "make mincemeat of you" might perhaps
be the modern equivalent for the phrase (New Cambridge).
27. *cullionly*   rascally; compare *2 Henry VI*, I.iii.38: "Away, base cul-
lions!". *barber-monger*   one who is always going to the barber's.
30. *Vanity*   a character in morality plays like *Lusty Juventus* or the
interlude adapted from it in *Sir Thomas More*, IV.i. These were sometimes
played by puppets, but puppet is also a term of contempt, usually for a
woman (compare *O.E.D.*, 1,1601: "Is it not a shame, that women . . . should
make themselves such pictures puppets and peacocks as they do?").
31. *carbonado*   flesh grilled after being scored across ("scotched"); compare *Coriolanus*, IV.v.187: "he scotch'd him and notch'd him like a carbonado."
32. *come your ways*   come on; Compare "away" = "*this* way," line 127
below.

OSWALD

Help, ho! murder! help!

KENT

Strike, you slave! Stand, rogue! Stand, you neat slave! Strike!
[*Beats him.*]

OSWALD

35   Help, ho! murder, murder!
Enter EDMUND, *with his rapier drawn;* CORNWALL, REGAN,
GLOUCESTER, *Servants.*

EDMUND

How now, What's the matter? Part!

KENT

With you goodman boy, if you please; come, I'll flesh ye; come
on young master!

GLOUCESTER

Weapons? Arms? What's the matter here?

CORNWALL

40   Keep peace, upon your lives!
He dies that strikes again. What is the matter?

REGAN

The messengers from our sister and the King.

CORNWALL

What is your difference? Speak.

OSWALD

I am scarce in breath, my lord.

---

35. S.D. *with ... drawn*   Q; not in F.
37. *With you*   I'm after you! Compare Lysander angrily pursuing De-
metrius in *A Midsummer Night's Dream*, III.ii.403: "I will be with thee
straight." *goodman*   used in addressing those below the rank of gentleman;
here meant as an insult. *flesh*   to initiate into bloodshed, as if he had never
fought before.
43. *difference*   See II.i.121 above.

KENT

45   No marvel, you have so bestirred your valour.
You cowardly rascal, Nature disclaims in thee; a tailor made
thee.

CORNWALL

Thou art a strange fellow; a tailor make a man?

KENT

A tailor sir; a stone-cutter or a painter could not have made
50   him so ill, though they had been but two years o'th'trade.

CORNWALL

Speak yet, how grew your quarrel?

OSWALD

This ancient ruffian sir, whose life I have spared
At suit of his grey beard—

KENT

Thou whoreson zed, thou unnecessary letter!
55   My lord, if you will give me leave, I will tread this unbolted
villain into mortar and daub the wall of a jakes with him.
Spare my grey beard, you wagtail?

---

46. *disclaims in thee*   gives up her claims in your begetting.

48. *tailor*   Cornwall is humoring him, for the expression was proverbial
(Tilley T 17).

50. *years*   Q has "hours", an actor's exaggeration.

53. *suit*   petition, i.e., pitying his age.

54. *zed . . . unnecessary*   The place of "z" could be taken by "s" in many
words; compare the variant forms in notes to I.i.65; II.i.118.

55–6. *tread . . . mortar*   like lumpy, unsifted lime which must be broken
up before it can be made into mortar. *unbolted*   unsifted, unrefined, un-
tried; compare *Henry V*, II.ii.127–37: "Show men dutiful? . . . of noble
family? . . . religious? . . . constant? . . . Such and so finely bolted didst thou
seem."

56. *jakes*   privy.

57. *wagtail*   a familiar or contemptuous form of address for a man or
a young woman; compare *O.E.D., sb.,* 3, 1607: "Wagtail, salute them all;
they are friends."

CORNWALL

Peace sirrah!
You beastly knave, know you no reverence?

KENT

60   Yes sir; but anger hath a privilege.

CORNWALL

Why art thou angry?

KENT

That such a slave as this should wear a sword,
Who wears no honesty. Such smiling rogues as these,
Like rats, oft bite the holy cords atwain
65   Which are too intrince t'unloose; smooth every passion
That in the natures of their lords rebel,
Being oil to fire, snow to the colder moods;
Renege, affirm, and turn their halcyon beaks
With every gale and vary of their masters,
70   Knowing naught (like dogs) but following.
A plague upon your epileptic visage!
Smile you my speeches, as I were a Fool?
Goose, if I had you upon Sarum Plain,
I'd drive ye cackling home to Camelot.

---

64. *holy cords* of matrimony (see IV.vi.243–4).

65. *too intrince* too intricate (from "intrinsicate," *Antony and Cleopatra*, V.ii.302–3: "this knot intrinsicate Of life ... untie"); F has "t'intrince", Q "to intrench" (misheard). *smooth* humor; compare *Titus Andronicus*, V.ii.140: "Yield to his humour, smooth and speak him fair."

67. *Being ... the* Q has "Bring oyle to stir, snow to their".

68. *Renege* deny; Q has "Reneag", F "Reuenge". *halcyon* kingfisher; believed to be a weather vane if dried and hung up.

69. *vary* change.

72. *Smile* F has "Smoile", Q "smoyle". The variation between "i" and "oi" in words with M.E. "ī" is not a matter of dialect; so Kent is not speaking in dialect here (as some editors, with I.iv.1–2 in mind, have thought). See Dobson, § 259.

73–4. *Sarum Plain ... Camelot* Salisbury Plain ... Winchester (where King Arthur kept his court).

CORNWALL

75   What, art thou mad, old fellow?

GLOUCESTER

How fell you out, say that.

KENT

No contraries hold more antipathy
Than I and such a knave.

CORNWALL

Why dost thou call him knave? What is his fault?

KENT

80   His countenance likes me not.

CORNWALL

No more perchance does mine, nor his, nor hers.

KENT

Sirs, 'tis my occupation to be plain:
I have seen better faces in my time
Than stands on any shoulder that I see
85   Before me at this instant.

CORNWALL

This is some fellow
Who having been praised for bluntness doth affect
A saucy roughness and constrains the garb
Quite from his nature. He cannot flatter, he!
An honest mind and plain, he must speak truth!
90   And they will take it, so; if not, he's plain.

---

80. *His . . . me*   See Appendix C, p. 225.

87. *saucy*   insolent towards superiors (*O.E.D.*); compare *As You Like It*,
III.ii.278: "a saucy lackey".

87-8. *and . . . nature*   and so forces this manner of doing things quite out
of its (see Appendix C, p. 224) honest nature; compare *O.E.D.*, "garb" *sb.*², 3,
1618: "Carrying himselfe . . . overloftily, and above the garb of a fellow-
citizen".

89. *An . . . plain*   Q has "he must be plaine".

90. *And*   if (Appendix C, p. 225).

These kind of knaves I know, which in this plainness
Harbour more craft and more corrupter ends
Than twenty silly-duckling observants
That stretch their duties nicely.

KENT

95   Sir, in good faith, in sincere verity,
Under th'allowance of your great aspéct,
Whose influence like the wreath of radiant fire
On flickering Phoebus' front—

CORNWALL

What mean'st by this?

KENT

To go out of my dialect which you discommend so much. I
100   know sir, I am no flatterer. He that beguiled you in a plain
accent was a plain knave, which for my part I will not be,
though I should win your displeasure to entreat me to't.

CORNWALL

What was th'offence you gave him?

OSWALD

I never gave him any:
105   It pleased the King his master very late

93–4. *silly-duckling . . . nicely*   foolishly bowing, overattentive servants
who exaggerate their responsibilities punctiliously (compare V.iii.141).

96. *under . . . aspéct*   subject to the approbation (compare I.iv.185) of
your eminent appearance, or (in the technical sense from astrology) the way
in which you as a star or sun look upon (and therefore influence) the earth.

98. *flickering Phoebus' front*   the forehead (compare I.iv.166) of the sun,
whose light is unsteady (like court favor); F has "flicking", Q "flitkering".

99. *dialect*   personal, not local, manner of speech (compare *Measure
for Measure*, I.ii.175–7: "in her youth There is a . . . dialect Such as move
men"). Kent has just been playing the flatterer, in parody.

100–2. *He that . . . to't.*   The "fellow" (line 85) who deceived you in the
frank terms you mention was an out-and-out rascal, which I will never be,
even though I should evoke your anger so much that it would beg me to
be one.

105. *late*   lately; compare I.iv.183.

To strike at me upon his misconstruction,
When he, compact and flattering his displeasure,
Tripped me behind; being down, insulted, railed,
And put upon him such a deal of man
110   That worthied him, got praises of the King
For him attempting who was self-subdued;
And in the fleshment of this dread exploit
Drew on me here again.

KENT

None of these rogues and cowards
But Ajax is their fool.

CORNWALL

Fetch forth the stocks.
115   You stubborn ancient knave, you reverend braggart,
We'll teach you.

KENT

Sir I am too old to learn;
Call not your stocks for me; I serve the King,
On whose employment I was sent to you.
You shall do small respect, show too bold malice

---

107. *compact*   leagued (with the King); see Appendix C, p. 223; Q has "conjunct" (compare V.i.12).

108. *being . . . insulted*   I being down, he showed scornful delight (compare *O.E.D.*, *v.*, 1, 1619: "The Lion being dead even Hares insult").

109–11. *put . . . self-subdued*   took upon himself so much manliness as to make him into one of the "worthies" or heroes, and was praised by the King for attacking a man who was self-controlled.

112. *fleshment*   the action of "fleshing" (compare II.ii.37), hence the excitement resulting from a first success (*O.E.D.*).

113–4. *None . . . fool.*   All rogues and cowards like the one who has been speaking, can make a fool of a "blockish Ajax" (*Troilus and Cressida*, I.iii.375), like Cornwall. The insult is worse if Ajax, "A'Iax" in Q, here = "a jakes," i.e., privy, as Jesperson believes (*Society for Pure English*, Clarendon Press, Oxford, England, 1929, Tract XXXIII, pp. 424–5).

115. *stubborn*   untameable. *ancient*   Q has "ausrent", miscorrected to "miscreant".

120   Against the grace and person of my master,
Stocking his messenger.

CORNWALL

Fetch forth the stocks;
As I have life and honour, there shall he sit till noon.

REGAN

Till noon? Till night my lord, and all night too.

KENT

Why madam, if I were your father's dog
125   You should not use me so.

REGAN

Sir, being his knave, I will.

Stocks brought out.

CORNWALL

This is a fellow of the self-same colour
Our sister speaks of. Come, bring away the stocks.

GLOUCESTER

Let me beseech your Grace not to do so.
His fault is much and the good King his master
130   Will check him for't. Your purposed low correction
Is such as basest and contemned'st wretches
For pilferings and most common trespasses
Are punished with. The King must take it ill

---

121. *stocking*   Q has "stobing", miscorrected to "stopping".

125. S.D.   The stocks would be brought downstage and well to one side to allow for the playing of the next two scenes.

126. *colour*   kind; Q has "nature".

127. *away*   along; compare *Measure for Measure*, II.i.41, where Elbow enters with the officers and Froth and Pompey, saying, "Come, bring them away."

129–33. *His . . . with.*   Q, not in F.

130. *check*   reprove; compare *Julius Caesar*, IV.iii.94–6: "Cassius is . . . Check'd like a bondman."

131. *contemned'st*   Capell; Q has "contaned" corrected to "temnest".

133. *must*   Q; F has "his master, needs must".

That he, so slightly valued in his messenger,
135 Should have him thus restrained.

CORNWALL
I'll answer that.

REGAN
My sister may receive it much more worse
To have her gentleman abused, assaulted,
For following her affairs. Put in his legs.
—[*To Cornwall*] Come my lord, away.
                    [*Exeunt all except* GLOUCESTER *and* KENT.]

GLOUCESTER
140 I am sorry for thee friend; 'tis the duke's pleasure,
Whose disposition, all the world well knows,
Will not be rubbed nor stopped. I'll entreat for thee.

KENT
Pray do not sir; I have watched and travelled hard;
Some time I shall sleep out, the rest I'll whistle;
145 A good man's fortune may grow out at heels.
Give you good morrow.

GLOUCESTER
The duke's too blame in this; 'twill be ill taken.   *Exit.*

---

134. *he, so*   F has "he so", Q "hee's so".
135. *answer*   take responsibility for.
138. Q, not in F.
139. *Come . . . away.*   Assigned to Cornwall in F; but Gloucester, thus addressed, remains. Q "Come my good Lord away?" continues Regan's speech as here.
142. *rubbed*   impeded: a common seventeenth-century sense of the noun is "an obstacle or hindrance" (*O.E.D.*, *sb.*[1], 3, 1590: "Some small rubs . . . cast in my way to hinder my coming forth . . .").
143. *watched*   stayed awake (compare II.i.19).
147. *too*   "Blame" was taken as an adjective meaning blameworthy. (See *O.E.D.*, *v.*, 6, 1594–1633.) The sense is not that it is the duke's fault, but that he has gone too far. Compare I.ii.41 and note.

KENT

Good King, that must approve the common saw,
Thou out of heaven's benediction com'st
150 To the warm sun.
Approach, thou beacon to this under globe,
That by thy comfortable beams I may
Peruse this letter. Nothing almost sees miracles
But misery. I know 'tis from Cordelia
155 Who hath most fortunately been informed
Of my obscurèd course: "And shall find time
From this enormous state, seeking to give
Losses their remedies." All weary and o'erwatched,
Take vantage, heavy eyes, not to behold
160 This shameful lodging.
Fortune good night; smile once more, turn thy wheel.   *Sleeps.*

---

148. *approve* prove, show to be true; compare II.iv.177.

149–50. *Thou ... sun* You go from good to worse, as from shade to heat; a common proverb (Tilley G 272).

152. *comfortable* comforting; see I.iv.282, n.

153. *miracles* Q has "my rackles" corrected to "my wracke" which is a guess. The whole sentence is awkward if it means "it takes misery to appreciate miracles"; Q may conceal a better reading and F show simply another guess.

156. *obscurèd* fallen into obscurity (because of my disguise).

156–8. *And ... remedies* extracts, imperfectly read by moonlight, from the letter which gives him the information he passes on in III.i.30ff. If, as seems necessary, we take it to have been sent to Kent at Albany's (whence he has been absent bearing letters since I.v., immediately after Lear's quarrel with Goneril), then it follows that the letter must have been written before the quarrels were known of in France and that the invasion must be planned in order to gain Cordelia's portion of the kingdom—not to defend her father. See Introduction p. xxvii and Greg *MLR* XXXV (1940), 442–3.

157. *from ... state* away from (compare II.i.122) this kingdom (compare IV.iii.3), which is abnormal, outrageous, wicked (compare *O.E.D.*, "enormous," 2, 1631: "The Pope's rapines and enormous proceedings").

158. *o'erwatched* Compare line 143 above.

159. *vantage* opportunity; compare *Macbeth*, I.ii.31–33: "But the Norweyan lord, surveying vantage, ... Began a fresh assault."

161. S.D. Q; not in F.

Scene iii: Enter EDGAR.

EDGAR

I heard myself proclaimed,
And by the happy hollow of a tree
Escaped the hunt. No port is free, no place
That guard and most unusual vigilance
5   Does not attend my taking. Whiles I may 'scape
I will preserve myself; and am bethought
To take the basest and most poorest shape
That ever penury in contempt of man
Brought near to beast. My face I'll grime with filth,
10 Blanket my loins, elf all my hairs in knots,
And with presented nakedness outface
The winds and persecutions of the sky.
The country gives me proof and precedent
Of Bedlam beggars who, with roaring voices,
15 Strike in their numbed and mortified bare arms
Pins, wooden pricks, nails, sprigs of rosemary;
And with this horrible object, from low farms,
Poor pelting villages, sheep-cotes, and mills,

Scene iii   The stage is big enough for Kent to sleep on one side while
Edgar, on the other, is assumed to be in another, unspecified place.

1. *proclaimed*   officially announced by word of mouth in public places
(Latin *proclamare* to cry out).

2. *happy*   lucky, suitable (from "hap" = "chance").

5. *attend my taking*   wait in readiness to capture me.

8. *in . . . man*   despising man; to show how despicable man is.

10. *elf*   tangle and twist as if an elf had done it; compare *O.E.D.*, "elf-
lock," 1637: "unkemb'd scattered hair . . . in long Elfe-locks".

11. *presented*   exhibited, enacted, as on stage. (The verb "present" is
used both of characters and of plays.)

13. *proof*   evidence, experience, knowledge.

15. *mortified*   deadened, insensible. *bare*   Q; not in F.

17. *object*   sight; compare V.iii.235.

18. *pelting*   mean (apparently related to the nouns "pelt, peltry, paltry"
= "trash"). *sheepcotes*   Q; F has "sheeps-coates".

Sometimes with lunatic bans, sometime with prayers,
20   Enforce their charity: "Poor Turlygod, poor Tom!"
That's something yet; Edgar I nothing am.   *Exit.*

Scene iv: Enter LEAR, FOOL, *and* GENTLEMAN, *[to* KENT *in the stocks].*

LEAR

'Tis strange that they should so depart from home
And not send back my messenger.

GENTLEMAN

            As I learned,
The night before there was no purpose in them
Of this remove.

KENT

Hail to thee noble master!

LEAR

5   Ha!
Mak'st thou this shame thy pastime?

KENT

             No my lord.

FOOL

Ha, ha! He wears cruel garters. Horses are tied by the heads,
dogs and bears by th' neck, monkeys by th' loins, and men by

---

19. *bans*   curses; compare the "blasphemous bannes" of the giantess in *The Faerie Queene*, III.vii.39.

20. *Turlygod*   unexplained.

Scene iv   1. *they*   Cornwall and Regan, to whom Kent was dispatched to announce Lear's coming (I.v.1). The Gentleman has gone on ahead after Kent; finding them away, he has returned to tell Lear, who has reached only the intermediate place where Gloucester lives. See I.v.1.

7. *cruel*   pun on "crewel" = "worsted"; compare II.ii.13–14.

th' legs. When a man's over-lusty at legs, then he wears
10   wooden nether-stocks.

LEAR

What's he that hath so much thy place mistook
To set thee here?

KENT

It is both he and she,
Your son and daughter.

LEAR

No.

KENT

15   Yes.

LEAR

No, I say.

KENT

I say yea.

LEAR

No no, they would not.

KENT

Yes, they have.

LEAR

20   By Jupiter, I swear no!

KENT

By Juno, I swear ay!

LEAR

They durst not do 't,
They could not, would not do't; 'tis worse than murder

---

9. *over-lusty at legs* given to running away, or to vagrancy. *nether-
stocks* stockings (in opposition to "upper-stocks" = "breeches").
18–19. *LEAR No no, ... have.* Q; not in F.
21. *KENT By Juno ... ay!* F; not in Q.

To do upon respect such violent outrage.
Resolve me with all modest haste which way
25   Thou mightst deserve or they impose this usage,
Coming from us.

KENT

My lord, when at their home
I did commend your Highness' letters to them,
Ere I was risen from the place that showed
My duty kneeling, came there a reeking post,
30   Stewed in his haste, half breathless, panting forth
From Goneril his mistress, salutations;
Delivered letters, spite of intermission,
Which presently they read; on whose contents
They summoned up their meiny, straight took horse,
35   Commanded me to follow and attend
The leisure of their answer, gave me cold looks;
And meeting here the other messenger
Whose welcome I perceived had poisoned mine—
Being the very fellow which of late
40   Displayed so saucily against your Highness—
Having more man than wit about me, drew.
He raised the house with loud and coward cries.
Your son and daughter found this trespass worth
The shame which here it suffers.

---

23. *upon respect*   on consideration, with deliberation; or (with Johnson)
upon the respect due to the King's messenger.

24. *modest*   moderate, i.e., sober; compare IV.vii.5.

27. *commend*   deliver (Latin *com* + *mandare* to commit into someone's
hands; compare III.i.19).

30. *panting*   Q; F has "painting".

32. *spite of intermission*   even though they were interrupting the receipt
and answer of my letters.

33. *whose*   Q; F has "those". *presently*   at once.

34. *meiny*   retinue, retainers; Q has "men".

40. *Displayed so saucily*   acted with such ostentation and insolence
(compare II.ii.87).

FOOL

45　Winter's not gone yet if the wild geese fly that way.

> Fathers that wear rags
> 　Do make their children blind,
> But fathers that bear bags
> 　Shall see their children kind.

50　　　　　Fortune, that arrant whore,
> 　Ne'er turns the key to th' poor.

But for all this thou shalt have as many dolours for thy daughters as thou canst tell in a year.

LEAR

O how this mother swells up toward my heart!
55　Hysterica passio, down, thou climbing sorrow;
Thy element's below. Where is this daughter?

KENT

With the earl sir, here within.

LEAR

Follow me not: stay here.　　　　　　　　　　　*Exit.*

GENTLEMAN

Made you no more offence but what you speak of?

---

45. *Winter's . . . way*　If the geese (which migrate as winter comes on)
are flying off (compare line 85)—i.e., revolting, deserting their father's interests—in that way, the time of trouble is not over yet. Lines 45–53 are
not in Q.

51. *turns the key*　unlocks the door.

52–3. *as many . . . year*　as many sorrows (with a pun on "dollars") as
you can recount, or count, in a year. *for thy daughters*　on account of them
(with "dolours") or to give to them (with "dollars"—as if he "bore bags"
of them).

54. *mother*　hysteria, from Greek ὑστέρα the womb, whence, as women
were more susceptible to the disease than men, it was thought to arise.

55. *Hysterica passio*　the old name (= "suffering belonging to the
womb") for hysteria. F and Q both have the mistaken form "*Historica*".

56. *thy element*　whichever of the four (earth, water, air, fire) is your
proper place.

KENT

60   None.

How chance the king comes with so small a number?

FOOL

And thou hadst been set i'th'stocks for that question, thou'dst
well deserved it.

KENT

Why, Fool?

FOOL

65   We'll set thee to school to an ant, to teach thee there's no
labouring i'th'winter. All that follow their noses are led by
their eyes but blind men, and there's not a nose among twenty
but can smell him that's stinking. Let go thy hold when a great
wheel runs down a hill, lest it break thy neck with following;
70   but the great one that goes upward, let him draw thee after.
When a wise man gives thee better counsel, give me mine
again. I would ha' none but knaves use it, since a fool gives it.

           That sir which serves and seeks for gain
              And follows but for form,
75   Will pack when it begins to rain
              And leave thee in the storm.
           But I will tarry, the Fool will stay
              And let the wise man fly;

65–8. *there's . . . stinking.* Nothing can be done about Lear's troubles
(compare line 45). All except the blind can see that (and desert him), and
even the blind can smell it out (and leave him too). Q exaggerates "twenty"
to "a 100" (compare II.ii.50).

69. *following*   Q has "following it,".

72. *ha' . . . use*   New Cambridge text. It is based on the plausible conjecture that the F reading ("hause . . . follow") is a conflation of the corrections "ha' " for Q "have" and "use" for Q "follow" (made side by side in
the margin), while, by either the collator's or the printer's oversight, "follow"
was printed too.

75. *pack*   leave (compare *Hamlet*, III.iv.211: "This man shall set me
packing.").

77–80. *But I . . . perdy.*   After his cynical play with the worldly wisdom
of deserting the king, the Fool shows how he stands himself; he calls the

The knave turns fool that runs away,

80   The Fool no knave, perdy.

KENT

Where learned you this, Fool?

FOOL

Not i'th'stocks, fool.
[Re-]enter LEAR, with GLOUCESTER.

LEAR

Deny to speak with me? They are sick, they are weary,
They have travelled all the night? Mere fetches,
85 The images of revolt and flying off.
Fetch me a better answer.

GLOUCESTER

My dear lord,

You know the fiery quality of the duke,
How unremovable and fixed he is
In his own course.

LEAR

90 Vengeance, plague, death, confusion!
Fiery? What quality? Why, Gloucester, Gloucester,
I'ld speak with the Duke of Cornwall and his wife.

GLOUCESTER

Well my good lord, I have informed them so.

LEAR

Informed them? Dost thou understand me man?

---

worldly wise man, who deserts, a knave and a fool, while he thinks the Fool who stays is no knave at all.
    82. S.D.   placed here in Q; after line 80 in F.
    84. *fetches*   dodges (compare *O.E.D.*, *sb.*[1], 2, 1635: "the crafty fetches of the wily Prince . . ."). Q has "Iustice," a mere guess.
    85. *flying off*   desertion.
    93–4. *Well . . . man?*   not in Q.

GLOUCESTER

95   Ay my good lord.

LEAR

The King would speak with Cornwall; the dear father
Would with his daughter speak, commands their service.
Are they informed of this? My breath and blood!
Fiery? the fiery duke? Tell the hot duke that—

100   No, but not yet; may be he is not well:
Infirmity doth still neglect all office
Whereto our health is bound, we are not ourselves
When ⌐nature⌐ being oppressed, commands the mind
To suffer with the body. I'll forbear

105   And am fallen out with my more headier will
To take the indisposed and sickly fit
For the sound man. Death on my state! Wherefore
Should he sit here? This act persuades me
That this remotion of the duke and her

110   Is practice only. Give me my servant forth.
Go tell the duke and 's wife I'ld speak with them
Now, presently; bid them come forth and hear me
Or at their chamber door I'll beat the drum
Till it cry sleep to death.

---

97. *commands their service*   Alexander; Q has "commands her service" corrected from "come and tends servise"; F has "commands, tends, service" from Q uncorrected. Greg takes "her" to be a guess and attempts to defend "tends" = "tenders, offers," as another instance of Lear's violent alteration of mood in the scene. But "their" could be misread as "tends" in what appears to have been a badly written passage.

98. *Are . . . blood!*   not in Q.

101. *office*   Compare II.i.104.

107. *state*   greatness, power, majesty (compare *Richard III*, III.vii.205: "I am unfit for state and majesty").

109. *remotion*   removal (compare line 4), departure; he means the excuse of their removal as in lines 84–5.

110. *practice*   See n. to I.ii.164 and to II.i.71.

112. *presently*   Compare line 33.

114. *cry . . . death*   shout sleep into non-existence, i.e., keep them awake.

GLOUCESTER

115   I would have all well betwixt you.   *Exit.*

LEAR

O me my heart, my rising heart! But down.

FOOL

Cry to it nuncle, as the cockney did to the eels when she put
'em i' th' paste alive. She knapped 'em o'th'coxcombs with a
stick and cried "Down wantons, down!" 'Twas her brother
120   that, in pure kindness to his horse, buttered his hay.
[*Re-*]*enter* GLOUCESTER, *with* CORNWALL, REGAN, *and Servants.*

LEAR

Good morrow to you both.

CORNWALL

Hail to your Grace!
                                    KENT *here set at liberty.*

REGAN

I am glad to see your Highness.

LEAR

Regan, I think you are. I know what reason
I have to think so; if thou shouldst not be glad,
125   I would divorce me from thy mother's tomb,
Sepulchring an adultress. [*To Kent*] O are you free?
Some other time for that.—Beloved Regan,
Thy sister's naught. O Regan, she hath tied

117–20. *Cry . . . hay.*   You are as foolish to try to quell your rising heart
by crying to it as was the cockney—the silly or squeamish woman—who
could not bear to kill the eels before putting them in a pie; she expected
them to lie down when she rapped them over the head and shouted, "Down,
you frisky things." In misguided tenderheartedness she was like the man
who buttered his horse's hay (with the result that the horse would not eat
it—ostlers sometimes did this so that they could then steal it themselves).
128. *naught*   worthless, wicked (compare *Romeo and Juliet*, III.ii.85–7:
"There's no . . . honesty in men; . . . all naught").

Sharp-toothed unkindness, like a vulture, here;
130   I can scarce speak to thee; thou'lt not believe
With how depraved a quality—O Regan—

REGAN

I pray you sir, take patience; I have hope
You less know how to value her desert
Than she to scant her duty.

LEAR

Say? How is that?

REGAN

135   I cannot think my sister in the least
Would fail her obligation. If sir perchance
She have restrained the riots of your followers,
'Tis on such ground, and to such wholesome end,
As clears her from all blame.

LEAR

140   My curses on her.

REGAN

O sir, you are old;
⌈Nature⌉in you stands on the very verge
Of his confine. You should be ruled and led

---

129. *like . . . here*   in my heart, as the vulture gnawed at the liver of Prometheus when he was punished by Zeus.

131. *With . . . quality*   in what a debased manner (compare *Merchant of Venice*, III.ii.6: "Hate counsels not in such a quality"); or with what a corrupted disposition or character (*O.E.D.*, "quality," 1, 1639: "He deserves no wife Of worthy quality . . .").

132–4. *I . . . duty*   I hope it is true that you are undervaluing her rather than that she is failing in her duty; Q "slacke" for "scant" perhaps anticipates line 239.

134–9. *Say . . . blame.*   not in Q.

137. *have*   See Appendix C, p. 225.

142. *confine*   place of confinement (compare *Tempest*, IV.i.120–1: "Spirits . . . I have from their confines call'd . . ."); or limit, boundary (compare *O.E.D.*, *sb.*², 1, b, 1599: ". . . the beginning and confine of the state and realm of Serifo . . .").

By some discretion that discerns your state
Better than you yourself; therefore I pray you
145   That to our sister you do make return;
Say you have wronged her.

LEAR

                              Ask her forgiveness?
Do you but mark how this becomes the house:
"Dear daughter, I confess that I am old;
Age is unnecessary; on my knees I beg
150   That you'll vouchsafe me raiment, bed, and food."

REGAN

Good sir, no more; these are unsightly tricks.
Return you to my sister.

LEAR

                              Never, Regan!
She hath abated me of half my train,
Looked black upon me, struck me with her tongue
155   Most serpent-like, upon the very heart.
All the stored vengeances of heaven fall
On her ingrateful top. Strike her young bones,
You taking airs, with lameness.

CORNWALL

                              Fie sir, fie!

LEAR

You nimble lightnings dart your blinding flames
160   Into her scornful eyes! Infect her beauty
You fen-sucked fogs, drawn by the pow'rful sun
To fall and blister her!

---

157. *young bones*   unborn child; compare *King Leir*, lines 844–7: "she breeds young bones, And that it is makes her so touchy sure."

158. *taking*   striking with disease, infecting, bewitching (compare *Merry Wives of Windsor*, IV.iv.27–31: "Herne the Hunter . . . blasts the tree, and takes the cattle . . .").

162. *blister her*   F has "blister", Q "blast her pride".

REGAN

O the blest gods!
So will you wish on me when the rash mood is on.

LEAR

No Regan, thou shalt never have my curse;
165   Thy tender-hefted nature shall not give
Thee o'er to harshness. Her eyes are fierce, but thine
Do comfort and not burn. 'Tis not in thee
To grudge my pleasures, to cut off my train,
To bandy hasty words, to scant my sizes,
170   And in conclusion to oppose the bolt
Against my coming in. Thou better know'st
The offices of nature, bond of childhood,
Effects of courtesy, dues of gratitude;
Thy half o' th' kingdom hast thou not forgot,
175   Wherein I thee endowed.

REGAN

Good sir, to th' purpose.

LEAR

Who put my man i'th'stocks?   *Tucket within.*

CORNWALL

What trumpet's that?

REGAN

I know't, my sister's. This approves her letter
That she would soon be here.
Enter OSWALD.
Is your lady come?

---

165. *tender-hefted*   set in a delicate . . . bodily frame (*O.E.D.*); to heft or
haft is to set in a handle.
169. *sizes*   legal allowances (for the necessities of life); compare *O.E.D.*,
sb.[1], 7, 1611: "A size is a portion of bread and ale."
172. *offices*   Compare II.i.104.
173. *effects*   Compare I.i.126.
177. *approves*   confirms; compare II.ii.148.

LEAR

This is a slave, whose easy, borrowed pride

180 Dwells in the sickly grace of her he follows.

Out varlet, from my sight!

CORNWALL

What means your Grace?

Enter GONERIL.

LEAR

Who stocked my servant? Regan I have good hope

Thou didst not know on't.—Who comes here? O heavens,

If you do love old men, if your sweet sway

185 Allow obedience, if you yourselves are old,

Make it your cause; send down and take my part.

[To Goneril] Art not ashamed to look upon this beard?—

O Regan will you take her by the hand?

GONERIL

Why not by th' hand sir? How have I offended?

190 All's not offence that indiscretion finds

And dotage terms so.

LEAR

O sides you are too tough!

Will you yet hold? How came my man i' th' stocks?

179–80. *whose . . . follows*   His arrogance is easy, i.e., compliant, is borrowed from his superiors, and depends upon Goneril's diseased favor (F has
"fickly"); compare II.ii.63–70; IV.vi.242–4. So New Cambridge; others hy-
phenate "easy-borrowed" and, with Q "fickle", take the meaning to be that
his haughtiness is borrowed too easily and will have to be given back when
Goneril's fickle favor is withdrawn.

182–3. *Who . . . on't.*   Assigned to Goneril in Q, with "struck" for
"stocked".

185. *Allow*   approve of; compare I.iv.185. Q omits "you" from this line.

188. Granville-Barker draws the producer's attention to the grouping as
Lear is "brought to a stand and to face the realities arrayed against him. . . .
On the one side stand Goneril and Regan and Cornwall in all authority. The
perplexed Gloucester hovers a little apart. On the other side is Lear, the Fool
at his feet, and his one servant, disarmed, freed but a minute since behind
him" (pp. 289–90).

CORNWALL

I set him there sir; but his own disorders
Deserved much less advancement.

LEAR

You? Did you?

REGAN

195   I pray you father, being weak, seem so.
If till the expiration of your month
You will return and sojourn with my sister,
Dismissing half your train, come then to me.
I am now from home, and out of that provision
200   Which shall be needful for your entertainment.

LEAR

Return to her? and fifty men dismissed?
No, rather I abjure all roofs and choose
To wage against the enmity o'th'air,
To be a comrade with the wolf and owl—
205   Necessity's sharp pinch! Return with her?
Why, the hot-blooded France, that dowerless took
Our youngest born, I could as well be brought
To knee his throne and, squire-like, pension beg
To keep base life afoot. Return with her?
210   Persuade me rather to be slave and sumpter
To this detested groom.

GONERIL

At your choice sir.

---

199. *provision*   condition of being prepared, having made arrangements in advance.

203. *wage*   struggle.

206. *hot-blooded*   passionate; compare *Merry Wives of Windsor*, V.v.3–4: "Now the hot-blooded gods assist me! Remember, Jove, thou wast a bull for thy Europa . . .", where, as here, F has "hot-bloodied". Q reads "the hot blood in *France*" here.

210–11. *sumpter . . . groom*   a pack horse, or its driver, for Oswald.

LEAR

I prithee daughter do not make me mad.
I will not trouble thee my child; farewell;
We'll no more meet, no more see one another.
215 But yet thou art my flesh, my blood, my daughter—
Or rather a disease that's in my flesh,
Which I must needs call mine. Thou art a boil,
A plague-sore or embossed carbuncle
In my corrupted blood. But I'll not chide thee:
220 Let shame come when it will, I do not call it;
I do not bid the thunder-bearer shoot
Nor tell tales of thee to high-judging Jove.
Mend when thou canst; be better at thy leisure;
I can be patient; I can stay with Regan,
225 I and my hundred knights.

REGAN

                    Not altogether so.
I looked not for you yet, nor am provided
For your fit welcome. Give ear sir to my sister;
For those that mingle reason with your passion
Must be content to think you old, and so—
230 But she knows what she does.

LEAR

                    Is this well spoken?

REGAN

I dare avouch it sir. What, fifty followers?
Is it not well? What should you need of more?
Yea, or so many, sith that both charge and danger
Speak 'gainst so great a number? How in one house

---

216. *that's in*   Q has "that lies within".
218. *embossed carbuncle*   swollen, protuberant tumor.
221. *thunder-bearer*   Jupiter or Jove.
228. *mingle . . . passion*   mix their own reason with, i.e., construe reasonably, your passionate outburst.
233. *charge*   expense; compare I.i.8.

91

235   Should many people under two commands
     Hold amity? 'Tis hard, almost impossible.

GONERIL

Why might not you my lord receive attendance
From those that she calls servants, or from mine?

REGAN

     Why not, my lord? If then they chanced to slack ye
240   We could control them. If you will come to me
     (For now I spy a danger) I entreat you
     To bring but five and twenty; to no more
     Will I give place or notice.

LEAR

I gave you all.

REGAN

And in good time you gave it.

LEAR

245   Made you my guardians, my depositaries,
     But kept a reservation to be followed
     With such a number. What, must I come to you
     With five and twenty? Regan, said you so?

REGAN

And speak't again my lord; no more with me.

LEAR

250   Those wicked creatures yet do look well-favoured
     When others are more wicked; not being the worst
     Stands in some rank of praise. [*To Goneril*] I'll go with thee.
     Thy fifty yet doth double five and twenty
     And thou art twice her love.

---

239. *slack ye*   neglect, be slack in attending you; Q has "slack you".

245. *my guardians, my depositaries*   wardens and trustees of the kingdom on my behalf.

GONERIL

Hear me my lord;

255 What need you five and twenty, ten, or five,
To follow, in a house where twice so many
Have a command to tend you?

REGAN

What need one?

LEAR

O reason not the need; our basest beggars
Are in the poorest thing superfluous.
260 Allow not nature more than nature needs,
Man's life is cheap as beast's. Thou art a lady;
If only to go warm were gorgeous,
Why, nature needs not what thou gorgeous wear'st,
Which scarcely keeps thee warm. But for true need—
265 You heavens, give me that patience; patience I need—
You see me here, you gods, a poor old man,
As full of grief as age, wretched in both;
If it be you that stirs these daughters' hearts
Against their father, fool me not so much
270 To bear it tamely; touch me with noble anger
And let not women's weapons, water drops,
Stain my man's cheeks. No you unnatural hags,
I will have such revenges on you both
That all the world shall—I will do such things—
275 What they are yet I know not, but they shall be

---

258. *reason* question; compare V.i.28.

259. *Are . . . superfluous* have something, even the meanest possession, over and above their bare necessities.

262–4. *If only . . . need—* If merely to be warm were to be sumptuously dressed [you would be poorly, because scantily, clothed]; your natural need is not for these sumptuous clothes, which hardly keep you warm at all. But true need on the other hand—(F has "need:") Lear breaks off to pray for self-control or fortitude, his own "true need".

266. *man* Q has "fellow".

The terrors of the earth! You think I'll weep;
No I'll not weep;   *Storm and Tempest.*
I have full cause of weeping, but this heart
Shall break into a hundred thousand flaws
280 Or ere I'll weep. O Fool I shall go mad.

> *Exeunt* [LEAR, GLOUCESTER, KENT, *and* FOOL.]

CORNWALL

Let us withdraw; 'twill be a storm.

REGAN

This house is little: the old man and's people
Cannot be well bestowed.

GONERIL

'Tis his own blame; hath put himself from rest,
285 And must needs taste his folly.

REGAN

For his particular I'll receive him gladly,
But not one follower.

GONERIL

So am I purposed.
Where is my Lord of Gloucester?

CORNWALL

Followed the old man forth.

> [*Re-*]*enter* GLOUCESTER.

He is returned.

GLOUCESTER

290 The King is in high rage.

---

279. *flaws* fragments; compare *O.E.D., sb.*[1], 2, 1607: "It will rankle worse, by reason of the flaw of iron remaining in the flesh."

284. *blame; hath* F and Q have "blame hath".

286. *For . . . particular* as far as he is concerned (compare *Coriolanus,* IV.vii.12–14: "Yet I wish, sir,—I mean for your particular—you had not Joined in commission with him . . .").

289. S.D. After line 288 in F, Q.

CORNWALL

Whither is he going?

GLOUCESTER

He calls to horse but will I know not whither.

CORNWALL

'Tis best to give him way; he leads himself.

GONERIL

My lord, entreat him by no means to stay.

GLOUCESTER

Alack the night comes on, and the high winds
295   Do sorely ruffle. For many miles about
There's scarce a bush.

REGAN

O sir, to wilful men
The injuries that they themselves procure
Must be their schoolmasters. Shut up your doors;
He is attended with a desperate train
300   And what they may incense him to, being apt
To have his ear abused, wisdom bids fear.

CORNWALL

Shut up your doors my lord, 'tis a wild night;
My Regan counsels well. Come out o' th' storm.   *Exeunt.*

Act III, Scene i: Storm still. Enter KENT *and a* Gentleman
severally.

KENT

Who's there besides foul weather?

290–1. *Whither . . . horse*   not in Q.
294. *high*   Q has "bleak".
295. *ruffle*   bluster (compare *O.E.D.*, v², 3. 1624: "Such an extreme gust
of wind and weather so ruffled in the trees and Church . . ."); Q has "russel".
296. *scarce*   Q has "not".
301. *abused*   Compare I.iii.20, IV.i.22.
Act III, scene i   S.D.   *severally*   separately; Q has "at severall doores"

GENTLEMAN

One minded like the weather, most unquietly.

KENT

I know you. Where's the King?

GENTLEMAN

Contending with the fretful elements;
5   Bids the wind blow the earth into the sea,
Or swell the curled waters 'bove the main,
That things might change or cease; tears his white hair,
Which the impetuous blasts with eyeless rage
Catch in their fury and make nothing of;
10   Strives in his little world of man to outscorn
The to-and-fro conflicting wind and rain.
This night, wherein the cub-drawn bear would couch,
The lion and the belly-pinched wolf
Keep their fur dry, unbonneted he runs,
15   And bids what will take all.

KENT

But who is with him?

(see Introduction, p. xxii). Each makes his way forward, one bearing right, the other left. They speak at first from opposite sides of the stage and meet eventually well downstage at line 17. The dialogue shows this to be out of doors; it was Rowe who first called the place "A Heath".

     6. *main*   mainland (compare *O.E.D.*, sb.[1], 4, 1600: "Not far from the main are certain dry and rocky isles").

     7–15. *tears . . . take all.*   Q; not in F.

     10. *little . . . man*   "because in the little frame of man's body there is a representation of the Universal [i.e., the universe], and (by allusion) a kind of participation of all the parts thereof [of the 'three sorts of living natures Angelical, Rational, and Brutal'], therefore was man called *Microcosmos*, or the little world" (Raleigh, *The History of the World*, 1614, I, chapter ii, § 5, "That Man is (as it were) a little world"). *outscorn*   defeat by scorning (*O.E.D.*)—exactly what Lear does (III.ii.16–21).

     12. *cub-drawn*   sucked dry by her cubs, and therefore fierce because hungry (Arden ed. compares *As You Like It*, IV.iii.125: "Food to the suck'd and hungry lioness"). *couch*   lie hidden (compare *Hamlet*, V.i.216: "Couch we awhile and mark").

     15. *bids . . . all*   calls for whatever *will* come, to overtake all things.

GENTLEMAN

None but the Fool, who labours to outjest
His heart-struck injuries.

KENT

Sir, I do know you,
And dare upon the warrant of my note
Commend a dear thing to you. There is division,
20   Although as yet the face of it is covered
With mutual cunning, 'twixt Albany and Cornwall,
Who have—as who have not, that their great stars
Throned and set high?—servants, who seem no less,
Which are to France the spies and speculations
25   Intelligent of our state. What hath been seen,
Either in snuffs and packings of the dukes,
Or the hard rein which both of them hath borne
Against the old kind King; or something deeper

---

16. *outjest* dispel by jesting.

17. *heart-struck* Compare II.iv.154–5. *Sir . . . you* The emphatic "do"·
and the repetition of "know you" from line 3 perhaps indicate that they now
meet at close quarters—well downstage if the "ring" of line 47 is to be
clearly seen.

18–19. *dare . . . you* on the assurance given by my knowledge (Q "Arte"),
I dare to entrust (compare II.iv.27) to you an important matter.

20. *face* outward appearance (compare Jonson *Bartholomew Fair*, 1614,
I.vi.66–9: "it . . . hath a face of offence with the weak, . . . but that face may
have a veil put over it . . .").

22–9. *Who . . . furnishings* not in Q.

23. *no less* i.e., merely servants, not spies.

24. *speculations* observers, spies (compare classical Latin *speculator*,
spy, and late Latin *speculatio*, spying).

25. *intelligent* bearing intelligence, information (compare III.v.9, III.vii.
10, and the noun "intelligencer" = "spy").

26. *snuffs and packings* resentments (compare IV.vi.39) and intrigues
(Arden ed. 1 compares Milton, *On the new Forcers of Conscience*, c. 1645,
lines 13–14: "your tricks, Your plots and packing . . .").

27–8. *the hard . . . King* the cruel curb or check they have kept upon
the King (compare, for the metaphor, *Julius Caesar*, I.ii.35–6: "You bear too
stubborn and too strange a hand Over your friend . . .") or the way they
have ridden, i.e., acted, against him.

Whereof perchance these are but furnishings—
30 But true it is from France there comes a power
Into this scattered kingdom, who already,
Wise in our negligence, have secret feet
In some of our best ports and are at point
To show their open banner. Now to you:
35 If on my credit you dare build so far
To make your speed to Dover, you shall find
Some that will thank you, making just report
Of how unnatural and bemadding sorrow
The King hath cause to plain.
40 I am a gentleman of blood and breeding,
And from some knowledge and assurance offer
This office to you.

GENTLEMAN

I will talk further with you.

KENT

No, do not.
For confirmation that I am much more
45 Than my outwall, open this purse and take
What it contains. If you shall see Cordelia
(As fear not but you shall) show her this ring,
And she will tell you who your fellow is
That yet you do not know. Fie on this storm!
50 I will go seek the King.

---

29. *furnishings*— embellishments (compare *Romeo and Juliet*, IV.ii.34–
5: ". . . ornaments . . . to furnish me tomorrow"); the rest of the speech,
which F ends here with a full stop, is from Q.

30–42. *But . . . to you.*   Q; not in F.

30. *power*   army.

33. *at point*   Compare I.iv.300.

35. *credit*   trustworthiness.

37. *making . . . report*   goes with "you," i.e., "if you make accurate
report".

39. *plain*   lament, deplore.

42. *office*   Compare II.i.104; iv.101.

GENTLEMAN

Give me your hand. Have you no more to say?

KENT

Few words, but, to effect, more than all yet—
That when we have found the King (in which your pain
That way, I'll this) he that first lights on him
55   Holla the other.   *Exeunt* [*separate ways*].

Scene ii: Storm still. Enter LEAR *and* FOOL.

LEAR

Blow winds, and crack your cheeks; rage, blow.
You cataracts and hurricanoes, spout
Till you have drenched our steeples, drowned the cocks.
You sulph'rous and thought-executing fires,
5   Vaunt-couriers of oak-cleaving thunderbolts,
Singe my white head. And thou all-shaking thunder,
Strike flat the thick rotundity o'th'world,

---

52. *to effect*   to the purpose.
53–4. *in . . . this*   In seeking him, let your efforts (compare I.iv.262) take
you that way, while I go this way. This looks like a brisk exit from opposite sides of the platform—for the King is to enter immediately through one
of the doors at the back of the stage.

Scene ii S.D.   *Storm*   See Introduction, p. xxiv.
1. *blow.*   F and Q omit the stop.
2. *cataracts . . . spout*   F has "Cataracts, and Hyrricano's spout," Q
"caterickes, & Hircanios spout"; a reference to the Flood, *Genesis* 7:11,
where the Vulgate has "cataractae caeli" and "fontes abyssi magnae".
"Hurricano" = "waterspout"; compare *Troilus and Cressida*, V.ii.169–70:
"the dreadful spout Which shipmen do the hurricano call".
3. *drowned*   Q; F reads "drown". *cocks*   weather-cocks.
4. *thought-executing*   carrying into effect the thought of the gods. This
seems more appropriate than New Cambridge "acting (? killing) as quick as
thought" (compare *Tempest*, I.ii.201–3: "lightning . . . momentary And sight-
outrunning" or *Hamlet*, I.v.29–30: "swift as meditation"), based on Johnson's "doing execution with rapidity equal to thought."
5. *Vaunt-couriers*   fore-runners; in Harsnett, p. 12.

Crack Nature's moulds, all germens spill at once
That makes ingrateful man!

FOOL

10 O nuncle, court holy water in a dry house is better than this
rain-water out o' door. Good nuncle, in; ask thy daughters
blessing. Here's a night pities neither wise men nor fools.

LEAR

Rumble thy bellyful. Spit fire, spout rain.
Nor rain, wind, thunder, fire are my daughters.
15 I tax not you, you elements, with unkindness:
I never gave you kingdom, called you children;
You owe me no subscription. Then let fall
Your horrible pleasure. Here I stand your slave,
A poor, infirm, weak, and despised old man;
20 But yet I call you servile ministers,
That will with two pernicious daughters join
Your high-engendered battles 'gainst a head
So old and white as this. O, ho! 'tis foul.

FOOL

He that has a house to put's head in has a good head-piece.
25   The codpiece that will house

---

8. *moulds* matrices; compare *O.E.D.*, *sb.*[3], 2.c., 1566: "I think dame
Nature her self hath broken the mould." *all germens spill* destroy all the
seeds (compare *Macbeth*, IV.i.58–60: "though the treasure Of nature's ger-
men[s] tumble all together, E'en till destruction sicken . . .").

10. *court holy-water* Malone cites Cotgrave: "*Eau beniste de Cour.*
Court holy-water . . . flattering speeches . . ."

11–12. *daughters blessing* for two objects after "ask", compare V.iii.10.

15. *tax . . . with* accuse of. Q has "taske"; compare I.iv.320.

17. *subscription* submission; see I.ii.24, n.

20. *servile ministers* slavishly obedient servants or agents; compare *2
Henry VI*, V.ii.33–4: "O war, thou son of hell, Whom angry heavens do make
their minister . . ."

21. *will . . . join* Q has "have . . . join'd".

22. *your . . . battles* your battalions born high in heaven.

24. *head-piece* both helmet and brain (compare *Winter's Tale*, I.ii.226–7:
". . . the finer natures, . . . Of head-piece extraordinary").

25. *codpiece* the appendage at the front of close-fitting breeches; here
both phallus and fool (line 38). So the Fool claims in the following lines that

Before the head has any,
The head and he shall louse;
So beggars marry many.
The man that makes his toe
30   What he his heart should make,
Shall of a corn cry woe
And turn his sleep to wake.

For there was never yet fair woman but she made mouths in
a glass.

Enter KENT.

LEAR

35   No, I will be the pattern of all patience,
I will say nothing.

KENT

Who's there?

FOOL

Marry, here's Grace and a codpiece; that's a wise man and
a fool.

KENT

40   Alas sir, are you here? Things that love night
Love not such nights as these. The wrathful skies
Gallow the very wanderers of the dark

---

to be such a fool as to copulate before taking a house (to give a home to the
penis before the head) brings on lice, as in the many "marriages" of vagrants
and beggars.

29–32. *The man . . . wake.* To treat as if it were a toe what should be
taken to the heart—to kick away Cordelia (compare *Merchant of Venice*,
I.iii.112–13: "You . . . foot me as you spurn a stranger cur")—will lead to
pain in the very part where the trouble began, and so to sleeplessness. New
Cambridge ed. compares Tilley, H 317.

33–4. *For . . . glass.* For all pretty women—like Goneril and Regan—pull
faces (expressing contempt for you—compare *Midsummer Night's Dream*,
III.ii.238: "Make mouths upon me when I turn my back") even if only in
the mirror.

38. *Grace*   the King's Grace, Lear.

40. *are*   Q has "sit".

42. *Gallow . . . dark*   frighten (O.E. *a-gælwan*) wandering animals; compare III.i.12–14.

And make them keep their caves. Since I was man,
Such sheets of fire, such bursts of horrid thunder,
45   Such groans of roaring wind and rain, I never
Remember to have heard. Man's nature cannot carry
Th'affliction nor the fear.

LEAR

Let the great gods,
That keep this dreadful pudder o'er our heads,
Find out their enemies now. Tremble, thou wretch
50   That hast within thee undivulged crimes
Unwhipped of justice. Hide thee, thou bloody hand,
Thou perjured, and thou simular of virtue
That art incestuous. Caitiff, to pieces shake,
That under covert and convenient seeming
55   Hast practised on man's life. Close pent-up guilts,
Rive your concealing continents, and cry

---

47. *fear*   Q has "force".

47–57. *Let . . . grace*   Commentators on Juvenal *Satires* XIII. 223–6 (about the guilty who tremble when it thunders) are struck by the similarity of this passage. See also Appendix B, p. 210.

48. *pudder*   This and Q "Powther" are variants of "pother," commotion.

49. *Find . . . now*   by the fear they show, like the guilty in Juvenal.

52. *simular*   simulator (compare *O.E.D.*, A, 1526: "Hypocrites, that is to saye Simulars"). Q has "simular man".

53. *Caitiff*   villain.

54. *covert*   not open, deceitful; compare *Richard III*, III.v.33: "the covert'st sheltered traitor." *convenient*   morally becoming, proper; compare A.V., Romans 1:28: "a reprobate mind, to do those things which are not convenient." Compare V.i.36.

55. *practised on*   plotted against; compare I.ii.164, n. *close*   secret; compare *Richard III*, I.i.158: "another secret close intent."

56. *Rive . . . continents*   break, split the containers that hide you; compare *Antony and Cleopatra*, IV.xiv.40–1: "Heart, once be stronger than thy continent, Crack thy frail case." Q has "concealed centers".

56–7. *cry . . . grace*   beg mercy from these awe-inspiring officials who summon you to the judgment of the gods (just as an official—called a summoner—still did bring offenders before ecclesiastical courts, though the word had for long been used in a nontechnical sense; compare *O.E.D.*, 2, 1580: "A messenger and summoner of us all to the dreadful Judgment-seat"). See Appendix C, p. 225, for the grammar here.

These dreadful summoners grace. I am a man
More sinned against than sinning.

KENT

Alack, bare-headed?
Gracious my lord, hard by here is a hovel;
60 Some friendship will it lend you 'gainst the tempest:
Repose you there, while I to this hard house
(More harder than the stones whereof 'tis raised;
Which even but now, demanding after you,
Denied me to come in) return, and force
65 Their scanted courtesy.

LEAR

My wits begin to turn.
Come on my boy. How dost my boy? Art cold?
I am cold myself. Where is this straw, my fellow?
The art of our necessities is strange
And can make vile things precious. Come, your hovel.
70 Poor Fool and knave, I have one part in my heart
That's sorry yet for thee.

FOOL

He that has and a little tiny wit—
With heigh-ho, the wind and the rain—
Must make content with his fortunes fit,
75   Though the rain it raineth every day.

---

60. *lend* grant, give; compare *Venus and Adonis*, 539: "Her arms do lend his neck a sweet embrace."

61. *hard house* cruel household (compare II.ii.1) = "Which," line 63.

65. *scanted* stinted; compare I.i.273.

68–69. *The art . . . precious* The practical skill (compare IV.vi.214) of an alchemist, which necessity teaches us, is extraordinary: it can turn base materials into precious ones.

72–5. *He that . . . day* The form and refrain of Feste's song at the end of *Twelfth Night*, adapted here to make the point that even a man with a small amount of understanding must make his desires fit in with his fortunes; compare *Richard II*, V.ii.37–8: "But heaven hath a hand in these events, To whose high will we bound our calm contents."

LEAR

True, boy. Come bring us to this hovel. *Exeunt* LEAR *and* KENT.

FOOL

This is a brave night to cool a courtesan. I'll speak a prophecy
ere I go:

> When priests are more in word than matter;
80 > When brewers mar their malt with water;
> When nobles are their tailors' tutors;
> No heretics burned, but wenches' suitors;
> Then comes the time, who lives to see't,
> That going shall be used with feet.

85 > When every case in law is right;
> No squire in debt nor no poor knight;
> When slanders do not live in tongues,
> Nor cutpurses come not to throngs;
> When usurers tell their gold i'th'field,
90 > And bawds and whores do churches build;
> Then shall the realm of Albion
> Come to great confusion.

This prophecy Merlin shall make, for I live before his time.

Exit.

79–92. *When . . . confusion* Warburton, New Cambridge. The two stanzas describe (1) the actual state of things when priests use more words than
their matter needs (79) or suitors (82) find that "light wenches will burn"
(i.e., give venereal disease; *Comedy of Errors*, IV.iii.51), then shall walking
(compare I.iv.104) be performed with the feet—as it is now; (2) the ideal
state of things when usurers count ("tell," compare II.iv.53) their gold
openly, or bawds and whores build churches in sign of repentance, then
Britain, which has got used to (1), will be ruined (compare *Macbeth*, III.v.27–
9: "sprites . . . Shall draw him on to his confusion"). The lines parody a
prophecy found in Thynne's edition of Chaucer (1532) and printed in Skeat's
edition (1894) VII, 450: "Whan feyth failleth in prestes sawes, And lordes
hestes ar holden for lawes, And robbery is holden purchas, And lechery is
holden solas, Than shal the lond of Albyon Be brought to grete confusion."
A similar set of verses quoted by Skeat VII, p. lxxxi is called a Prophecy
of Merlin, the seer of the time of King Arthur—much later, of course,
than that of King Lear. (See Terence Hawkes, *Notes and Queries*, N.S. VII

Scene iii: Enter GLOUCESTER *and* EDMUND, *with lights.*

GLOUCESTER

Alack, alack Edmund, I like not this⌐unnatural⌐dealing. When
I desired their leave that I might pity him, they took from me
the use of mine own house, charged me on pain of perpetual
displeasure neither to speak of him, entreat for him, or any
5   way sustain him.

EDMUND

Most savage and⌐unnatural.⌐

GLOUCESTER

Go to; say you nothing. There is division between the dukes,
and a worse matter than that: I have received a letter this night
—'tis dangerous to be spoken—I have locked the letter in my
10   closet. These injuries the King now bears will be revenged
home. There is part of a power already footed; we must incline
to the King. I will look him and privily relieve him; go you
and maintain talk with the duke, that my charity be not of
him perceived; if he ask for me, I am ill and gone to bed. If I
15   die for it (as no less is threatened me), the King my old master
must be relieved. There is strange things toward, Edmund;
pray you be careful.   *Exit.*

[Sept., 1960], 331–2.) Shakespeare's two stanzas are printed as one in F, with
lines 83–4 after line 90; New Cambridge ed. ends stanza 1 with lines 91–2.
The lines are not in Q and have been thought to be mere actor's gag: Lear,
after his "new-found care" for the Fool (66–7), should not "leave the Fool
behind him" (Granville-Barker, p. 312).

   Scene iii   S.D.   *with lights*   Q; not in F. Gloucester is on his way back
to help Lear.
   5. *sustain*   provide with the necessities of life (compare IV.iv.6).
   7. *Go to*   enough!
   11. *home*   thoroughly. *footed*   See III.i.30–32; Q has "landed".
   12. *look*   look for; Q has "seeke".
   16. *toward*   coming.

EDMUND

This courtesy, forbid thee, shall the duke
Instantly know, and of that letter too.
20 This seems a fair deserving and must draw me
That which my father loses—no less than all.
The younger rises when the old doth fall.   *Exit.*

Scene iv: Enter LEAR, KENT, *and* FOOL.

KENT

Here is the place, my lord; good my lord, enter:
The tyranny of the open night's too rough
For [nature] to endure.   *Storm still.*

LEAR

Let me alone.

KENT

Good my lord, enter here.

LEAR

Wilt break my heart?

KENT

5 I had rather break mine own. Good my lord, enter.

LEAR

Thou think'st 'tis much that this contentious storm
Invades us to the skin; so 'tis to thee,
But where the greater malady is fixed,

---

20. *a fair deserving*   an action which deserves well (compare V.iii.301).

Scene iv S.D. They enter by one door; the other is taken to be that of the "hovel." Lear moves further downstage each time the others try to make him go in, until he delivers lines 28–36 from the very front, directly to the audience.

4. *Wilt . . . heart?* by asking me inside, where I shall no longer have the storm to distract me from thoughts of ingratitude.

6. *contentious* Q has "crulentious", corrected to "tempestious".

The lesser is scarce felt. Thou'dst shun a bear;
10   But if thy flight lay toward the roaring sea,
Thou'dst meet the bear i'th'mouth. When the mind's free
The body's delicate; this tempest in my mind
Doth from my senses take all feeling else
Save what beats there, filial ingratitude;
15   Is it not as this mouth should tear this hand
For lifting food to't? But I will punish home.
No, I will weep no more. In such a night
To shut me out? Pour on; I will endure.
In such a night as this? O Regan, Goneril,
20   Your old kind father, whose frank heart gave all—
O that way madness lies; let me shun that;
No more of that.

                          KENT

                Good my lord, enter here.

                          LEAR

Prithee go in thyself, seek thine own ease;
This tempest will not give me leave to ponder
25   On things would hurt me more, but I'll go in.
[*To the Fool*] In boy, go first. You houseless poverty—
Nay, get thee in; I'll pray, and then I'll sleep—   *Exit* FOOL.
Poor naked wretches, whereso'er you are,
That bide the pelting of this pitiless storm,
30   How shall your houseless heads and unfed sides,

---

11. *free*   not burdened, untroubled; compare III.vi.98.

12. *delicate*   fastidious, sensitive (Latin *delicatus*, charming, voluptuous).

16. *home*   Compare III.iii.11, n.; Q has "sure".

17–18. *In . . . endure*   not in Q.

20. *frank*   bounteous (compare *Coriolanus*, III.i.130: "our so frank do-
nation") or open, ingenuous (compare *Othello*, I.iii.38: "with frank appearance"). *gave*   Q has "gave you"; compare II.iv.244.

24–5. *This . . . in*   Unless I go in, this tempest will not allow me to think
of what would hurt me more, i.e., if I do not go in, this tempest will keep
me from thinking (compare lines 8–9).

26–7. *In . . . sleep*   not in Q.

29. *storm*   Q has "night"; compare III.ii.12.

Your looped and windowed raggedness, defend you
From seasons such as these? O I have ta'en
Too little care of this! Take physic, pomp;
Expose thyself to feel what wretches feel,

35   That thou mayst shake the superflux to them,
And show the heavens more just.

Enter EDGAR and FOOL.

EDGAR

Fathom and half, fathom and half! Poor Tom!

FOOL

Come not in here nuncle, here's a spirit. Help me, help me!

KENT

Give me thy hand. Who's there?

FOOL

40   A spirit, a spirit, he says his name's poor Tom.

KENT

What art thou that dost grumble there i'th'straw?
Come forth!

EDGAR

Away! the foul fiend follows me!

Through the sharp hawthorn blow the cold winds.
Humh! Go to thy bed and warm thee.

28–36. *Poor . . . just.* "The supreme moment for Lear himself, the turning point, therefore, of the play's main theme" (Granville-Barker, p. 274). Compare IV.i.64–9.

31. *looped* full of holes; compare *O.E.D.*, sb.[2], 1, 1628: "holes or loops in walls to shoot out against the Assailants".

35. *superflux* surplus.

36–7. S.D. *Enter . . . Tom!* not in Q; in F Edgar is held to have entered as soon as he speaks, probably while crouching just within the tiring-house door; he comes into view at line 42. *Fathom and half* as if he is sounding the depth of the storm-waters.

43. *blow the cold winds* F has "blow the windes", Q "blowes the cold wind". The adjective makes up a metrical line and the snatch of a song, as in line 87 of "The Friar of Orders Grey," in Percy's *Reliques of Ancient English Poetry*, 1765.

LEAR

                  Didst thou give

45 All to thy daughters? And art thou come to this?

EDGAR

Who gives anything to poor Tom? whom the foul fiend hath
led through fire and through flame, through ford and whirl-
pool, o'er bog and quagmire; that hath laid knives under his
pillow and halters in his pew; set ratsbane by his porridge;

50 made him proud of heart, to ride on a bay trotting horse over
four-inched bridges, to course his own shadow for a traitor.
Bless thy five wits! Tom's a-cold. O, do de, do de, do de. Bless
thee from whirlwinds, star-blasting, and taking! Do poor Tom
some charity, whom the foul fiend vexes. There could I have

55 him now—and there—and there again—and there.

                                 Storm still.

LEAR

What, has his daughters brought him to this pass?
Couldst thou save nothing? Wouldst thou give 'em all?

44–5. *Didst . . . daughters*   Q reads "Hast thou given all to thy two
daughters"; compare I.i.123; III.ii.21.

48–9. *knives . . . halters*   to tempt him to suicide; compare Harsnett,
p. 219, and Marlowe, *Dr. Faustus*, ed. Greg, vi.650–2 or II.ii.591–2: ". . .
knives . . . halters . . . Are laid before me to dispatch myself."

49. *pew*   seat in church, or else his station or allotted place; compare
O.E.D., *sb.*[1], 3b, 1607: "The Elisian Gardens . . . scarce one amongst five
hundred has her pew there." *porridge*   broth; Q has "pottage".

51. *four-inched bridges*   bridges only four inches wide; compare Jonson, *The Magnetick Lady*, V.viii.15–16: "Run over two-inch bridges; With
his eyes fast, and i' the dead of night!" *course*   to hunt.

52. *Bless*   hallow by making the sign of the cross, and hence defend
against evil. *five wits*   five mental faculties; in Hawes, *The Pastime of
Pleasure*, XXIV, 2 (*E.E.T.S.*, No. 173, p. 108): "These are the five wits . . .
common wit, . . . imagination, Fantasy [perception] and estimation [judg-
ment] . . . And memory."

52. *do . . . de*   shivering; compare Cotgrave "*Friller*, to shiver . . . or
didder for cold"; not in Q.

53. *star-blasting*   blighting by the influence of a star; compare I.iv.275.
taking   Compare II.iv.158, n.

56. *What, has his*   Duthie, from F "Ha's his" and Q "What, his".

FOOL

Nay, he reserved a blanket; else we had been all shamed.

LEAR

Now all the plagues that in the pendulous air
60 Hang fated o'er men's faults light on thy daughters!

KENT

He hath no daughters, sir.

LEAR

Death, traitor! Nothing could have subdued ⌐nature⌐
To such a lowness, but his unkind daughters.
Is it the fashion that discarded fathers
65 Should have thus little mercy on their flesh?
Judicious punishment! 'Twas this flesh begot
Those pelican daughters.

EDGAR

Pillicock sat on Pillicock Hill.
Alow, alow, loo, loo!

FOOL

70 This cold night will turn us all to fools and madmen.

---

59. *pendulous*   menacingly hanging overhead.

60. *fated*   preordained; compare *Tempest*, I.ii.128–30: "one midnight
Fated to th' purpose, did Antonio open The gates of Milan."

67. *pelican*   attacking their parent, as the children of the pelican were
said to do (compare John of Gaunt's charge that Richard II had spilt the
blood of his grandfather's line, *Richard II*, II.i.126–7: "That blood already,
like the pelican, Hast thou tapp'd out, and drunkenly carous'd"). In return,
the pelican was said to "repast them with [her] blood" (*Hamlet*, IV.v.143–4);
compare *Leir*, 512–3: "I am as kind as is the pelican, That kills itself to save
her young ones' lives."

68. *Pillicock*   phallus (in Florio under *puga, pinco*, etc.); or darling
(Florio, under *zugo*), "pretty rogue" (Cotgrave, under *mistigouri*); suggested
to Edgar in sound by "pelican" and in sense by "this flesh begot"; perhaps
echoing an older rhyme, *Oxford Dictionary of Nursery Rhymes*, 1952, p. 432.

69. *Alow . . . loo*   cries as to a hawk or a dog; Q has "a lo lo lo"; compare *Hamlet*, I.v.116: "Hillo, ho, ho, boy! Come, bird, come," *Troilus and
Cressida*, V.vii.9–10: ". . . now dog! 'Loo, Paris, 'loo!"

EDGAR

Take heed o'th'foul fiend, obey thy parents, keep thy words justly, swear not, commit not with man's sworn spouse, set not thy sweet heart on proud array. Tom's a-cold.

LEAR

What hast thou been?

EDGAR

75 A servingman, proud in heart and mind; that curled my hair, wore gloves in my cap; served the lust of my mistress' heart, and did the act of darkness with her; swore as many oaths as I spake words, and broke them in the sweet face of heaven; one that slept in the contriving of lust, and waked to do it.
80 Wine loved I deeply, dice dearly; and in woman, out-paramoured the Turk. False of heart, light of ear, bloody of hand; hog in sloth, fox in stealth, wolf in greediness, dog in madness, lion in prey. Let not the creaking of shoes nor the rustling of silks betray thy poor heart to woman. Keep thy
85 foot out of brothels, thy hand out of plackets, thy pen from lenders' books, and defy the foul fiend.
Still through the hawthorn blows the cold wind,
Says suum, mun, hey nonny nonny.
Dolphin my boy, boy, sessa! let him trot by.   *Storm still.*

---

71. *foul* similar in sound to "fool," line 70; compare *3 Henry VI*, V.vi.19–20: Icarus was "taught . . . the office of a fowl! And yet, for all his wings, the fool was drown'd."

72. *justly* Q; F has "Iustice". Compare Deuteronomy, 23:23. *commit* commit adultery. *sworn* taken by an oath.

73. *sweet heart* Q; F has "Sweet-heart".

76. *gloves* mistresses' favors (as in *Troilus and Cressida*, IV.iv.70).

80. *deeply* Q; F has "deerely".

81. *light* frivolous, unthinking; compare *O.E.D.*, *a.*1, 14, 1610: "If light ears incline to light lips, harm ensueth."

88. *Says suum, mun* imitating the sound of the wind; not in Q. *hey nonny nonny* F has "nonny", Q "hay no on ny".

89. *Dolphin* perhaps a devil; Arden ed. quotes the Newcastle Play of Noah (ed. Waterhouse, *The Non-Cycle Mystery Plays*, 1909, p. 25): "I pray to Dolphin, prince of dead, Scald you all in his lead." *sessa* Malone, from

LEAR

90 Thou wert better in a grave than to answer with thy uncov-
ered body this extremity of the skies. Is man no more than
this? Consider him well. Thou ow'st the worm no silk, the
beast no hide, the sheep no wool, the cat no perfume. Ha!
Here's three on's are sophisticated; thou art the thing itself.
95 Unaccommodated man is no more but such a poor, bare, forked
animal as thou art. Off off you lendings! Come, unbutton
here.

Enter GLOUCESTER *with a torch.*

FOOL

Prithee nuncle be contented; 'tis a naughty night to swim in.
Now a little fire in a wild field were like an old lecher's heart—
100 a small spark, all the rest on's body cold. Look, here comes a
walking fire.

EDGAR

This is the foul Flibbertigibbet. He begins at curfew, and walks
till the first cock. He gives the web and the pin, squenes the

---

The Taming of the Shrew, Induction 5; F has "Sesey", Q "caese". Unexplained; compare III.vi.68; IV.vi.195.

90. *Thou wert better* See Appendix C, p. 225.

93. *cat* civet; compare IV.vi.127.

95. *unaccommodated* unprovided with "accommodations" or comforts
(compare *Measure for Measure*, III.i.14).

96. *lendings* things borrowed from worm, beast and sheep, i.e., clothes;
compare Florio's Montaigne (Tudor Translations, 1893) ii.184: "borrowing
. . . wool, . . . hair, . . . feathers, . . . silk to shroud us." *unbutton here* a
command to a servant (compare V.iii.306) which he begins to carry out himself; Q has "on bee true" corrected to "on".

98. *naughty* wicked; compare "naught" II.iv.128.

102. *the foul Flibbertigibbet* from Harsnett, p. 49. Q has "the foule fiend
fliberdegibek", corrected from "Sriberdegibit".

103. *till the* Q; F has "at". *the web and the pin* cataract. *squenes*
makes squint; Greg's conjecture (pp. 165–7) from Q "squemes" (corrected
from "-queues"), citing two occurrences (*O.E.D.*, "squean" 1608–9) in works
by Armin, actor of the Fool here. F "squints", not found elsewhere in Shakespeare, appears to be a sophistication.

eye, and makes the harelip; mildews the white wheat, and
105 hurts the poor creature of earth.

> S'Withold footed thrice the 'old:
> He met the Nightmare and her nine-fold;
>   Bid her alight
>   And her troth plight—
110   And aroint thee witch, aroint thee!

KENT

How fares your Grace?

LEAR

What's he?

KENT

Who's there? What is't you seek?

GLOUCESTER

What are you there? Your names?

EDGAR

115 Poor Tom, that eats the swimming frog, the toad, the tadpole,
the wall-newt and the water; that in the fury of his heart,
when the foul fiend rages, eats cow-dung for sallets, swallows
the old rat and the ditch-dog, drinks the green mantle of the

---

104. *white*   ripening, and hence light in color.

106. *S'Withold*   Saint Withold; New Cambridge ed. compares *Trouble-some Raigne of King John*, xi. 4: "Sweet S. Withold of thy lenity defend us from extremity." *'old*   Q has "wold", open country.

107. *Nightmare . . . nine-fold*   a female spirit (O.E. *mare*, which was thought to trouble sleepers by settling upon them) and her nine offspring.

109. *troth plight*   Q; promise, after getting off the sleeper's chest, not to return; F has "troth-plight". Warburton quoted Scot, *Discoverie of Witchcraft* (1584) IV, xi, where St. George beats the Nightmare "Until her troth she to him plight She would not come to her [the sufferer] that night."

110. *aroint thee*   be off!

116. *wall-newt*   probably the wall lizard.

117. *sallets*   savory mixture; compare *Hamlet*, II.ii.435: ". . . there was [F] no sallets in the lines to make the matter savoury."

120 standing pool; who is whipped from tithing to tithing, and
stock-punished and imprisoned; who hath had three suits to
his back, six shirts to his body,

> Horse to ride, and weapon to wear;
> But mice and rats and such small deer
> Have been Tom's food for seven long year.

125 Beware my follower. Peace Smulkin, peace thou fiend.

GLOUCESTER

What, hath your Grace no better company?

EDGAR

The Prince of Darkness is a gentleman!
Modo he's called, and Mahu.

GLOUCESTER

Our flesh and blood, my lord, is grown so vile,
130 That it doth hate what gets it.

EDGAR

Poor Tom's a-cold.

GLOUCESTER

Go in with me; my duty cannot suffer
T'obey in all your daughters' hard commands.
Though their injunction be to bar my doors
135 And let this tyrannous night take hold upon you,
Yet have I ventured to come seek you out
And bring you where both fire and food is ready.

---

119. *tithing*　a district (of ten families).

120. *stock-punished*　punished by being put in the stocks; Q; F has "stockt, punish'd". *hath . . . suits*　Q; F reads "hath three Suites". Compare II.ii.13.

123. *deer*　animals. The lines are adapted from *Sir Beves of Hamtoun* (c. 1320): "Rattes and myce and such small dere Was his mete that seven yere" E.E.T.S., Extra series No. 46, p. 75.

125–8. *Smulkin . . . Modo . . . Mahu*　from devils' names in Harsnett, pp. 46–7.

130. *gets*　begets.

LEAR

First let me talk with this philosopher.
What is the cause of thunder?

KENT

                    Good my lord,
140 Take his offer; go into the house.

LEAR

I'll talk a word with this same learned Theban.
What is your study?

EDGAR

How to prevent the fiend and to kill vermin.

LEAR

Let me ask you one word in private.

KENT

145 Impórtune him once more to go, my lord;
His wits begin t'unsettle.

GLOUCESTER

                   Canst thou blame him?   *Storm still.*
His daughters seek his death. Ah, that good Kent,
He said it would be thus, poor banished man.
Thou sayest the King grows mad; I'll tell thee friend
150 I am almost mad myself. I had a son,
Now outlawed from my blood: he sought my life
But lately, very late. I loved him, friend,
No father his son dearer: true to tell thee,

---

138. *philosopher*   Kings used to keep a wise man at court, just as they kept a Fool.

143. *prevent*   balk, forestall (by acting first, Latin *praevenire* to come before; compare Brutus, meditating the murder of Caesar who may "abuse . . . greatness," *Julius Caesar*, II.i.28: "Then lest he may, prevent").

145. *once more*   not in Q.

115

The grief hath crazed my wits. What a night's this!—
155 I do beseech your Grace—

                    LEAR

                    O cry you mercy, sir.
Noble philosopher, your company.

                    EDGAR

Tom's a-cold.

                    GLOUCESTER

In fellow there, into th' hovel; keep thee warm.

                    LEAR

Come let's in all.

                    KENT

                    This way, my lord.

                    LEAR

                                        With him;
160 I will keep still with my philosopher.

                    KENT

Good my lord, soothe him; let him take the fellow.

                    GLOUCESTER

Take him you on.

                    KENT

Sirrah, come on; go along with us.

                    LEAR

Come, good Athenian.

                    GLOUCESTER

165 No words, no words, hush.

---

155. *cry you mercy* by your leave (compare III.vi.47 and Appendix C,
p. 225); he wishes not to be separated from his "philosopher," with whom
he forms a group, now, distinct from the sane.
161. *soothe* humor.

EDGAR

Childe Roland to the dark tower came.
His word was still "Fie, foh, and fum.
I smell the blood of a British man."   *Exeunt.*

Scene v: Enter CORNWALL *and* EDMUND.

CORNWALL

I will have my revenge ere I depart his house.

EDMUND

How, my lord, I may be censured, that ⌐nature⌐ thus gives way
to loyalty, something fears me to think of.

CORNWALL

I now perceive it was not altogether your brother's evil dispo-
5   sition made him seek his death; but a provoking merit, set
awork by a reproveable badness in himself.

EDMUND

How malicious is my fortune, that I must repent to be just!

---

166. *Childe*   a youth not yet knighted. *Roland*   Charlemagne's nephew.
tower   Q has "towne". The line is commonly taken to be from a lost ballad, here incongruously juxtaposed with the words of the Giant in *Jack the
Giant-Killer.*

168. *blood*   Compare line 151 above and III.v.19; Edgar fears his "blood"
(his relationship to his father) will be smelled out (New Cambridge).

Scene v   S.D.   using the opposite door from that by which Lear has just
entered the hovel.

1. *his house*   Gloucester's; compare III.vii.29, 37.

2. *censured*   judged, estimated (not "criticized"); compare *Julius Caesar*,
III.ii.17: "Censure me in your wisdom, and awake your senses, that you may
better judge." *nature*   my feeling for my father.

3. *something . . . me*   somewhat frightens me.

4–6. *it was . . . himself*   it was not only Edgar's wickedness that made
him plan to murder Gloucester but Gloucester's own deserts: a virtue was
provoking Edgar, a virtue which was moved by a reprehensible wickedness
in Gloucester himself.

7. *repent . . . just*   repent of doing right.

This is the letter which he spoke of; which approves him an intelligent party to the advantages of France. O heavens; that
10   this treason were not—or not I the detector!

CORNWALL

Go with me to the duchess.

EDMUND

If the matter of this paper be certain, you have mighty business in hand.

CORNWALL

True or false, it hath made thee Earl of Gloucester. Seek out
15   where thy father is, that he may be ready for our apprehension.

EDMUND

[*Aside*] If I find him comforting the King, it will stuff his suspicion more fully.—[*To Cornwall*] I will perséver in my course of loyalty, though the conflict be sore between that and my blood.

CORNWALL

20   I will lay trust upon thee; and thou shalt find a dearer father in my love.   *Exeunt.*

Scene vi: Enter GLOUCESTER *and* KENT.

GLOUCESTER

Here is better than the open air; take it thankfully. I will piece

---

8–9. *approves . . . France* proves that he was well-informed about the favorable opportunities of the King of France; or (compare III.i.25) that he was an informer and an ally, to the benefit of the King of France.

15. *for our apprehension* for us to arrest him.

16. *comforting* relieving; compare IV.i.16.

20. *dearer* Q; F has "deere".

Scene vi S.D. They enter by the door they had used at the end of Scene iv to go into the hovel. Some cushions (line 31) or a pallet of straw (IV.vii.40) show that the platform represents the inside of this.

1–2. *piece out* add to; compare I.i.194.

out the comfort with what addition I can: I will not be long
from you.   *Exit.*

KENT

All the power of his wits have given way to his impatience.
5 The gods reward your kindness!

Enter LEAR, EDGAR, *and* FOOL.

EDGAR

Frateretto calls me, and tells me Nero is an angler in the lake
of darkness. Pray, innocent, and beware the foul fiend.

FOOL

Prithee nuncle tell me, whether a madman be a gentleman or a
yeoman.

LEAR

10 A king, a king!

FOOL

No, he's a yeoman that has a gentleman to his son; for he's a
mad yeoman that sees his son a gentleman before him.

LEAR

To have a thousand with red burning spits
Come hizzing in upon 'em!

EDGAR

15 The foul fiend bites my back.

---

4. *impatience*   lack of endurance, inability to bear suffering; compare
II.iv.265.

6–7. *Frateretto*   another devil, Harsnett p. 49; compare III.iv.102, 125,
127. *Nero . . . darkness*   suggested by phrases ("stygian lake," "Caesars
humor") in Harsnett pp. 45, 47, and by Chaucer, *The Monk's Tale* (*Works*,
ed. Robinson, VII, 2475–76), where Nero has "nettes of gold threed . . . To
fisshe in Tybre whan him liste pleye." The link is the mention of a "Fidler"
soon after *Frateretto* on p. 49 of Harsnett. (See *RES*, XI (1935), 421–29.)
innocent   Fool; compare *All's Well that Ends Well*, IV.iii.173–5: "the
sheriff's fool . . . a dumb innocent."

11–12. *FOOL. No . . . him. LEAR*   F; not in Q.

13–14. *To have . . . 'em!*   Lear has been prompted by Edgar to think of
Goneril and Regan in the torments of hell.

FOOL

He's mad that trusts in the tameness of a wolf, a horse's health,
a boy's love, or a whore's oath.

LEAR

It shall be done; I will arraign them straight.—
[*To Edgar*] Come sit thou here most learned justicer.—
20   [*To the Fool*] Thou sapient sir, sit here.—Now you she-foxes—

EDGAR

Look where he stands and glares! Want'st thou eyes at trial
madam?
                    Come o'er the burn, Bessy, to me.

FOOL

                    Her boat hath a leak,
25   And she must not speak
            Why she dares not come over to thee.

EDGAR

The foul fiend haunts poor Tom in the voice of a nightingale.
Hoppedance cries in Tom's belly for two white herring. Croak
not, black angel; I have no food for thee.

KENT

30   How do you sir? Stand you not so amazed.
Will you lie down and rest upon the cushions?

15–51. *The foul fiend . . . 'scape?*   Q; not in F.
16. *a horse's health*   i.e., as reported by a horse dealer.
18. *arraign . . . straight*   indict them from a tribunal at once.
19. *justicer*   Compare III.vi.51 and IV.ii.79; Q has "Iustice".
20. *Now*   Q2; Q has "No".
21. *eyes*   spectators.
23. *burn*   brook; Q has "broome". Capell noted the song "Come over
the Boorne besse to me" in Wager's play *The Longer thou Livest the More
Fool thou Art*, c. 1559.
28. *Hoppedance*   "Hoberdidance" in Harsnett, p. 49. *cries . . . belly*   like
the rumbling of a fasting woman's belly, Harsnett, p. 195. *croak*   rumble.

LEAR

I'll see their trial first. Bring in their evidence.—
[*To Edgar*] Thou robèd man of justice, take thy place;—
[*To the Fool*] And thou, his yoke-fellow of equity,
35   Bench by his side.—[*To Kent*] You are o'th'commission;
Sit you too.

EDGAR

Let us deal justly.
        Sleepest or wakest thou, jolly shepherd?
          Thy sheep be in the corn;
40   And for one blast of thy minikin mouth
          Thy sheep shall take no harm.
Purr the cat is gray.

LEAR

Arraign her first; 'tis Goneril. I here take my oath before this
honourable assembly, she kicked the poor King her father.

FOOL

45   Come hither mistress; is your name Goneril?

LEAR

She cannot deny it.

FOOL

Cry you mercy, I took you for a joined stool.

---

32. *evidence* witnesses.

33. *robèd* Pope; Q has "robbed".

34. *equity* a system of precedents based on natural justice, supplementing common and statute law.

35. *commission* authority given under the Great Seal to empower persons to act as justices.

37–8. *justly. Sleepest* Q has "justly sleepest".

40. *minikin* high-pitched treble; compare *O.E.D.*, *sb.*, 2, c, 1601: ". . . what treble minikin squeaks there, ha?"; *adj.*, 2, 1602: "a high stretched minikin voice."

47. *Cry . . . stool* Compare III.iv.155; a mock apology for not noticing someone (Tilley M 897), funnier if there is a stool there, of course. *joined* make by a joiner; Q has "joyne", Q2 "joynt".

LEAR

And here's another, whose warped looks proclaim
What store her heart is made on. Stop her there!
50 Arms, arms, sword, fire, corruption in the place!
False justicer why hast thou let her 'scape?

EDGAR

Bless thy five wits!

KENT

O pity! Sir, where is the patience now
That you so oft have boasted to retain?

EDGAR

55 [*Aside*] My tears begin to take his part so much,
They mar my counterfeiting.

LEAR

The little dogs and all,
Tray, Blanche, and Sweetheart; see, they bark at me.

EDGAR

Tom will throw his head at them. Avaunt you curs!
60   Be thy mouth or black or white,
            Tooth that poisons if it bite;
            Mastiff, greyhound, mongrel grim,
            Hound or spaniel, brach or lym,
            Or bobtail tyke or trundle-tail,
65   Tom will make him weep and wail;

48–49. *whose . . . made on*   whose distorted face shows what emotions
are stored up within her.

52. *five wits*   Compare III.iv.52.

53–4. *where . . . retain?*   Compare III.ii.35.

63. *brach*   Compare I.iv.96. *lym*   a kind of bloodhound held in by a
lyam or leather thong (compare Jonson, *Bartholomew Fair*, 1614, I.iii.12–13:
". . . all the lyam-hounds . . . should have drawn after you by the scent");
F has "Hym", Q "him".

64. *tyke*   cur; F has "tight", Q "tike". *trundle-tail*   curly-tailed; F has
"Troudle taile", Q "trūndletaile".

For, with throwing thus my head,
Dogs leaped the hatch, and all are fled.
Do, de, de, de. Sessa! Come, march to wakes and fairs and market towns. Poor Tom, thy horn is dry.

LEAR

70 Then let them anatomize Regan; see what breeds about her heart. Is there any cause in ⌈nature⌉ that makes these hard hearts? [*To Edgar*] You, sir, I entertain for one of my hundred; only, I do not like the fashion of your garments. You will say they are Persian; but let them be changed.

KENT

75 Now good my lord, lie here and rest awhile.

LEAR

Make no noise, make no noise; draw the curtains. So, so; we'll go to supper i'th'morning.

FOOL

And I'll go to bed at noon.

[*Re-*]*enter* GLOUCESTER.

GLOUCESTER

Come hither friend. Where is the King my master?

KENT

80 Here sir: but trouble him not; his wits are gone.

---

67. *hatch*　half-door.

68. *Do . . . de*　See III.iv.52, note; Q has "loudla doodla". *Sessa*　Compare III.iv.89; F has "sese"; not in Q.

69. *horn*　ox horn used by the Bedlam beggar to call for alms and to drink from when he got them.

70. *Regan*　who has no alms for beggars, or for her father.

71–2. *these . . . hearts*　Q has "this hardnes".

72. *entertain*　take into service (as one of my hundred knights, I.i.128); compare *Much Ado About Nothing*, I.iii.50: "Being entertain'd for a perfumer . . ."

74. *Persian*　Q has "Persian attire"; compare Horace *Odes*, I. xxxviii. 1: "Persicos odi, puer, apparatus"—"Persian luxury I hate . . ."

78. *go . . . noon*　Proverbial for "act the fool" (compare Tilley B 197); his last words in the play. Q omits the line. S.D.　here in Q, after line 74 in F.

GLOUCESTER

Good friend, I prithee take him in thy arms.
I have o'erheard a plot of death upon him.
There is a litter ready; lay him in't,
And drive toward Dover friend, where thou shalt meet
85   Both welcome and protection. Take up thy master;
If thou should'st dally half an hour, his life,
With thine and all that offer to defend him,
Stand in assured loss. Take up, take up,
And follow me, that will to some provision
90   Give thee quick conduct.

KENT

                    Oppressed ⌈nature⌉ sleeps.
This rest might yet have balmed thy broken sinews,
Which, if convenience will not allow,
Stand in hard cure.—[*To the Fool*] Come help to bear thy
      master;
Thou must not stay behind.

GLOUCESTER

              Come, come, away!
              [*Exeunt* GLOUCESTER, KENT, *and* FOOL, *carrying* LEAR.]

EDGAR

95   When we our betters see bearing our woes,
We scarcely think our miseries our foes.
Who alone suffers, suffers most i'th'mind,

---

89. *provision*   necessaries for the journey, compare II.iv.199.
90–4. *Oppressed . . . behind.*   Q, not in F.
91. *sinews*   nerves.
93. *Stand . . . cure*   will be difficult to cure.
95–108. *When . . . lurk.*   Q, not in F. Granville-Barker (274n, 319, 331)
justifies the cut, because the lines (a) lower dramatic tension and so perhaps
damage III.vii; (b) mar the purpose of giving Edgar "a fresh start in his
dramatic career," which is better served by IV.i.1–9 alone, after the violence
of Gloucester's blinding.
97. *alone, most*   These are the words emphasized.

Leaving free things and happy shows behind;
But then the mind much sufferance doth o'erskip,
100   When grief hath mates, and bearing fellowship.
How light and portable my pain seems now,
When that which makes me bend makes the King bow.
He childed as I fathered. Tom, away!
Mark the high noises, and thyself bewray
105   When false opinion, whose wrong thoughts defile thee,
In thy just proof repeals and reconciles thee.
What will hap more tonight, safe 'scape the King!
Lurk, lurk.   *Exit.*

Scene vii: Enter CORNWALL, REGAN, GONERIL, EDMUND, *and Servants.*

CORNWALL

[*To Goneril*] Post speedily to my lord your husband; show him
this letter: the army of France is landed. Seek out the traitor
Gloucester.

REGAN

Hang him instantly.

GONERIL

5   Pluck out his eyes.

CORNWALL

Leave him to my displeasure. Edmund, keep you our sister
company. The revenges we are bound to take upon your trai-

---

100. *bearing* endurance (compare line 95).

103. *He . . . fathered* See Appendix C, p. 226.

104. *high noises* rumors from high places, or about those in high estate.
bewray Compare II.i.105.

106. When you are proved just, opinion will recall you and reconcile you
with your father.

107. *What* whatever; compare V.iii.98.

Scene vii 2. *letter* See III.iii.8, 19; v.8.

torous father are not fit for your beholding. Advise the duke,
where you are going, to a most festinate preparation: we are
10 bound to the like. Our posts shall be swift and intelligent betwixt us. Farewell dear sister, farewell my Lord of Gloucester.
                    Enter OSWALD.
How now? Where's the King?

OSWALD

My Lord of Gloucester hath conveyed him hence.
Some five or six and thirty of his knights,
15 Hot questrists after him, met him at gate,
Who, with some other of the lord's dependants,
Are gone with him toward Dover, where they boast
To have well-armed friends.

CORNWALL

                Get horses for your mistress.

GONERIL

Farewell sweet lord, and sister.

CORNWALL

20 Edmund farewell.   [*Exeunt* GONERIL, EDMUND, *and* OSWALD.]
                Go seek the traitor Gloucester;
Pinion him like a thief, bring him before us.
                                    [*Exeunt Servants.*]
Though well we may not pass upon his life
Without the form of justice, yet our power
Shall do a curtsy to our wrath, which men
25 May blame, but not control.

---

9. *festinate*   speedy; F has "festiuate", Q "festuant".

10. *bound to*   intending, or ready, to do. *posts . . . intelligent*   swift messengers will carry information.

13. See III.vi.84. Cornwall, in line 11 above, refers to Edmund, the new Earl (III.v.14).

15. *questrists*   seekers—ever since Lear left Albany's house.

22. *pass*   pass sentence.

24. *do a curtsy*   defer, give way (Q has "curtesie", F "curt'sie").

Enter GLOUCESTER *and Servants.*
                    Who's there? The traitor?

REGAN

Ingrateful fox, 'tis he.

CORNWALL

Bind fast his corky arms.

GLOUCESTER

What means your graces? Good my friends consider,
You are my guests. Do me no foul play friends.

CORNWALL

30 Bind him I say.   [*Servants bind him.*]

REGAN

Hard, hard. O filthy traitor!

GLOUCESTER

Unmerciful lady as you are, I'm none.

CORNWALL

To this chair bind him. Villain, thou shalt find—
                    [REGAN *plucks his beard.*]

GLOUCESTER

By the kind gods, 'tis most ignobly done
To pluck me by the beard.

REGAN

35 So white, and such a traitor?

GLOUCESTER

                    Naughty lady,
These hairs which thou dost ravish from my chin

---

25. S.D. *and Servants*   Q has "*brought in by two or three*"; see Appendix
E, p. 229.
27. *corky*   like cork or bark, therefore dry, withered; compare Harsnett,
p. 23: "an old corkie woman".
35. *naughty*   Compare III.iv.98.

127

Will quicken and accuse thee. I am your host:
With robbers' hands my hospitable favors
You should not ruffle thus. What will you do?

CORNWALL

40 Come sir. What letters had you late from France?

REGAN

Be simple-answered, for we know the truth.

CORNWALL

And what confederacy have you with the traitors
Late footed in the kingdom?

REGAN

             To whose hands
You have sent the lunatic King: speak.

GLOUCESTER

45 I have a letter, guessingly set down,
Which came from one that's of a neutral heart,
And not from one opposed.

CORNWALL

             Cunning.

REGAN

                  And false.

CORNWALL

Where hast thou sent the King?

GLOUCESTER

             To Dover.

REGAN

Wherefore to Dover? Wast thou not charged at peril—

---

37. *quicken* come to life.
38. *favors* features; compare *O.E.D.*, *sb.*, 9, c, 1598: "In thy Face, one
Favour from the rest I singled forth."
49. *at peril*— Q; F has "at perill."; under penalty.

CORNWALL

50 Wherefore to Dover? Let him answer that.

GLOUCESTER

I am tied to th' stake, and I must stand the course.

REGAN

Wherefore to Dover?

GLOUCESTER

Because I would not see thy cruel nails
Pluck out his poor old eyes, nor thy fierce sister
55 In his anointed flesh rash boarish fangs.
The sea, with such a storm as his bare head
In hell-black night endured, would have buoyed up
And quenched the stellèd fires;
Yet, poor old heart, he holp the heavens to rain.
60 If wolves had at thy gate howled that dearn time,
Thou shouldst have said, "Good porter turn the key."
All cruels else subscribe: but I shall see
The winged Vengeance overtake such children.

---

51. *course*   attack (by the dogs upon a bear; compare *Macbeth*, V.vii.1–2: "They have tied me to a stake; I cannot fly, But bear-like I must fight the course").

55. *anointed*   as King. *rash*   Q, = "slash" (compare *Faerie Queene*, IV.ii.17: "They . . . mailes did rash, and helmes did hew"); "sticke" in F is probably a sophistication.

56. *as his bare*   Q has "on his lowd" corrected from "of his lou'd". New Cambridge ed. reads "as his loved", regarding F "bare" as a substitution by the prompter or a misreading of "lou'd".

57. *buoyed*   risen; Q "bod" corrected from "layd".

58. *stellèd*   formed into stars (compare "stellate" from *stellatus*); or else fixed, contrasted with "wandering" fires, i.e., planets (O.E. *stellan*).

59. *holp*   helped (by weeping).

60. *dearn*   Q; dark, drear (O.E. *derne* secret, evil); F has "sterne" (compare line 55, n. for the sophistication).

61. *shouldst*   wouldst certainly; see Appendix C, p. 225.

62. *All . . . subscribe*   Countenance, acquiesce in all other cruelties; compare *Measure for Measure*, II.iv.88–9: "Admit no other way to save his life, As I subscribe not that, nor any other . . ."; Q has "subscrib'd" (compare

CORNWALL

See 't shalt thou never. Fellows, hold the chair.
65   Upon these eyes of thine I'll set my foot.

GLOUCESTER

He that will think to live till he be old,
Give me some help—O cruel! O you gods.

REGAN

One side will mock another. Th'other too!

CORNWALL

If you see Vengeance—

FIRST SERVANT

Hold your hand, my lord!
70   I have served you ever since I was a child,
But better service have I never done you
Than now to bid you hold.

REGAN

How now, you dog?

FIRST SERVANT

If you did wear a beard upon your chin,
I'd shake it on this quarrel.

REGAN

What do you mean?

I.ii.24). If, on the other hand, "cruels" are cruel creatures and if the phrase is
still not part of the preceding quotation, which F and Q do not mark off,
then either the antithesis is between "all other cruel creatures" and "I" immediately following—which is nonsense—or else there is a very strained
ellipsis, as in Duthie's interpretation: "All cruel creatures yield to feelings
of compassion under strong provocation: you alone do not," giving to the
verb alone a sense caught from a whole context in *Troilus and Cressida*,
IV.v.105–6: "Hector in his blaze of wrath subscribes To tender objects."

    69. *Vengeance*—   Compare line 63; Q has "vengeance—"; F "ven-
geance."

    74. *What . . . mean?*   Assigned to Regan by Kittredge; the conclusion
of the First Servant's speech in F and Q.

CORNWALL

75 My villain?   [*They*] *draw and fight.*

FIRST SERVANT

Nay then come on, and take the chance of anger.

REGAN

[*To another Servant*] Give me thy sword. A peasant stand up
thus?   *She takes a sword and runs at him behind.*

FIRST SERVANT

O, I am slain. My lord, you have one eye left
80 To see some mischief on him. O!   [*Dies.*]

CORNWALL

Lest it see more, prevent it. Out vile jelly!
Where is thy lustre now?

GLOUCESTER

All dark and comfortless! Where's my son Edmund?
Edmund, enkindle all the sparks of ⌈nature⌉
85 To quit this horrid act.

REGAN

      Out, treacherous villain!
Thou call'st on him that hates thee. It was he
That made the overture of thy treasons to us,
Who is too good to pity thee.

GLOUCESTER

O my follies! Then Edgar was abused.
90 Kind gods, forgive me that, and prosper him.

---

75. *villain* serf, as well as scoundrel (compare "peasant" below). S.D.
Q, not in F.
76. *chance of anger* risk of fighting while you are angry, and/or your
adversary is.
78. S.D. Q; F has "Kills him."
84. *nature* filial affection; compare III.v.2.
85. *quit* requite, avenge.
87. *overture* disclosure.
89. *abused* deceived; compare IV.vii.77.

REGAN

Go thrust him out at gates, and let him smell
His way to Dover.   *Exit [a Servant] with* GLOUCESTER.
          How is't my lord? How look you?

CORNWALL

I have received a hurt. Follow me, lady.
Turn out that eyeless villain. Throw this slave
95   Upon the dunghill. Regan, I bleed apace.
Untimely comes this hurt. Give me your arm.

          [*Exeunt* CORNWALL *and* REGAN.]

SECOND SERVANT

I'll never care what wickedness I do,
If this man come to good.

THIRD SERVANT

          If she live long
And in the end meet the old course of death,
100   Women will all turn monsters.

SECOND SERVANT

Let's follow the old earl, and get the bedlam
To lead him where he would; his roguish madness
Allows itself to anything.

THIRD SERVANT

Go thou; I'll fetch some flax and whites of eggs
105   To apply to his bleeding face. Now heaven help him.

          [*Exeunt.*]

97–105. Q, not in F.

99. *old* normal.

101–2. *get . . . him* Perhaps Shakespeare's earlier intention; Gloucester
is led by one of his own tenants (IV.i.13) until Edgar finds him.

102–3. *his . . . anything* The madness of a rogue and vagabond like Tom
will lend itself to any commission.

104. *flax . . . eggs* prescribed in the sixteenth and seventeenth centuries
as a plaster for a hurt eye.

Act IV, Scene i: Enter EDGAR.

EDGAR

Yet better thus, and known to be contemned,
Than still contemned, and flattered. To be worst,
The lowest and most dejected thing of Fortune,
Stands still in esperance, lives not in fear:
5   The lamentable change is from the best;
The worst returns to laughter. Welcome then,
Thou unsubstantial air that I embrace:
The wretch that thou hast blown unto the worst
Owes nothing to thy blasts. But who comes here?
            Enter GLOUCESTER, *led by an Old Man.*
10   My father, poorly-eyed? World, world, O world!

Act IV, scene i   1–6. *Yet . . . laughter.*   It is better to be a beggar, openly
scorned, than, like a courtier, to be openly flattered but scorned in secret.
To be worst of all, the most humbled plaything of Fortune, still gives cause
for hope, not dread: the change to be lamented is not from the worst but
from the best; the worst can change only for the better. For line 2, F has
"Then still contemn'd and flatter'd, to be worst:" and Q "Then still contemn'd and flattered to be worst," but clearly the occurrences of "worst" in
lines 2, 6, and 8 must all correspond, in opposition to "best" in line 5. It
seems too confusing to follow the F and Q punctuation and interpret "The
worst is to be secretly scorned and openly flattered, not to be a beggar and
openly scorned," for it is not *this* state which can change only for the better, but rather the state of beggary itself, that of the lowest thing, most
humbled by Fortune.

6–9. *Welcome . . . But*   not in Q. The wind has done all it can to him
in bringing him to the worst; having paid all he can, he owes it no more—
or owes it no deference (as the courtier would to his flatterers).

9. S.D. *led by*   Q; F has "and".

10. *poorly-eyed*   New Cambridge, but without hyphen; Q has "parti,
eyd" corrected from "poorlie, leed". The hyphen seems to me to be necessary in order to explain why the corrector of Q should need to rewrite the
word (and so lead to the compositor's misreading "parti,")—i.e., not only
to cut out the comma between the two words but to make them into one
compound adjective. Of course the result brings us closer only to the corrector's MS, not necessarily to Shakespeare's (see Appendix E, p. 229–230).
F has "poorely led", from Q uncorr.

But that thy strange mutations make us hate thee,
Life would not yield to age.

OLD MAN

O my good lord,
I have been your tenant, and your father's tenant,
These fourscore years.

GLOUCESTER

15 Away, get thee away; good friend, be gone:
Thy comforts can do me no good at all;
Thee, they may hurt.

OLD MAN

You cannot see your way.

GLOUCESTER

I have no way, and therefore want no eyes;
I stumbled when I saw. Full oft 'tis seen,
20 Our means secure us, and our mere defects
Prove our commodities. Oh dear son Edgar,
The food of thy abusèd father's wrath,
Might I but live to see thee in my touch,
I'd say I had eyes again,

OLD MAN

How now! Who's there?

10–12. *World . . . age*   No one would submit to old age (which brings us nearer to death) but for the fact that the inexplicable changes of the world make us hate it.

13–14. An important dramatic contrast to the treatment of Gloucester and Lear by their dependents in III.

16. *comforts*   Compare III.v.16.

20. *Our . . . us*   Our wealth makes us overconfident or careless (Latin *securus*; compare *Merry Wives of Windsor*, II.i.208: "a secure fool").

20–1. *mere . . . commodities*   sheer (Latin *merus*, unmixed) what proves to be an advantage (compare *2 Henry IV*, I.ii. conclusion: "I will turn diseases to commodity").

22. *The food . . . wrath*   who fed the wrath of your deluded (compare I.iii.20; II.iv.301) father.

EDGAR

25 [*Aside*] O gods! Who is't can say, "I am at the worst"?
I am worse than e'er I was.

OLD MAN

'Tis poor mad Tom.

EDGAR

[*Aside*] And worse I may be yet; the worst is not
So long as we can say, "This is the worst."

OLD MAN

Fellow, where goest?

GLOUCESTER

Is it a beggar-man?

OLD MAN

30 Madman, and beggar too.

GLOUCESTER

He has some reason, else he could not beg.
I' th' last night's storm I such a fellow saw,
Which made me think a man a worm. My son
Came then into my mind; and yet my mind
35 Was then scarce friends with him. I have heard more since:
As flies to wanton boys, are we to th' gods;
They kill us for their sport.

EDGAR

[*Aside*] How should this be?
Bad is the trade that must play fool to sorrow,

---

31. *He . . . reason* He is not quite mad.

33. *worm* Compare *Psalm* 22:6: "But I am a worme & not a man; a shame of men, and the contempt of the people" (Breeches Bible, 1599).

35. *I . . . since* See III. vii.86–9.

36–7. *As . . . sport* Contrast V.iii.167–8. See Introduction, p. xiii. *wanton* playful.

38. *Bad . . . sorrow* Edgar's deprecation of his own role in befooling his suffering father (compare "O fault!" V. iii.189). The only reason why he

Angering itself, and others.—[*To Gloucester*] Bless thee
    master!

GLOUCESTER

40 Is that the naked fellow?

OLD MAN

    Ay my lord.

GLOUCESTER

Then prithee get thee away. If, for my sake,
Thou wilt o'ertake us hence a mile or twain
I' th' way toward Dover, do it for ancient love;
And bring some covering for this naked soul,
45 Which I'll entreat to lead me.

OLD MAN

        Alack sir, he is mad.

GLOUCESTER

'Tis the time's plague, when madmen lead the blind.
Do as I bid thee, or rather do thy pleasure;
Above the rest, be gone.

OLD MAN

I'll bring him the best 'parel that I have,
50 Come on't what will.   *Exit.*

GLOUCESTER

    Sirrah, naked fellow.

EDGAR

Poor Tom's a-cold. [*Aside*] I cannot daub it further.

"must" (line 53) is that the parallelism of plot and subplot must be continued
into Act V.

    39. *Angering* troubling, afflicting—if this sense is still possible: it is
not recorded in *O.E.D.* later than the fifteenth century.

    41. *Then prithee* Q; not in F.

    46. *the time's plague* the calamity of the present state of affairs; compare *Hamlet*, I.v.189: "The time is out of joint."

    48. *Above the rest* above all.

    51. *daub it* dissemble (O.F. *dauber*, Lat. *de-albare*, to whitewash); com-

GLOUCESTER

Come hither fellow.

EDGAR [*Aside*]

And yet I must. Bless thy sweet eyes, they bleed.

GLOUCESTER

Know'st thou the way to Dover?

EDGAR

55 Both stile and gate, horse-way and foot-path. Poor Tom hath
been scared out of his good wits; bless thee, good man's son,
from the foul fiend! Five fiends have been in poor Tom at
once: of lust, as Obidicut, Hoberdidence prince of dumbness,
Mahu of stealing, Modo of murder, Flibbertigibbet of mopping
60 and mowing, who since possesses chambermaids and waiting-
women. So, bless thee master.

GLOUCESTER

Here take this purse, thou whom the heavens' plagues
Have humbled to all strokes: that I am wretched
Makes thee the happier: heavens deal so still!
65 Let the superfluous and lust-dieted man,
That slaves your ordinance, that will not see

---

pare *Richard III*, III.v.29: "So smooth he daub'd his vice with show of virtue." Q has "dance".

53. *And ... must* not in Q.

57–61. *Five ... master.* Q; not in F. Again the names of the devils, with
some variations (e.g. Maho, Modu, Hoberdicut), are in Harsnett, pp. 46, 49,
119.

59–61. *Flibbertigibbet ... mowing.* Q has "Stiberdigebit of Mobing, &
Mohing"; (compare F "Flibbertigibbet" III.iv.102, n.); "mopping and mowing" = "making faces" (compare Harsnett, p. 136: "to ... make antic faces,
... mow, and mop like an Ape"). *who ... waiting-women* as was alleged
to have happened to the three in Harsnett; the general reference is to servants who, when so possessed, make faces behind their mistresses' backs.

64–9. *heavens ... enough* Compare III.iv.33–6.

65. *superfluous and lust-dieted* who has more than his needs (compare
II.iv.259) and whose feeding is subjected only to the regimen of pleasure
(compare Bacon, *Advancement of Learning*, Book I,II.3, ed. Wright, 1900, p.
14: "There will be seldom use of ... physic in a sound or well dieted body"),

Because he does not feel, feel your power quickly;
So distribution should undo excess
And each man have enough. Dost thou know Dover?

EDGAR

70   Ay master.

GLOUCESTER

There is a cliff whose high and bending head
Looks fearfully in the confined deep;
Bring me but to the very brim of it
And I'll repair the misery thou dost bear
75   With something rich about me. From that place
I shall no leading need.

EDGAR

Give me thy arm;
Poor Tom shall lead thee.   *Exeunt.*

Scene ii: Enter GONERIL *and* EDMUND.

GONERIL

Welcome my lord. I marvel our mild husband
Not met us on the way.

---

or perhaps whose course of life is determined by pleasure (compare *O.E.D.*, *sb.*[1], 1, 1612–5: "Worldly minds think no man can be of any other than their own diet"). The explanation "whose desires are fed to the full" overlooks the fact that "dieted" does not mean "fed to the full" and that "lust" in such compounds is commonly objective or instrumental, particularly when there is another noun (here "man") to stand in subjective relation to the participle "dieted" (as in, for instance, *Othello*, V.i.36: "Thy bed, lust-stain'd . . ."). See Appendix C, p. 224.

66. *slaves*   makes a slave of (instead of deferring to); compare *O.E.D.*, v.[1], 1, 1602: "Thou canst not slave Or banish me." Q has "stands".

67. *quickly*   sensitively (even as late as 1800 in *O.E.D.*, *adv.*, 1: "to feel rather quickly"). See Appendix C, p. 222.

71. *bending*   overhanging (compare *Hamlet*, I.iv.70–71).

Scene ii   1. *Welcome*   to the Duke of Albany's. See III.vii.1.

Enter OSWALD.
Now, where's your master?

OSWALD

Madam, within, but never man so changed.
I told him of the army that was landed;
5   He smiled at it. I told him you were coming;
His answer was, "The worse." Of Gloucester's treachery
And of the loyal service of his son
When I informed him, then he called me sot,
And told me I had turned the wrong side out:
10   What most he should dislike seems pleasant to him;
What like, offensive.

GONERIL

[*To Edmund*] Then shall you go no
further.
It is the cowish terror of his spirit
That dares not undertake; he'll not feel wrongs
Which tie him to an answer. Our wishes on the way
15   May prove effects. Back, Edmund, to my brother;
Hasten his musters and conduct his powers.
I must change arms at home and give the distaff
Into my husband's hands. This trusty servant
Shall pass between us; ere long you are like to hear
20   (If you dare venture in your own behalf)

---

9. *turned . . . out*   got the matter the wrong way round; compare *Much Ado About Nothing*, III.i.68–70: "So turns she every man the wrong side out, And never gives to truth and virtue that Which simpleness and merit purchaseth."

12. *cowish*   cowardly.

13. *undertake*   to enter upon an enterprise.

14. *tie . . . answer*   oblige him to retaliate.

15. *effects*   things accomplished, fulfilled; i.e., Edmund may supplant my husband (perhaps by murder, as may be hinted in line 20). *Edmund*   Q has "Edgar".

17. *arms*   Q; F has "names". Compare the wife of Chaucer's Host who cries, "False coward, . . . I wol have thy knyf, And thou shalt have my distaf and go spynne!" (*Works*, ed. Robinson, VII. 1905–7).

A mistress's command. Wear this; spare speech;

        [*Giving a favour.*]

Decline your head: this kiss, if it durst speak,
Would stretch thy spirits up into the air.
Conceive, and fare thee well.

      EDMUND

25 Yours in the ranks of death.   *Exit.*

      GONERIL

     My most dear Gloucester.

O, the difference of man and man.
To thee a woman's services are due:
A fool usurps my bed.

      OSWALD

    Madam, here comes my lord. *Exit.*
    Enter ALBANY.

      GONERIL

I have been worth the whistling.

      ALBANY

      O Goneril,

30 You are not worth the dust which the rude wind
Blows in your face. I fear your disposition:
That ⌈nature⌉ which contemns it origin

---

24. *conceive* Compare I.i.10.

28. *A fool . . . bed* Q corr., New Cambridge; F has "My Foole usurpes my body", from Q uncorr. "My foote usurps my body", where the first "my" may be accounted for as an accidental anticipation of the second.

29. *whistling* Q corr., New Cambridge; "whistle" F, from Q uncorr.; compare Tilley, D 488, 1611: "A poor dog that is not worth the whistling". She means she was once worth more attention than this (compare lines 1–2).

31–50. *I . . . deep.* Q; not in F.

31. *fear* fear for; compare *Richard III*, I.i.136–7: "The King is sickly . . . And his physicians fear him mightily."

32. *contemns* spurns; compare IV.i.1. *it* its; Q uncorr. (wrongly corrected to "ith").

Cannot be bordered certain in itself;
She that herself will sliver and disbranch
35 From her material sap, perforce must wither
And come to deadly use.

GONERIL

No more; the text is foolish.

ALBANY

Wisdom and goodness to the vile seem vile;
Filths savour but themselves. What have you done?
40 Tigers, not daughters, what have you performed?
A father, and a gracious agèd man
Whose reverence even the head-lugged bear would lick,
Most barbarous, most degenerate, have you madded.
Could my good brother suffer you to do it?
45 A man, a prince, by him so benefited!
If that the heavens do not their visible spirits
Send quickly down to tame these vile offences,
It will come
Humanity must perforce prey on itself
50 Like monsters of the deep.

GONERIL

Milk-livered man!

---

33. *bordered . . . itself*   kept reliably within its own natural bounds.

34–5. *sliver . . . sap*   tear off and cut away, like a splinter or a branch, from the sap which forms her own material or substance.

36. *deadly use*   destruction; compare V.iii.287.

37. *text*   topic or quotation, for a sermon.

39. *Filths . . . themselves*   The filthy like only what is filthy, as they are; compare Jonson, *Cynthia's Revels*, III.iv.12–15: ". . . a proud, and spangled sir, . . . Savours himself alone, is only kind And loving to himself."

42. *reverence*   reverend person. *head-lugged*   hauled along by the head.

46. *If that*   See Appendix C, p. 225. *visible spirits*   the "high-engendered" battalions of thunder and lightning as in III.ii.21–2, 48.

47. *these*   Q uncorr. has "this", Q corr. "the". *vile*   Q has "vild"; perhaps with a quibble on "wild" (Arden)?

49–50. *Humanity . . . deep*   Greg compares *Sir Thomas More* (Alexander, p. 1348, lines 86–7): "men like ravenous fishes would feed on one another."

50. *milk-livered*   cowardly; compare "lily-livered" II.ii.14, n.

That bearest a cheek for blows, a head for wrongs;
Who hast not in thy brows an eye discerning
Thine honour from thy suffering; that not knowest
Fools do those villains pity who are punished
55   Ere they have done their mischief. Where's thy drum?
France spreads his banners in our noiseless land,
With plumed helm thy state begins to threat,
Whil'st thou, a moral fool, sits still and cries,
"Alack, why does he so?"

ALBANY

See thyself, devil!
60   Proper deformity shows not in the fiend
So horrid as in woman.

GONERIL

O vain fool!

ALBANY

Thou changèd and self-covered thing, for shame,
Be-monster not thy feature. Were't my fitness
To let these hands obey my blood,
65   They are apt to dislocate and tear

---

52. *eye discerning*   hyphenated in F; Q has "eye deseruing".

53–9. *that . . . so?"*   Q; not in F.

54. *Fools do*   only fools will.

57. *thy . . . threat*   Jennens, 1770; i.e., France threatens Britain with war; Q has "thy state begins thereat" corrected from "thy slayer begin threats".

58. *moral*   preaching; compare *Much Ado About Nothing*, V.i.21–30 where to "counsel and speak . . . patience" is "to be so moral".

60–61. *Proper . . . woman*   The fiend's deformity is proper to him and less horrid than deformity in a woman, which is not proper to her; F, Q uncorr. have "seemes", Q corr. "shows".

62–9. *Thou . . . news?*   Q; not in F.

62. *changèd and self-covered*   changed into a fiend so that your proper (womanly) self is covered up, or so that you are covered over by what is now seen to be your true self.

63. *Be-monster . . . feature*   Do not make your form or appearance (compare *O.E.D.*, sb., 1, 1600: "Horses of a fine feature") that of a monster (compare I.iv.237). *my fitness*   fitting for me, as a man.

Thy flesh and bones; howe'er thou art a fiend,
A woman's shape doth shield thee.

GONERIL

Marry, your manhood mew—

> *Enter a* Messenger.

ALBANY

What news?

MESSENGER

70 O my good lord, the Duke of Cornwall's dead,
Slain by his servant, going to put out
The other eye of Gloucester.

ALBANY

Gloucester's eyes!

MESSENGER

A servant that he bred, thrilled with remorse,
Opposed against the act, bending his sword
75 To his great master, who, thereat enraged,
Flew on him, and amongst them felled him dead;
But not without that harmful stroke which since
Hath plucked him after.

ALBANY

This shows you are above,
You justicers, that these our nether crimes

---

66. *howe'er* however much.

68. *mew*— Q, corrected from "now—"; a challenge = cast off your manly "fitness" (like a hawk "mewing," i.e., moulting its feathers)—or pen it up (as in a "mew" or cage)—and I will face you!

73. *thrilled* penetrated, moved; Q has "thrald". *remorse* pity; compare *King John*, IV.iii.50: "the tears of soft remorse."

74. *bending* Compare II.i.44.

75. *thereat enraged* Q; F has "threat-enrag'd".

76. *amongst . . . dead* between them Cornwall and Regan killed him; compare III.vii.75–80 and *2 King Henry IV*, V.iv.18: "The man is dead that you and Pistol beat amongst you."

79. *you justicers* Q, corrected from "your Iustices". F has "You Iustices".

80 So speedily can venge! But (O poor Gloucester)
Lost he his other eye?

MESSENGER

Both, both, my lord.
This letter, madam, craves a speedy answer;
'Tis from your sister.

GONERIL

[*Aside*] One way I like this well;
But being widow, and my Gloucester with her,
85 May all the building in my fancy pluck
Upon my hateful life: another way,
The news is not so tart.—I'll read, and answer.   *Exit.*

ALBANY

Where was his son when they did take his eyes?

MESSENGER

Come with my lady hither.

ALBANY

He is not here.

MESSENGER

90 No my good lord; I met him back again.

ALBANY

Knows he the wickedness?

MESSENGER

Ay my good lord; 'twas he informed against him,
And quit the house on purpose that their punishment
Might have the freer course.

ALBANY

Gloucester, I live
95 To thank thee for the love thou showedst the King,
And to revenge thine eyes. Come hither friend,
Tell me what more thou knowest.   *Exeunt.*

---

87. S.D.   Q; not in F.
90. *back*   on his way back; see line 15.

Scene iii: Enter KENT *and a* Gentleman.

KENT

Why the King of France is so suddenly gone back know you
no reason?

GENTLEMAN

Something he left imperfect in the state, which since his coming forth is thought of; which imports to the kingdom so much
5   fear and danger that his personal return was most required and
necessary.

KENT

Who hath he left behind him general?

GENTLEMAN

The Marshal of France, Monsieur La Far.

KENT

Did your letters pierce the queen to any demonstration of
10   grief?

GENTLEMAN

Ay sir; she took them, read them in my presence,
And now and then an ample tear trilled down
Her delicate cheek; it seemed she was a queen
Over her passion, who most rebel-like
15   Sought to be king o'er her.

Scene iii   Q; not in F; an attempt to avoid presenting the invasion as by
the King of France (compare Cordelias' claim in iv.27–9). Granville-Barker
considered that "the Folio gives the producer a good lead", on the theatrical
principle "Never explain, never apologize" (p. 273, n.). But the account of
Cordelia (lines 16ff.) does seem necessary dramatic preparation for her final
role. S.D.   Kent has found here, near Dover, the "welcome" which Gloucester promised in III.vi.85. The Gentleman is the one he had sent on in III.i.36,
46.

4. *imports*   carries as consequence; compare *Richard III*, III.vii.67–8:
"matter of great moment, No less importing than our general good".

11. *sir*   Theobald; Q has "say".

KENT

O then it moved her.

GENTLEMAN

Not to a rage; patience and sorrow strove
Who should express her goodliest. You have seen
Sunshine and rain at once; her smiles and tears
Were like, a better way: those happy smilets
20   That played on her ripe lip seemed not to know
What guests were in her eyes, which parted thence
As pearls from diamonds dropped. In brief,
Sorrow would be a rarity most beloved,
If all could so become it.

KENT

Made she no verbal question?

GENTLEMAN

25   Faith, once or twice she heaved the name of "father"
Pantingly forth, as if it pressed her heart;
Cried, "Sisters, sisters, shame of ladies, sisters!
Kent! father! sisters! What, i' th' storm? i' th' night?
Let pity not be believed!" There she shook
30   The holy water from her heavenly eyes,
And clamour moistened, then away she started
To deal with grief alone.

KENT

It is the stars,

---

16. *rage*   violent emotion. *patience*   ability to bear suffering, self-control
(compare III.vi.4).

19. *like . . . way*   like sun and rain together, but in a better manner;
Q has no comma.

20. *seemed*   Q has "seeme".

24. *become*   grace, adorn; compare *Cymbeline,* V.v.406–7: "He would
have well becom'd this place and grac'd The thankings of a king." *verbal
question*   comment in words.

31. *clamour moistened*   wet, with tears, her outcry; Q has "clamour
moystened her".

The stars above us, govern our conditions,
Else one self mate and make could not beget
35   Such different issues. You spoke not with her since?

GENTLEMAN

No.

KENT

Was this before the King returned?

GENTLEMAN

                              No, since.

KENT

Well sir, the poor distressed Lear's i' th' town,
Who sometime in his better tune remembers
40   What we are come about, and by no means
Will yield to see his daughter.

GENTLEMAN

                              Why good sir?

KENT

A sovereign shame so elbows him: his own unkindness,
That stripped her from his benediction, turned her
To foreign casualties, gave her dear rights
45   To his dog-hearted sisters, these things sting

---

33. *conditions*   dispositions, characters; compare *Merchant of Venice*,
I.ii.116–8: "the condition of a saint and the complexion of a devil".

34. *one . . . make*   the one pair.

38. *town*   a group of farm buildings or a hamlet; compare *2 Henry IV*,
Induction 33: "This have I rumour'd through the peasant towns." Lear is
found in the fields, between the two armies (vi.181, 201–6).

39. *tune*   frame of mind; compare *Much Ado About Nothing*, III.iv.36:
"Why, . . . do you speak in the sick tune?"

42. *sovereign*   supreme. *elbows*   keeps him back from meeting Cordelia,
elbows him out of his way towards her; parallel to "detains" in line 47.

44. *casualties*   hazards, chances; compare the similar cast-off situation of
Marina in *Pericles*, V.i.91–3: "time hath rooted out my parentage, And to the
world and awkward casualties Bound me in servitude."

45. *dog-hearted*   Compare "O inhuman dog!", Roderigo's cry as Iago
stabs him, *Othello*, V.i.62.

His mind so venomously that burning shame
Detains him from Cordelia.

GENTLEMAN

        Alack poor gentleman.

KENT

Of Albany's and Cornwall's powers you heard not?

GENTLEMAN

'Tis so; they are afoot.

KENT

50 Well sir, I'll bring you to our master Lear
And leave you to attend him. Some dear cause
Will in concealment wrap me up awhile;
When I am known aright, you shall not grieve
Lending me this acquaintance. I pray you
55 Go along with me.   *Exeunt.*

Scene iv: Enter with drum and colours, CORDELIA, *Doctor, Gentlemen, and Soldiers.*

CORDELIA

Alack, 'tis he: why, he was met even now
As mad as the vexed sea, singing aloud,
Crowned with rank fumiter and furrow-weeds,
With hardocks, hemlock, nettles, cuckoo-flowers,

---

48. *powers* forces.
51. *dear* important; compare III.i.19. Does he refer to the sentence of banishment which might still be used against him if he revealed his identity? But compare IV.vii.9.

Scene iv S.D. "Doctor" from Q; not in F.
2. *mad . . . sea* Compare *Hamlet*, IV.i.7: "Mad as the sea and wind, when both contend . . ." The action is still near Dover and the coast.
3. *fumiter* fumitory, formerly a medicinal herb, from *fumus terrae*, smoke of the earth; Q has "femiter", F "Fenitar".
4. *hardocks* Q has "hordocks"; unidentified. *cuckoo-flowers* flowers which come with the cuckoo.

5   Darnel, and all the idle weeds that grow
    In our sustaining corn. A century send forth;
    Search every acre in the high-grown field
    And bring him to our eye.   [*Exit a Gentleman.*]
                        What can man's wisdom
    In the restoring his bereaved sense?
10 He that helps him take all my outward worth.

                        DOCTOR

    There is means madam;
    Our foster-nurse of (nature) is repose,
    The which he lacks; that to provoke in him
    Are many simples operative, whose power
15 Will close the eye of anguish.

                        CORDELIA

                        All blessed secrets,
    All you unpublished virtues of the earth,
    Spring with my tears, be aidant and remediate
    In the good man's distress. Seek, seek for him,
    Lest his ungoverned rage dissolve the life
20 That wants the means to lead it.

                Enter Messenger.

                        MESSENGER

                        News madam:
    The British powers are marching hitherward.

                        CORDELIA

    'Tis known before; our preparation stands

---

5. *Darnel*   Wyclif's translation, in *Matthew* 13:25, of what appears in
A.V. as "tares."

6. *century*   a force of a hundred.

10. *worth*   wealth; compare *Othella*, I.ii.28: "the seas' worth." DOC-
TOR Q; F has "Gent."

16. *virtues*   (healing) powers; compare *Sonnets*, 81, 13: "You still shall
live, such virtue hath my pen . . ."

18. *distress*   Q; F has "desires".

19. *rage*   madness; compare iii.16, vii.78.

In expectation of them. O dear father,
It is thy business that I go about;
25   Therefore great France
My mourning and impórtuned tears hath pitied.
No blown ambition doth our arms incite,
But love, dear love, and our aged father's right.
Soon may I hear, and see him!   *Exeunt.*

Scene v: Enter REGAN *and* OSWALD.

REGAN

But are my brother's powers set forth?

OSWALD

                              Ay madam.

REGAN

Himself in person there?

OSWALD

                    Madam, with much ado:
Your sister is the better soldier.

REGAN

Lord Edmund spake not with your lord at home?

OSWALD

5   No madam.

REGAN

What might import my sister's letter to him?

---

26. *impórtuned*   importunate. Q has "important".
27. *blown*   inflated. *incite*   Q has "in sight".

Scene v   Located wherever the widowed Regan may be living, probably
still at Gloucester's castle; Oswald has been sent there with a letter from
Goneril to Edmund.
4. *lord*   Q has "Lady".

OSWALD

I know not, lady.

REGAN

Faith, he is posted hence on serious matter.
It was great ignorance, Gloucester's eyes being out,
10 To let him live; where he arrives he moves
All hearts against us. Edmund, I think, is gone,
In pity of his misery, to dispatch
His nighted life; moreover, to descry
The strength o' th' enemy.

OSWALD

15 I must needs after him, madam, with my letter.

REGAN

Our troops set forth to-morrow; stay with us;
The ways are dangerous.

OSWALD

                    I may not, madam;
My lady charged my duty in this business.

REGAN

Why should she write to Edmund? Might not you
20 Transport her purposes by word? Belike,
Some things, I know not what. I'll love thee much,
Let me unseal the letter.

OSWALD

               Madam, I had rather—

---

9. *ignorance*   lack of skill; compare Pisanio, after receiving his instructions to kill Imogen, *Cymbeline*, III.ii.23: "I am ignorant in what I am commanded."

11. *Edmund*   Q has "and now".

13. *nighted*   plunged in night, blinded.

18. *charged*   commanded.

21. *love thee*   favor you; compare *King John*, III.iii.66–7: "Hubert, I love thee. Well, I'll not say what I intend for thee."

22. *Madam . . . rather*   a courteous refusal.

REGAN

I know your lady does not love her husband,
I am sure of that; and at her late being here
25   She gave strange œilliads and most speaking looks
To noble Edmund. I know you are of her bosom.

OSWALD

I, madam?

REGAN

I speak in understanding; y' are, I know't:
Therefore I do advise you, take this note:
30   My lord is dead; Edmund and I have talked,
And more convenient is he for my hand
Than for your lady's. You may gather more.
If you do find him, pray you give him this,
And when your mistress hears thus much from you,
35   I pray desire her call her wisdom to her.
So fare you well.
If you do chance to hear of that blind traitor,
Preferment falls on him that cuts him off.

OSWALD

Would I could meet him, madam! I should show
40   What party I do follow.

REGAN

Fare thee well.   *Exeunt.*

---

25. *œilliads*   amorous looks.
26. *bosom*   confidence; compare *Julius Caesar*, V.i.7–8: "I am in their
[the enemy's] bosoms, and I know Wherefore they do it."
29. *take this note*   take note of this.
31. *convenient*   proper, becoming; compare V.i.36.
33. *this*   a token of some sort.
39. *him*   Q; not in F.

Scene vi: Enter GLOUCESTER *and* EDGAR.

GLOUCESTER

When shall I come to th' top of that same hill?

EDGAR

You do climb up it now; look how we labour.

GLOUCESTER

Methinks the ground is even.

EDGAR

                Horrible steep.

Hark, do you hear the sea?

GLOUCESTER

            No truly.

EDGAR

5   Why then your other senses grow imperfect
By your eyes' anguish.

GLOUCESTER

            So it may be indeed.
Methinks thy voice is altered, and thou speak'st
In better phrase and matter than thou didst.

EDGAR

Y'are much deceived; in nothing am I changed
10 But in my garments.

GLOUCESTER

            Methinks y'are better spoken.

Scene vi 1. *hill* See IV.i.71–2. In the lines which follow (2–11) they
make their way to the front of the platform, as if climbing.
10. *garments* See IV.i.44.

EDGAR

Come on sir; here's the place: stand still. How fearful
And dizzy 'tis to cast one's eyes so low!
The crows and choughs that wing the midway air
Show scarce so gross as beetles. Half way down
15 Hangs one that gathers sampire, dreadful trade!
Methinks he seems no bigger than his head.
The fishermen that walk upon the beach
Appear like mice, and yond tall anchoring bark
Diminished to her cock; her cock, a buoy
20 Almost too small for sight. The murmuring surge
That on th' unnumbered idle pebble chafes
Cannot be heard so high. I'll look no more,
Lest my brain turn, and the deficient sight
Topple down headlong.

GLOUCESTER

Set me where you stand.

EDGAR

25 Give me your hand; you are now within a foot
Of th' extreme verge: for all beneath the moon
Would I not leap upright.

GLOUCESTER

Let go my hand.
Here friend's another purse; in it a jewel

11–22. *How fearful . . . high* New Cambridge ed. compares the death of
Malbecco, Spenser, *Faerie Queene*, III.x.56–7.

13. *choughs* jackdaws, grackles.

15. *sampire* herb of Saint Peter (Pierre), the fleshy leaves of which are
used in pickles.

17. *walk* Q; F has "walk'd".

19. *cock* small boat, especially one towed behind a coaster.

21. *idle* useless: of moss in *Comedy of Errors*, II.ii.177, weeds in *Richard
III*, III.i.103, and deserts in *Othello*, I.iii.140.

22. *heard . . . I'll* Q has "heard, its so hie ile".

23. *deficient* failing.

27. *upright* right up; straight up, even where I am standing.

28. *another* See IV.i.62.

Well worth a poor man's taking: fairies and gods
30 Prosper it with thee. Go thou further off;
Bid me farewell, and let me hear thee going.

EDGAR

Now fare ye well, good sir.

GLOUCESTER

With all my heart.

EDGAR

[*Aside*] Why I do trifle thus with his despair
Is done to cure it.

GLOUCESTER

[*Kneeling*]   O you mighty gods!
35 This world I do renounce, and in your sights
Shake patiently my great affliction off;
If I could bear it longer, and not fall
To quarrel with your great opposeless wills,
My snuff and loathèd part of nature should
40 Burn itself out. If Edgar live, O bless him!
Now fellow, fare thee well. [*Falls forward.*]

EDGAR

Gone sir,

farewell.—

[*Aside*] And yet I know not how conceit may rob
The treasury of life, when life itself
Yields to the theft. Had he been where he thought,
45 By this had thought been past.—[*To Gloucester, with altered*

---

29. *fairies*   said to multiply treasure after it had been found.

37–40. *If . . . out*   Even if I could suffer any longer without rebelling
against your will which cannot be opposed, the smoldering remnant of my
hateful life would soon burn out.

39. *snuff*   part of the wick of a candle, not quite burnt away and needing
to be trimmed off with "snuffers"; compare III.i.26.

41. S.D.   not in F; Q has "He *fals*."

42–4. *And yet . . . theft*   Nevertheless I do not know if imagination may
kill him, seeing that he wants to die (following on from lines 33–4).

45   *voice*] Alive or dead?
Ho, you sir! Friend, hear you sir, speak!—
Thus might he pass indeed; yet he revives.—
What are you sir?

GLOUCESTER

Away, and let me die.

EDGAR

Hadst thou been aught but gossamer, feathers, air,
50   So many fathom down precipitating,
Thou'dst shivered like an egg; but thou dost breathe,
Hast heavy substance, bleed'st not, speak'st, art sound.
Ten masts at each make not the altitude
Which thou hast perpendicularly fell:
55   Thy life's a miracle. Speak yet again.

GLOUCESTER

But have I fall'n, or no?

EDGAR

From the dread summit of this chalky bourn.
Look up a-height; the shrill-gorged lark so far
Cannot be seen or heard: do but look up.

GLOUCESTER

60   Alack, I have no eyes.
Is wretchedness deprived that benefit
To end itself by death? 'Twas yet some comfort
When misery could beguile the tyrant's rage
And frustrate his proud will.

EDGAR

Give me your arm:
65   Up, so; how is't? Feel you your legs? You stand.

---

53. *at each*   end to end.
57. *bourn*   boundary, limit.
58. *shrill-gorged*   shrill-throated.
63. *beguile*   cheat; compare V.iii.151.

GLOUCESTER

Too well, too well.

EDGAR

       This is above all strangeness.
Upon the crown o' th' cliff what thing was that
Which parted from you?

GLOUCESTER

         A poor unfortunate beggar.

EDGAR

As I stood here below methought his eyes
70 Were two full moons; he had a thousand noses,
Horns whelked and waved like the enridgèd sea:
It was some fiend; therefore thou happy father,
Think that the clearest gods, who make them honours
Of men's impossibilities, have preserved thee.

GLOUCESTER

75 I do remember now: henceforth I'll bear
Affliction till it do cry out itself,
"Enough, enough," and die. That thing you speak of
I took it for a man: often 'twould say,
"The fiend, the fiend." He led me to that place.

EDGAR

80 Bear free and patient thoughts. But who comes here?

---

    67. *cliff what* Q; F has "cliff. What".

    71. *whelked* convoluted like the shell of a whelk; F has "wealk'd", Q "welk't". *enridgèd* Q; F has "enraged".

    72. *father* old man; compare V.ii.1.

    73. *clearest* most glorious, or free from evil; compare *Macbeth*, I.vii.16–18: "Duncan . . . So clear in his great office".

    73–4. *who . . . impossibilities* who find honor in doing what men cannot.

    77. *die* I.e., affliction will tire first.

    80. *free* untroubled (compare III.iv.11), innocent (compare *Hamlet*, II.ii.557: "Make mad the guilty, and appal the free"). *patient* able to "bear Affliction"; compare III.vi.4, n. S.D. Q has *"Enter Lear mad"* (after line 82); he is obviously crowned with wild flowers as in IV.iv.3ff.

Enter LEAR.

The safer sense will ne'er accommodate
His master thus.

LEAR

No, they cannot touch me for coining; I am the King himself.

EDGAR

O thou side-piercing sight!

LEAR

85　Nature's above art, in that respect. There's your press-money.
That fellow handles his bow like a crow-keeper: draw me a
clothier's yard. Look, look, a mouse: peace, peace, this piece of
toasted cheese will do't. There's my gauntlet; I'll prove it on a
giant. Bring up the brown bills. O well flown, bird: i' th' clout,
90　i' th' clout—hewgh! Give the word.

EDGAR

Sweet marjoram.

LEAR

Pass.

81–2. The sane mind (compare IV.iv.9 and *Othello*, IV.i.266: "Are his
wits safe?") would never dress up (compare III.iv.95) its possessor like this.

83. *coining*　Q; counterfeiting money (which the King alone had the
right to coin); F has "crying".

85. *Nature's . . . respect*　In coining, a king who does it by natural right
is above a forger who does it by skill. *press-money*　payment made in advance to a soldier or sailor pressed into service.

86–7. *like a crow-keeper . . . yard*　no better than a scarecrow might, or a
mere boy using a bow for the same purpose: let him rather draw the bow
back for me a full yard (the length of the arrow).

88–9. *There's . . . giant*　I throw my glove down as a challenge; I'll prove
my contention in a duel even with a giant.

89. *brown bills*　the soldiers with halberds (consisting of a blade and a
spearhead at the end of a long shaft) painted brown to prevent rust.

89–90. *O . . . hewgh!*　spoken to the arrow flying to the mark ("clout")
with a whizz ("hewgh"). Q has "O . . . bird in the ayre, hagh,".

90. *word*　password.

91. *marjoram*　an herb considered a medicine against mental diseases
and common in limestone country like that near Dover; so, very likely, Lear
is decked with it.

GLOUCESTER

I know that voice.

LEAR

Ha! Goneril with a white beard? They flattered me like a dog,
95 and told me I had the white hairs in my beard ere the black
ones were there. To say "ay" and "no" to every thing that I
said! "Ay" and "no" too was no good divinity. When the rain
came to wet me once and the wind to make me chatter, when
the thunder would not peace at my bidding, there I found 'em,
100 there I smelt 'em out. Go to, they are not men o' their words:
they told me I was every thing; 'tis a lie, I am not ague-proof.

GLOUCESTER

The trick of that voice I do well remember.
Is't not the King?

LEAR

Ay, every inch a King.
When I do stare, see how the subject quakes.
105 I pardon that man's life. What was thy cause?
Adultery?
Thou shalt not die. Die for adultery? No,
The wren goes to 't, and the small gilded fly
Does lecher in my sight.
110 Let copulation thrive; for Gloucester's bastard son
Was kinder to his father than my daughters
Got 'tween the lawful sheets.

94-6. *Goneril . . . there* He mistakes the bearded Gloucester for
Goneril. This reminds him of the flattery of I.i.—and before, when, even as
a beardless boy, he was credited with age and wisdom. Q has "Ha *Gonorill*,
ha *Regan*, they . . ."

97. *divinity* theology, as in James 5:12: ". . . swear not . . . but let your
yea be yea; and your nay, nay . . ."

106-29. *Adultery . . . for thee* Q prints as prose and F as misdivided
verse down to "soldiers" in line 113, and thereafter as prose.

110-12. *Gloucester's . . . sheets* "Gloucester knows better . . . A slight
unconscious turn of the sightless eyes toward him [Lear], a simple gesture—
unseen—in response from Edgar, patiently biding his time, will illuminate
the irony and the pathos" (Granville-Barker, p. 296).

　　　To 't, luxury, pell-mell, for I lack soldiers.
　　　Behold yond simpering dame,
115　Whose face between her forks presages snow;
　　　That minces virtue, and does shake the head
　　　To hear of pleasure's name;
　　　The fitchew nor the soilèd horse goes to 't
　　　With a more riotous appetite.
120　Down from the waist they are centaurs,
　　　Though women all above;
　　　But to the girdle do the gods inherit,
　　　Beneath is all the fiend's.
　　　There's hell, there's darkness, there is the sulphurous pit—
125　Burning, scalding, stench, consumption.
　　　Fie, fie, fie! pah, pah!
　　　Give me an ounce of civet, good apothecary,
　　　To sweeten my imagination.
　　　There's money for thee.

GLOUCESTER

O let me kiss that hand.

LEAR

130　Let me wipe it first; it smells of mortality.

---

113. *luxury*　lasciviousness.

115. *forks*　legs; or, possibly, ornaments for holding up the hair. *snow* frigidity, chastity; compare *Timon of Athens*, IV.iii.383–4: ". . . thaw the consecrated snow That lies on Dian's lap."

116. *minces virtue*　makes affectation of chastity.

118. *fitchew*　polecat, perhaps also prostitute; compare Cassio, of Bianca, in *Othello*, IV.i.144: " 'Tis such another fitchew!" *soilèd* richly fed; *O.E.D.*, *v.*⁴, 1736: "To soil horses, is to . . . purge 'em, by giving 'em . . . green clover . . ."

120. *centaurs*　with animals' bodies (and lusts).

122. *inherit*　possess, dwell; compare *O.E.D.*, *v.*, 5.b, 1600: "O, where can life celestial inherit?"

125. *consumption*　Q has "consumation".

127–8. *civet . . . To sweeten*　from Q; F has "Civet; good Apothecary sweeten". Civet is a perfume, secreted by the animal of that name.

GLOUCESTER

O ruined piece of Nature! This great world
Shall so wear out to naught. Dost thou know me?

LEAR

I remember thine eyes well enough. Dost thou squiny at me?
No, do thy worst, blind Cupid; I'll not love.
135   Read thou this challenge; mark but the penning of it.

GLOUCESTER

Were all thy letters suns, I could not see.

EDGAR

[*Aside*] I would not take this from report; it is,
And my heart breaks at it.

LEAR

Read.

GLOUCESTER

140   What, with the case of eyes?

LEAR

O ho, are you there with me? No eyes in your head, nor no
money in your purse? Your eyes are in a heavy case, your
purse in a light; yet you see how this world goes.

GLOUCESTER

I see it feelingly.

---

131. *this great world*   the universe; compare III.i.10, n.
133. *squiny*   peer (as still in Midland dialects of England at the time of
Onions, *Shakespeare Glossary*, 1911).
134. *blind Cupid*   Compare *Much Ado About Nothing*, I.i.219: ". . . hang
me up at the door of a brothel-house for the sign of blind Cupid."
135. *challenge*   Compare line 88.
140. *case*   casing: sockets and lids; compare *Pericles*, III.ii.104: "Her
eyelids, cases to those heavenly jewels".
141. *are . . . me?*   Is that what I am to understand? Compare *2 Henry
VI*, II.i.48: "I am with you" = "I understand."
144. *feelingly*   (a) by the sense of feeling (b) with strong emotion; compare *Rape of Lucrece*, 1492: "Here feelingly she weeps Troy's painted woes."

LEAR

145   What, art mad? A man may see how this world goes, with no
eyes. Look with thine ears: see how yond justice rails upon
yond simple thief. Hark in thine ear: change places, and handy-
dandy, which is the justice, which is the thief? Thou hast seen
a farmer's dog bark at a beggar?

GLOUCESTER

150   Ay sir.

LEAR

And the creature run from the cur? There thou might'st behold
the great image of authority: a dog's obeyed in office.
Thou rascal beadle, hold thy bloody hand.
Why dost thou lash that whore? Strip thine own back;
155   Thou hotly lusts to use her in that kind
For which thou whip'st her. The usurer hangs the cozener.
Through tattered clothes small vices do appear;
Robes and furred gowns hide all. Plate sin with gold,
And the strong lance of justice hurtless breaks;
160   Arm it in rags, a pigmy's straw does pierce it.
None does offend, none—I say none; I'll able 'em:
Take that of me, my friend, who have the power

147–8. *handy-dandy*   take your choice, from the children's game of
guessing which hand holds an object behind the back. Compare Jonson,
Bartholomew Fair, III.v.119: "handy-dandy, which hand will he have?"
change . . . and   not in Q.

152. *dog's obeyed*   Q has "dogge, so bade".

153. *beadle*   a parish officer who kept order in church and whipped petty
offenders.

153–66. *Thou . . . so*   prose in F and Q.

155. *kind*   fashion.

156. *The . . . cozener*   The man who takes excessive interest on his money
will sentence, in his position as magistrate, one who merely cheats.

157. *clothes*   Q has "rags". *small*   Q; F has "great".

158. *Plate sin*   Theobald; F has "Place sinnes". Lines 158–63, "Plate . . .
lips", are not in Q.

161. *able*   impower, authorize; compare *O.E.D.*, *v.*, 4.b, 1600: "That none
be abled in law to receive any benefice . . . unless he be a preacher."

162. *that*   what I have just said.

To seal th' accuser's lips. Get thee glass eyes
And like a scurvy politician seem
165   To see the things thou dost not. Now, now, now, now.
Pull off my boots; harder, harder; so.

EDGAR

[*Aside*] O matter and impertinency mixed;
Reason in madness.

LEAR

If thou wilt weep my fortunes, take my eyes.
170   I know thee well enough; thy name is Gloucester.
Thou must be patient; we came crying hither:
Thou know'st, the first time that we smell the air,
We wawl and cry. I will preach to thee: mark.

GLOUCESTER

Alack, alack the day.

LEAR

175   When we are born, we cry that we are come
To this great stage of fools. This a good block!
It were a delicate stratagem to shoe
A troop of horse with felt; I'll put 't in proof,
And when I have stol'n upon these son-in-laws,
180   Then, kill, kill, kill, kill, kill, kill!
                    Enter a Gentleman [*, with Attendants*].

GENTLEMAN

O here he is; lay hand upon him. Sir,
Your most dear daughter—

---

164. *scurvy politician*   vile schemer; see I.ii.45, n.
167. *impertinency*   what is not pertinent or relevant.
171. *patient*   Compare line 80, n.
176. *block*   a mold for a hat, hence shape or fashion of hat, i.e., the weeds
he is "crowned" with, which he takes off before beginning to preach; compare *Much Ado About Nothing*, I.i.63: "He wears his faith but as the fashion
of his hat; it ever changes with the next block."
177. *delicate*   ingenious.
177–8. *shoe . . . felt*   Q has "shoot . . . fell".
181. *him. Sir,*   Q has "him sirs,"; F "him, Sir."

LEAR

No rescue? What, a prisoner? I am even
The natural fool of fortune. Use me well;
185   You shall have ransom. Let me have surgeons;
I am cut to th' brains.

GENTLEMAN

You shall have anything.

LEAR

No seconds? all myself?
Why this would make a man a man of salt,
To use his eyes for garden water-pots,
190   Ay, and laying autumn's dust. I will die bravely,
Like a smug bridegroom. What! I will be jovial:
Come, come, I am a King, masters, know you that?

GENTLEMAN

You are a royal one, and we obey you.

LEAR

Then there's life in't. Come, and you get it, you shall get it by
195   running. Sa, sa, sa, sa.   *Exit running.* [*Attendants follow.*]

GENTLEMAN

A sight most pitiful in the meanest wretch,

---

184. *natural*   born.
187. *seconds*   supporters; compare *Tempest*, III.iii.103: "I'll fight their
legions o'er. *Antonio:* I'll be thy second."
188. *salt*   salt tears.
189–90. *water-pots . . . I will*   Q has "waterpots . . . dust. *Lear.* I will";
F "water-pots. I wil".
190. *bravely*   (a) valiantly (b) in fine clothes.
191. *smug*   not in Q; smart, spruce; compare Shylock, of Antonio, *Merchant of Venice*, III.i.39: ". . . a beggar, that was us'd to came so smug upon
the mart."
194. *Then . . . it*   Then my cause is not lost. Come, if you are to get
the ransom (line 185) . . .
195. *Sa . . . sa*   not in Q; French "çà, çà!" Here, here! (to encourage, for
instance, hounds). S.D.   F has "*Exit*."; Q "*Exit King running*."

Past speaking of in a king! Thou hast one daughter
Who redeems⌈Nature⌉from the general curse
Which twain have brought her to.

EDGAR

200   Hail gentle sir.

GENTLEMAN

Sir, speed you; what's your will?

EDGAR

Do you hear aught, sir, of a battle toward?

GENTLEMAN

Most sure, and vulgar; every one hears that,
Which can distinguish sound.

EDGAR

But by your favour,
How near's the other army?

GENTLEMAN

205   Near, and on speedy foot; the main descry
Stands on the hourly thought.

EDGAR

I thank you sir: that's all.

GENTLEMAN

Though that the queen on special cause is here,
Her army is moved on.   *Exit.*

---

197. *one*   Q; F has "a".

200. *gentle*   well-born. *speed you*   May God prosper you; compare I.ii.19 and *Julius Caesar*, I.ii.88: ". . . let the gods so speed me . . ."

202. *vulgar*   commonly known; compare *Hamlet*, I.ii.98–9: "For what we know must be, and is as common As any the most vulgar thing to sense . . ."

203. *sound*   Q has "sense".

205–6. *the main . . . thought*   Sight of the main body is expected any hour now; Q has ". . . on speed fort the main descryes, Standst on the howerly thoughts".

EDGAR

I thank you sir.

GLOUCESTER

You ever-gentle gods, take my breath from me;
210   Let not my worser spirit tempt me again
To die before you please.

EDGAR

Well pray you, father.

GLOUCESTER

Now good sir, what are you?

EDGAR

A most poor man, made tame to Fortune's blows,
Who, by the art of known and feeling sorrows,
215   Am pregnant to good pity. Give me your hand,
I'll lead you to some biding.

GLOUCESTER

Hearty thanks;
The bounty and the benison of Heaven
To boot, and boot!

Enter OSWALD.

OSWALD

A proclaimed prize! Most happy!
That eyeless head of thine was first framed flesh
220   To raise my fortunes. Thou old unhappy traitor,

---

210. *worser spirit*   bad angel; compare *Sonnets*, 144, 2–4: "... two spirits
do suggest me still; The better angel is a man right fair, The worser spirit a
woman colour'd ill."

213. *tame to*   Q has "lame by".

214–5. *Who ... pity.*   Through the skill (compare III.ii.67) given by the
experience of keenly-felt sorrows, I am ready to pity (compare *Twelfth
Night*, III.i.86: "your ... pregnant and vouchsafed ear").

216. *biding*   abode.

218. *To ... boot*   in addition (to my thanks) and as compensation; Q
has "to boot, to boot", corrected from "to save thee".

Briefly thyself remember: the sword is out
That must destroy thee.

GLOUCESTER

Now let thy friendly hand
Put strength enough to 't.   [EDGAR *interposes.*]

OSWALD

Wherefore, bold peasant,
Dar'st thou support a published traitor? Hence;
225 Lest that th' infection of his fortune take
Like hold on thee. Let go his arm.

EDGAR

Chill not let go zir, without vurther 'casion.

OSWALD

Let go slave, or thou diest.

EDGAR

Good gentleman go your gate and let poor volk pass. And
230 'chud ha' bin zwagger'd out of my life, 'twould not ha' bin zo
long as 'tis by a vortnight. Nay, come not near th' old man;
keep out, che vor' ye, or ise try whether your costard or my
ballow be the harder. Chill be plain with you.

---

221. *thyself remember*   Survey your life (in preparation for death).

224. *published*   proclaimed; compare I.i.38; II.iii.1.

227. I will not let go without further occasion, i.e., reason. Edgar's language down to line 235 is "a patchwork of current colloquialisms and conventional stage dialect" (Kökeritz, *Shakespeare's Pronunciation*, 1953, p. 39) adopted to disguise himself as a countryman, in the presence of a servant of his father's enemies.

229. *gate*   way.

229–31. *And . . . vortnight.*   If I would have been killed by mere swaggering, my life would have been a fortnight shorter at least; "as 'tis" is not in Q.

232. *che vor' ye*   I warrant you; a mere expression of strong belief or emphasis.

232–3. *ise . . . harder*   I shall try which is harder, your head (literally, apple) or my cudgel (Q has "bat", miscorrected from "battero").

OSWALD

Out, dunghill!

EDGAR

235   Chill pick your teeth, zir. Come; no matter vor your foins.

They fight.

OSWALD

Slave thou hast slain me; villain, take my purse.
If ever thou wilt thrive, bury my body;
And give the letters which thou find'st about me
To Edmund Earl of Gloucester; seek him out
240   Upon the English party: O untimely death!
Death.

He dies.

EDGAR

I know thee well: a serviceable villain,
As duteous to the vices of thy mistress
As badness would desire.

GLOUCESTER

What, is he dead?

EDGAR

245   Sit you down father; rest you.
Let's see these pockets; the letters that he speaks of
May be my friends. He's dead; I am only sorry
He had no other deathsman. Let us see:
Leave, gentle wax; and, manners, blame us not:
250   To know our enemies' minds, we rip their hearts;

---

235. *foins* fencing thrusts (compare *2 Henry IV*, II.i.17: "He will foin like any devil"), the aristocratic way of fighting. S.D.   Q; not in F.

236. *villain* See III.vii.75, n.

238. *letters* a letter (*litterae*).

240. *party* side; compare II.i.25. *English* Q has "British"; compare III.iv.168.

241. S.D.   Q; not in F.

248. *deathsman* executioner, i.e., he should have been hanged.

249–50. *Leave . . . To* Q punctuates "leave gentle waxe, and manners blame us not To"; F "Leave gentle waxe, and manners: blame us not To". Compare *Twelfth Night*, II.v.87: "By your leave, wax."

Their papers is more lawful.   *Reads the letter.*

"Let our reciprocal vows be remembered. You have many
opportunities to cut him off; if your will want not, time and
place will be fruitfully offered. There is nothing done if he re-
255 turn the conqueror; then am I the prisoner, and his bed my
gaol; from the loathed warmth whereof deliver me, and supply
the place for your labour.

                    Your (wife, so I would say) affectionate servant,
                                        Goneril."

260 O indistinguished space of woman's will!
A plot upon her virtuous husband's life,
And the exchange my brother! Here in the sands
Thee I'll rake up, the post unsanctified

                    [*Letting* OSWALD *down through a trap*]

Of murtherous lechers; and in the mature time
265 With this ungracious paper strike the sight
Of the death-practised duke. For him 'tis well
That of thy death and business I can tell.

                    GLOUCESTER

The King is mad: how stiff is my vile sense
That I stand up, and have ingenious feeling
270 Of my huge sorrows! Better I were distract:

---

254. *fruitfully* copiously, fully.

254–5. *done . . . then* The punctuation in F "done. If hee returne the
Conqueror, then" seems to derive from Q "done, If . . . conqueror, then".

258. *affectionate servant* Q has "your affectionate servant and for you
her owne for *Venter*" for "and your own for venture", i.e., your own lady
if you are willing to venture in your own behalf; compare IV.ii.20.

263. *rake up* cover up; compare *O.E.D., v.*¹, 4.b, 1576: "The dead body
. . . raked up in clods of earth." Presumably the body is either dragged off
here, or disposed of through a trap (Introduction, p. xxiii). *post* courier,
messenger.

265. *strike* blast, destroy; compare *Hamlet*, I.i.162: ". . . no planets
strike."

266. *death-practised* whose death has been plotted (compare III.ii.55).

268. *stiff* obstinate, stubborn.

269. *ingenious* quick, sensitive; compare *Hamlet*, V.i.242: "thy most
ingenious sense."

So should my thoughts be severed from my griefs
And woes by wrong imaginations lose
The knowledge of themselves.   *Drum afar off.*

EDGAR
                              Give me your hand.
Far off methinks I hear the beaten drum.
275 Come father, I'll bestow you with a friend.   *Exeunt.*

Scene vii: Enter CORDELIA, KENT, Doctor, *and* Gentleman.

CORDELIA

O thou good Kent, how shall I live and work
To match thy goodness? My life will be too short
And every measure fail me.

KENT

To be acknowledged, madam, is o'erpaid.
5   All my reports go with the modest truth,
Nor more nor clipped, but so.

CORDELIA

                    Be better suited;
These weeds are memories of those worser hours;
I prithee put them off.

---

271. *severed* Q has "fenced".
272–3. *woes . . . themselves* my sorrows would be forgotten in false fantasies [of madness].
274. *drum* Empson suggests that the drum should be continued, getting steadily louder, throughout the next scene, showing the threat of the advancing enemy from whom Lear "is no longer in a condition to save his daughter's life" (*Critical Quarterly* III [Spring 1961], 67).
275. *bestow* Compare II.iv.283.

Scene vii "*Scena Septima*" in F, even though the one before is "Scena Quinta"; compare IV.iii., headnote. S.D. *Doctor* Q, not in F.
3. *measure fail* because Kent's goodness cannot be measured.
6. *Nor . . . clipped* without addition or curtainment. *suited* clothed.
7. *weeds* clothes.

KENT

Pardon dear madam;
Yet to be known shortens my made intent:
10 My boon I make it that you know me not
Till time and I think meet.

CORDELIA

Then be't so my good lord.—[*To the Doctor*]
How does the King?

DOCTOR

Madam, sleeps still.

CORDELIA

O you kind gods,
15 Cure this great breach in his abusèd nature!
Th' untuned and jarring senses, O wind up,
Of this child-changed father.

DOCTOR

So please your Majesty
That we may wake the King? he hath slept long.

CORDELIA

Be governed by your knowledge, and proceed
20 I' th' sway of your own will. Is he arrayed?
Enter LEAR *in a chair carried by Servants.*

GENTLEMAN

Ay madam; in the heaviness of sleep
We put fresh garments on him.

---

9. *Yet . . . intent* To be known as Kent yet, would curtail the plan I have made. Kent's plan remains unknown (compare IV.iii.52) but Shakespeare's is clear enough: see V.iii.279–80.

16. *jarring* Q has "hurrying". *wind up* tune up, by tightening the strings.

17. *child-changed* changed by his children; or changed to a child, i.e., entering his second childhood or dotage.

DOCTOR

Be by, good madam, when we do awake him;
I doubt not of his temperance.

CORDELIA

Very well. [*Music.*]

DOCTOR [*moving towards Lear*]

25 Please you draw near. Louder the music there!

CORDELIA

O my dear father, restoration hang
Thy medicine on my lips, and let this kiss
Repair those violent harms that my two sisters
Have in thy reverence made.

KENT

Kind and dear princess.

CORDELIA

30 Had you not been their father, these white flakes
Did challenge pity of them. Was this a face
To be opposed against the warring winds?
To stand against the deep dread bolted thunder?
In the most terrible and nimble stroke
35 Of quick cross lightning? to watch—poor *perdu!*—

---

24. *not* Q; not in F. *temperance* self-control; compare *O.E.D.*, 1, 1654:
"Yet it pleased God to give me much patience and temperance to bear this
. . . ingratitude."

24–5. CORDELIA *Very . . . there* Q; not in F. S.D. *music* "best com-
forter To an unsettled fancy" (*Tempest*, V.i.58–9).

29. *thy reverence* the respect due to you.

30. *flakes* tufts, locks (of hair).

31. *challenge* claim (compare I.i.48); Q has "had challengd".

32. *opposed* Q has "exposd". *warring* Q; F has "iarring" (compare
line 16 above).

33–6. *To . . . helm?* Q; not in F.

35. *cross* forked; compare *Julius Caesar*, I.iii.50–1: "And when the cross
blue lightning seem'd to open The breast of heaven . . ." *watch . . . perdu* to
keep awake, as if on the lookout like a "lost" sentinel (French *sentinelle
perdue*) in an advanced and perilous position.

With this thin helm? Mine enemy's dog,
Though he had bit me, should have stood that night
Against my fire. And wast thou fain, poor father,
To hovel thee with swine and rogues forlorn,
40   In short and musty straw? Alack, alack,
'Tis wonder that thy life and wits at once
Had not concluded all.—He wakes; speak to him.

DOCTOR

Madam do you; 'tis fittest.

CORDELIA

How does my royal lord? How fares your Majesty?

LEAR

45   You do me wrong to take me out o' th' grave;
Thou art a soul in bliss; but I am bound
Upon a wheel of fire, that mine own tears
Do scald like molten lead.

CORDELIA

Sir, do you know me?

LEAR

You are a spirit I know; where did you die?

CORDELIA

50   Still, still, far wide.

DOCTOR

He's scarce awake; let him alone awhile.

---

36. *thin helm*   scanty hair. *enemy's*   Q has "iniurious".
38. *fain*   glad.
42. *all*   Compare I.i.99.
47. *wheel of fire*   traditionally one of the torments of hell (where Lear
believes he is). *that*   with the result that.
48. *scald*   Q; F has "scal'd".
50. *wide*   mistaken; compare *O.E.D., a.,* 10.b, 1592: " 'Tis neither as you
think, nor as you think . . . you're wide all."

LEAR

Where have I been? Where am I? Fair daylight?
I am mightily abused; I should e'en die with pity
To see another thus. I know not what to say.
55   I will not swear these are my hands: let's see;
I feel this pin prick. Would I were assured
Of my condition.

CORDELIA

O look upon me sir,
And hold your hand in benediction o'er me.
No sir, you must not kneel.   [*Kneels.*]

LEAR

Pray do not mock me:
60   I am a very foolish fond old man,
Fourscore and upward, not an hour more, nor less;
And to deal plainly,
I fear I am not in my perfect mind.
Methinks I should know you, and know this man;
65   Yet I am doubtful: for I am mainly ignorant
What place this is; and all the skill I have
Remembers not these garments; nor I know not
Where I did lodge last night. Do not laugh at me;
For (as I am a man) I think this lady
To be my child Cordelia.

CORDELIA

70   And so I am, I am.

LEAR

Be your tears wet? Yes faith. I pray weep not;

---

53. *abused*   Compare IV.i.22.

59. *No sir*   Q; not in F. *you*   emphatic, as Lear makes a move as if to get up from his chair and kneel himself. Compare Appendix B, p. 212.

60. *fond*   Compare I.ii.47.

61. *not . . . less*   not in Q, which is perhaps right, for "Fourscore and upward, and to deal plainly" would make a complete, although not a very good, line.

65. *mainly*   quite, perfectly.

If you have poison for me, I will drink it.
I know you do not love me; for your sisters
Have (as I do remember) done me wrong:
75   You have some cause, they have not.

CORDELIA

No cause, no cause.

LEAR

Am I in France?

KENT

In your own kingdom sir.

LEAR

Do not abuse me.

DOCTOR

Be comforted good madam; the great rage,
You see, is killed in him; and yet it is danger
80   To make him even o'er the time he has lost.
Desire him to go in; trouble him no more
Till further settling.

CORDELIA [*rising*]

Will't please your Highness walk?

LEAR

You must bear with me.
Pray you now forget, and forgive; I am old and foolish.

Exeunt [*all but* KENT *and* Gentleman].

GENTLEMAN

85   Holds it true, sir, that the Duke of Cornwall was so slain?

KENT

Most certain sir.

---

78. *rage*   Compare IV.iv.19.
79–80. *and . . . lost*   Q; not in F. *even o'er*   smooth over, fill in.
82. *settling*   calming down.
84. S.D.   Q has *"Exeunt. Manet Kent and Gent.",* F *"Exeunt."* The rest
of the scene is not in F.

GENTLEMAN

Who is conductor of his people?

KENT

As 'tis said, the bastard son of Gloucester.

GENTLEMAN

They say Edgar, his banished son, is with the Earl of Kent in
90 Germany.

KENT

Report is changeable. 'Tis time to look about; the powers of
the kingdom approach apace.

GENTLEMAN

The arbitrement is like to be bloody. Fare you well sir.   [*Exit.*]

KENT

My point and period will be thoroughly wrought,
95 Or well or ill, as this day's battle's fought.   *Exit.*

Act V, Scene i: Enter, with drum and colours, EDMUND, REGAN,
Gentlemen, and Soldiers.

EDMUND

Know of the duke if his last purpose hold,
Or whether, since, he is advised by aught
To change the course; he's full of alteration
And self-reproving; bring his constant pleasure.

[*Exit a Gentleman.*]

---

93. *arbitrement*   decision between the two "powers" (armies); compare
Henry V, IV.i.158: "the arbitrement of swords."

94. *point and period*   Both words mean full stop or conclusion and goal
or culmination; compare *Merry Wives of Windsor*, III.iii.38: "This is the
period of my ambition."

Act V, scene i   1. *his last purpose*   Compare IV.v.1ff.
4. *constant*   settled, fixed; compare I.i.38.

REGAN

5 Our sister's man is certainly miscarried.

EDMUND

'Tis to be doubted, Madam.

REGAN

                              Now sweet lord,
You know the goodness I intend upon you;
Tell me but truly, but then speak the truth,
Do you not love my sister?

EDMUND

                              In honoured love.

REGAN

10 But have you never found my brother's way
To the forfended place?

EDMUND

                    That thought abuses you.

REGAN

I am doubtful that you have been conjunct
And bosomed with her, as far as we call hers.

EDMUND

No by mine honour, madam.

REGAN

15 I never shall endure her; dear my lord
Be not familiar with her.

---

6. *doubted* suspected; compare "doubtful", line 12, and *Hamlet*, I.ii.255:
"I doubt some foul play."

11. *forfended* forbidden (in *Exodus*, 20:14, the commandment against
adultery). *abuses* dishonors.

11–13. *That . . . hers* Q (as prose); not in F; "conjunct" (= "conjoined")
is the Q reading at II.ii.107.

EDMUND

Fear me not.

She and the duke her husband!

Enter, with drum and colours, ALBANY, GONERIL, *Soldiers.*

GONERIL

[*Aside*] I had rather lose the battle than that sister
Should loosen him and me.

ALBANY

20   Our very loving sister, well be-met.
Sir, this I heard: the King is come to his daughter
With others whom the rigor of our state
Forced to cry out. Where I could not be honest,
I never yet was valiant; for this business

25   It touches us as France invades our land,
Not bolds the King, with others whom, I fear,
Most just and heavy causes make oppose.

EDMUND

Sir you speak nobly.

REGAN

Why is this reasoned?

GONERIL

Combine together 'gainst the enemy;

---

16. *Fear me*   Compare IV.ii.31, n.; F omits "me".

17. S.D.   by the opposite door to that used by the first army.

18–19.   Q; not in F.

22. *rigor . . . state*   strictness of our government.

23–8. *Where . . . nobly*   Q; not in F and possibly corrupt. "I have never fought in a cause I could not honestly support; in this case I fight not because the business (of my intervention) makes bold, and so supports, the King and others who have just cause to oppose us, but because the business is resisting an invader"; "with others" is repeated from line 22, and "whom . . . oppose" looks like a second attempt on Shakespeare's part at lines 22–3 "whom . . . cry out", so that one or the other should perhaps be deleted.

28. *reasoned*   questioned, argued about; compare II.iv.258 and *1 Henry IV*, II.iii.100–101: "I must not have you henceforth question me Whither I go, nor reason whereabout."

30   For these domestic and particular broils
Are not the question here.

ALBANY

Let's then determine
With th' ancient of war on our proceeding.

EDMUND

I shall attend you presently at your tent.

REGAN

Sister you'll go with us?

GONERIL

35   No.

REGAN

'Tis most convenient; pray go with us.

GONERIL

[*Aside*] O ho, I know the riddle. I will go.
     [*As they are going out,*] *enter* EDGAR [*, disguised*].

EDGAR

If e'er your grace had speech with man so poor,
Hear me one word.

ALBANY

[*To Goneril*]   I'll overtake you.
         [*Exeunt all but* ALBANY *and* EDGAR.]
            —Speak.

---

30. *and . . . broils*   Q has "dore particulars".

31. *the*   Q has "to".

31–2. *determine . . . proceeding*   come to a decision with the senior or experienced soldiers, as to what to do.

33. Q; not in F. This is perhaps taken by Goneril to carry a hint of private conversation first.

36. *convenient*   Compare III.ii.54.

37. *riddle*   hidden meaning; i.e., you do not want to leave me alone with Edmund. S.D.   Theobold; F has "*Exeunt both the Armies. / Enter Edgar.*"

EDGAR

40   Before you fight the battle, ope this letter.
      If you have victory, let the trumpet sound
      For him that brought it; wretched though I seem,
      I can produce a champion that will prove
      What is avouchèd there. If you miscarry,
45   Your business of the world hath so an end,
      And machination ceases. Fortune love you!

ALBANY

Stay till I have read the letter.

EDGAR

                              I was forbid it.
When time shall serve, let but the herald cry,
And I'll appear again.   *Exit.*

ALBANY

                    Why, fare thee well;
50   I will o'erlook thy paper.
                    [*Re-*]*enter* EDMUND.

EDMUND

The enemy's in view; draw up your powers.
[*Giving a paper*] Here is the guess of their true strength
      and forces
By diligent discovery; but your haste
Is now urged on you.

ALBANY

                    We will greet the time.   *Exit.*

EDMUND

55   To both these sisters have I sworn my love;
      Each jealous of the other, as the stung

---

46. *And . . . ceases*   not in Q. *love*   Q; F has "loves".
52. *Here . . . true*   Q has "Hard is the quesse of their great . . ."
54. *greet the time*   welcome the occasion.
56. *jealous*   *Compare*   I.iv.59, n.

Are of the adder. Which of them shall I take?
Both? one? or neither? Neither can be enjoyed
If both remain alive: to take the widow
60　Exasperates, makes mad her sister Goneril;
And hardly shall I carry out my side,
Her husband being alive. Now then, we'll use
His countenance for the battle; which being done,
Let her who would be rid of him devise
65　His speedy taking off. As for the mercy
Which he intends to Lear and to Cordelia—
The battle done, and they within our power,
Shall never see his pardon; for my state
Stands on me to defend, not to debate.　　　　　　*Exit.*

Scene ii: Alarum within. Enter, with drum and colours, LEAR,
CORDELIA, *and Soldiers, over the stage, and exeunt.*

Enter EDGAR *and* GLOUCESTER.
EDGAR

Here father, take the shadow of this tree
For your good host; pray that the right may thrive.
If ever I return to you again
I'll bring you comfort.

---

61. *side*　of the bargain (with Goneril), or of the game (to win the crown).

63. *countenance*　favor, sanction, authority; compare *2 Henry IV*, IV.ii.
24–5: "Employ the countenance and grace of heav'n As a false favourite
doth his prince's name . . ."

68–9. *for . . . debate*　for my position depends on my defending it, not
discussing it.

Scene ii S.D.　Probably a march from the level of the yard (see Introduction, p. xxiii), up and across the stage, and out by one of the doors at the
back of it, beyond which the battle is taken to occur (between lines 4 and
5). *Alarum*　call to arms (compare II.i.51 and *O.E.D.*, *sb.*, 4, 1609: ". . . the
drum did sound an all-arm").

1. *father*　Compare IV.vi.72.

4. S.D. *retreat*　the trumpet call to retreat.

GLOUCESTER

        Grace go with you sir.   *Exit* [EDGAR].
    Alarum and retreat within. [*Re-*]*enter* EDGAR.

EDGAR

5   Away old man; give me thy hand; away!
King Lear hath lost, he and his daughter ta'en,
Give me thy hand; come on.

GLOUCESTER

No further sir; a man may rot even here.

EDGAR

What, in ill thoughts again? Men must endure
10 Their going hence, even as their coming hither:
Ripeness is all. Come on.

GLOUCESTER

        And that's true too.   *Exeunt*

Scene iii: Enter, in conquest with drum and colours, EDMUND;
LEAR *and* CORDELIA, *as prisoners; Soldiers,* Captain.

EDMUND

Some officers take them away: good guard,
Until their greater pleasures first be known
That are to censure them.

CORDELIA

        We are not the first
Who with best meaning have incurred the worst.
5   For thee, oppressed King, I am cast down;
Myself could else out-frown false fortune's frown.
Shall we not see these daughters and these sisters?

---

11. *Ripeness is all.*   The state of maturity in which we die is more important than the time. Compare *Hamlet*, V.ii.215–16: ". . . the readiness is all."

Scene iii   2–3. *Until . . . them*   until first (Q "best") the wishes be known of those of higher rank who are to pass judgment on Lear and Cordelia.

LEAR

No, no, no, no! Come, let's away to prison;
We two alone will sing like birds i' th' cage;
10 When thou dost ask me blessing, I'll kneel down,
And ask of thee forgiveness; so we'll live,
And pray, and sing, and tell old tales, and laugh
At gilded butterflies, and hear poor rogues
Talk of court news, and we'll talk with them too—
15 Who loses and who wins; who's in, who's out—
And take upon 's the mystery of things,
As if we were God's spies; and we'll wear out
In a walled prison packs and sects of great ones
That ebb and flow by th' moon.

EDMUND

Take them away.

LEAR

20 Upon such sacrifices, my Cordelia,
The gods themselves throw incense. Have I caught thee?
He that parts us shall bring a brand from heaven

---

9. *cage*   a common seventeenth-century word for prison.

10. Compare IV.vii.59.

13–14. *hear . . . talk*   Q; F has "heere (poor Rogues) talk".

16. *take upon's*   profess, pretend (to understand); compare *Cymbeline*, V.iv.180: "You must . . . be directed by some that take upon them to know, or take upon yourself that which I am sure you do not know . . ."

17. *God's spies*   F and Q have "Gods"; in the theatre it is not clear whether this is "God's" or "gods' ", though it is perhaps most commonly heard as "God's". These spies are the "spirits" of IV.ii.46, "Daemons . . . or angels and ministers of the gods" "which are their espies and escouts, going to and fro throughout all parts, some to oversee and direct the sacrifices [compare line 21 below], and sacred rites and ceremonies performed to the gods: others to . . . punish . . . offences" (Plutarch *Morals*, translated by Holland, 1603, pp. 1331, 1329.) See M. Lloyd, *Notes and Queries*, N.S., VII (Sept. 1960), 324.

17–19. *wear . . . moon*   outlive, in our prison, whole conspiring gangs and parties of those in high rank who rise and fall like the tides.

20. *such sacrifices*   such sacrifice, i.e., renunciation, of the world.

21. *Have . . . thee?*   echoing the second song from Sidney's *Astrophil and Stella*: "Have I caught my heavenly Jewel?" Ed. Feuillerat, II, 287.

22. *shall*   Compare I.i.27.

And fire us hence like foxes. Wipe thine eyes;
The good years shall devour them, flesh and fell,
25 Ere they shall make us weep! We'll see 'em starved first.
Come.   [*Exeunt* LEAR *and* CORDELIA, *guarded*.]

EDMUND

Come hither captain, hark. [*Giving a paper*]
Take thou this note; go follow them to prison.
One step I have advanced thee; if thou dost
30 As this instructs thee, thou dost make thy way
To noble fortunes. Know thou this, that men
Are as the time is; to be tender-minded
Does not become a sword. Thy great employment
Will not bear question; either say thou'lt do 't,
35 Or thrive by other means.

CAPTAIN

I'll do 't my lord.

EDMUND

About it; and write happy when th' hast done.
Mark—I say, instantly; and carry it so
As I have set it down.

CAPTAIN

I cannot draw a cart nor eat dried oats;
40 If it be man's work I'll do't.   *Exit.*

Flourish. Enter ALBANY, GONERIL, REGAN, *Soldiers.*

---

23. *fire . . . foxes*   drive us from each other with fire, as foxes were from
their holes—and at that only fire from heaven will do it.

24. *good years*   usually explained as misfortune (compare O.E.D., "good-
year," 1639: "Wishing their books burned, and the authors at the goodyere")
but the ordinary meaning gives the stronger total sense that our enemies are
more likely to be destroyed by good fortune than to make us weep. Q has
"The good shall . . ." *flesh and fell*   entirely—flesh and skin.

26. S.D.   Theobald; F has "*Exit.*"

34. *question*   comment, discussion; compare IV.iii.24.

36. *write happy*   call yourself fortunate.

39–40. Q; not in F.

ALBANY

Sir, you have showed to-day your valiant strain
And fortune led you well. You have the captives
Who were the opposites of this day's strife;
I do require them of you, so to use them
45 As we shall find their merits and our safety
May equally determine.

EDMUND

Sir, I thought it fit
To send the old and miserable King
To some retention and appointed guard;
Whose age had charms in it, whose title more,
50 To pluck the common bosom on his side
And turn our impressed lances in our eyes
Which do command them. With him I sent the queen—
My reason all the same—and they are ready
To-morrow, or at further space, t'appear
55 Where you shall hold your session. At this time
We sweat and bleed; the friend hath lost his friend;
And the best quarrels, in the heat, are cursed
By those that feel their sharpness.
The question of Cordelia and her father
60 Requires a fitter place.

ALBANY

Sir, by your patience,

---

41. *strain* disposition (compare *Timon of Athens*, IV.iii.212–3: ". . . praise his most vicious strain, And call it excellent") or descent, pedigree (compare *O.E.D.*, *sb.*1, 5, 1615: "From noble Crete I fetch my Native strain").

43. *opposites* opponents.

45. *their merits* what they deserve.

48. *and . . . guard* Q corr.; not in F or Q uncorr.

49. *Whose* since his; see Appendix C, p. 225.

50. *To . . . side* to draw on to his side the hearts of the common people.

51–2. *turn . . . them* turn the lances of our conscripted soldiers into the eyes of us who command them.

55–60. *At . . . place* Q ("session at . . ."), not in F.

57–8. *And . . . sharpness* And the best causes are cursed by those who

I hold you but a subject of this war,
Not as a brother.

REGAN

That's as we list to grace him;
Methinks our pleasure might have been demanded
Ere you had spoke so far. He led our powers,
65 Bore the commission of my place and person,
The which immediacy may well stand up
And call itself your brother.

GONERIL

Not so hot;
In his own grace he doth exalt himself
More than in your addition.

REGAN

In my rights,
70 By me invested, he compeers the best.

ALBANY

That were the most, if he should husband you.

REGAN

Jesters do oft prove prophets.

GONERIL

Holla, holla,
That eye that told you so looked but asquint.

---

still feel the sharp wounds they inflict—Q uncorr. "sharpes" makes this even
clearer and may well be right (Greg, p. 179)—as if, at such a time, Lear
would not get a fair trial (Arden).

62. *list* please.

65. *Bore . . . person* exercised command by my authority as daughter of
the King and widow of Cornwall.

66. *immediacy* freedom from any intermediary, i.e., from subordination.
Q has "imediate".

69. *addition* Compare I.i.131. Q has "advancement".

69–70. *In . . . best* By virtue of my claims (compare *A Midsummer
Night's Dream*, I.i.91–2: ". . . yield Thy crazed title to my certain right") and
clothed with authority by me, he equals the best.

73. *asquint* with jealousy or prejudice; compare O.E.D., 2.b, 1605: "Men
will impartially, and not asquint, look toward the office . . . of a Poet."

REGAN

Lady I am not well, else I should answer

75 From a full-flowing stomach. General,

Take thou my soldiers, prisoners, patrimony;

Dispose of them, of me; the walls is thine;

Witness the world, that I create thee here

My lord and master.

GONERIL

Mean you to enjoy him?

ALBANY

80 The let-alone lies not in your good will.

EDMUND

Nor in thine, lord.

ALBANY

Half-blooded fellow, yes.

REGAN

[*To Edmund*] Let the drum strike, and prove my title thine.

ALBANY

Stay yet; hear reason. Edmund, I arrest thee

On capital treason; and, in thy attaint, [*Pointing to Goneril*]

85 This gilded serpent. For your claim, fair sister,

I bar it in the interest of my wife;

'Tis she is sub-contracted to this lord,

---

75. *stomach* resentment; compare *Titus Andronicus*, III.i.233–4: ". . . losers will have leave To ease their stomachs with their bitter tongues."

77. not in Q. *walls* of the fortress of my person.

80. *The let-alone* the power to hinder or not (not hyphenated in F or Q).

82. *REGAN Let . . . thine* Q has "*Bast*. Let . . . good." Edmund, not the drum, is being ordered to prove by combat that the title of line 79 is rightly his.

84. *attaint* Q; conviction, but connected through false etymology with "stain", so that the phrase means "as dishonoured by you, as your accomplice"; F has "arrest".

87. *sub-contracted* affianced or contracted to one man after being contracted to another: ironical, for the second contract would be valid only after abrogation of the first.

And I, her husband, contradict your banns.

If you will marry, make your loves to me;

90   My lady is bespoke.

GONERIL

An interlude!

ALBANY

Thou art armèd, Gloucester; let the trumpet sound:

If none appear to prove upon thy person

Thy heinous, manifest, and many treasons,

There is my pledge; [*Throwing down a glove*] I'll make it on
     thy heart,

95   Ere I taste bread, thou art in nothing less

Than I have here proclaimed thee.

REGAN

Sick, O sick!

GONERIL

[*Aside*] If not, I'll ne'er trust medicine.

EDMUND

There's my exchange. [*Throwing down a glove*] What in the
     world he is

That names me traitor, villain-like he lies.

100   Call by the trumpet: he that dares approach,

On him, on you, who not, I will maintain

My truth and honour firmly.

ALBANY

A herald, ho!

Trust to thy single virtue; for thy soldiers,

---

90. *interlude*   farce; Q omits the interjection.

94. *make it*   show, allege it to be so; Q has "prove it".

97. *medicine*   Q has "poyson".

98. *he is*   Q; F has "hes".

102. *A herald, ho!*   Q adds "*Bast.* A Herald ho, a Herald."

103. *virtue*   courage; compare O.E.D., 7, 1579: "He fought with great
virtue."

All levied in my name, have in my name
105   Took their discharge.

REGAN

My sickness grows upon me.

ALBANY

She is not well; convey her to my tent.   [*Exit* REGAN, *led.*]
          Enter a Herald.
Come hither herald—let the trumpet sound—
And read out this.   *A trumpet sounds.*

HERALD [*reads*]

"If any man of quality or degree within the lists of the army
110   will maintain upon Edmund, supposed Earl of Gloucester, that
he is a manifold traitor, let him appear by the third sound of
the trumpet. He is bold in his defence."

          1 trumpet.
Again!   *2 trumpet.*
Again!   *3 trumpet.*
          Trumpet answers within.
      Enter EDGAR, *armed, a trumpet before him.*

ALBANY

115   Ask him his purposes, why he appears
Upon this call o' th' trumpet.

HERALD

          What are you?
Your name, your quality, and why you answer
This present summons?

EDGAR

          Know my name is lost,

---

106. S.D. *Enter a Herald.* F after "firmly", line 102.
107. *trumpet* Q; F has "Trumper" (M.E. for "trumpeter").
108. Q adds "*Cap.* Sound trumpet?"
113–14. Q has "*Bast.* Sound? Againe?"
114. S.D. *a . . . him* Q; not in F.
117. *quality* rank.

By treason's tooth bare-gnawn, and canker-bit;
120 Yet am I noble as the adversary
I come to cope.

ALBANY

Which is that adversary?

EDGAR

What's he that speaks for Edmund Earl of Gloucester?

EDMUND

Himself; what say'st thou to him?

EDGAR

Draw thy sword,
That, if my speech offend a noble heart,
125 Thy arm may do thee justice; here is mine.
Behold it is the privilege of mine honours,
My oath, and my profession. I protest,
Maugre thy strength, place, youth, and eminence,
Despite thy victor sword and fire-new fortune,
130 Thy valour and thy heart, thou art a traitor,
False to thy gods, thy brother, and thy father,
Conspirant 'gainst this high illustrious prince,
And from th' extremest upward of thy head
To the descent and dust below thy foot,
135 A most toad-spotted traitor. Say thou "No",
This sword, this arm, and my best spirits are bent

---

119. *canker-bit*   worm-eaten; compare A.V. *Joel*, 1:4: "That which the locust hath left, hath the canker-worm eaten."

126–7. *it . . . profession*   To challenge an adversary to single combat is a privilege I have earned by my titles, my oath of initiation, and my profession as a knight. *honours*   Q has "tongue".

128. *maugre*   despite.

129. *Despite*   Q; F has "Despise". *fire-new fortune*   the position in life which you have newly acquired, like metal fresh from forge or mint; F has "fire new Fortune", Q "fire new fortun'd".

132. *conspirant*   conspiring; Q has "Conspicuate".

135. *toad-spotted*   your honor stained as a toad (proverbially venomous) is with spots.

To prove upon thy heart, whereto I speak,
Thou liest.

EDMUND

    In wisdom I should ask thy name,
But since thy outside looks so fair and war-like
140 And that thy tongue some say of breeding breathes,
What safe and nicely I might well delay
By rule of knighthood, I disdain and spurn;
Back do I toss these treasons to thy head,
With the hell-hated lie o'erwhelm thy heart,
145 Which, for they yet glance by and scarcely bruise,
This sword of mine shall give them instant way
Where they shall rest for ever. Trumpets, speak.
      Alarums. [*They fight.* EDMUND *falls.*]

ALBANY

Save him! save him!
    [*Soldiers intervene and escort* EDMUND *to a bench.*]

GONERIL

    This is practice, Gloucester:
By th' law of war thou wast not bound to answer
150 An unknown opposite; thou art not vanquished,
But cozened and beguiled.

---

138. *In wisdom*   in case he is a man of lower rank whom Edmund should refuse to fight (see lines 149–50 below).

140. *say*   assay, sample, smack; compare *O.E.D.*, *sb.*², 9, 1530: "To give you a say or a taste . . ." F has "tongue (some say) of", Q "being some say of".

141. Q omits. *nicely*   punctiliously.

144. Q has "With the hell hatedly, oreturnd thy heart".

145. *scarcely*   Q; F has "scarely".

147. S.D. *Alarums*   the trumpets' call to arms. Q has no S.D., F "*Alarums. Fights.*" after "save him!" line 148.

148. *Save . . . him*   Does Albany wish Edmund to be saved for a state trial or at least for questioning about the letter, or merely to be saved from falling, and escorted to a bench whence he may take his important part in the dialogue which follows? *practice*   treachery.

ALBANY

                Shut your mouth dame,
Or with this paper shall I stop it.—Hold sir,

                 [*Offering the paper to* EDMUND]

Thou worse than any name, read thine own evil.—
No tearing, lady; I perceive you know it.

GONERIL

155   Say if I do, the laws are mine, not thine;
Who can arraign me for't?

ALBANY

                Most monstrous! O!
Know'st thou this paper?

GONERIL

           Ask me not what I know.   *Exit.*

ALBANY

Go after her: she's desperate; govern her.   [*Exit an Officer.*]

EDMUND

What you have charged me with, that have I done,
160   And more, much more; the time will bring it out.
'Tis past, and so am I. But what art thou
That hast this fortune on me? If thou'rt noble,
I do forgive thee.

    151–3. *Shut . . . evil.*—   Q has "Stop . . . stople it, thou worse than any thing . . . evill", missing the change of person addressed, which is clearly indicated by F punctuation "stop it: hold". *this paper*   the letter of IV.vi. 252ff. *Hold*   here! take it! (*O.E.D.*, 15.b). For the whole episode see Introduction, p. xii.

    157. *Ask . . . Exit.*   Q; in F the speech is Edmund's and Goneril's exit is after "arraign me for't?" But it seems pointless for Edmund to defy Albany here only to confess two lines later, or for Albany to ask Edmund if he "knows" a paper which was intercepted before being received. Compare Iago's final words, *Othello*, V.ii.306: "Demand me nothing. What you know, you know."

EDGAR

Let's exchange charity.
I am no less in blood than thou art, Edmund;
65 If more, the more th' hast wronged me.
My name is Edgar, and thy father's son.
The gods are just, and of our pleasant vices
Make instruments to plague us;
The dark and vicious place where thee he got
Cost him his eyes.

EDMUND

Th' hast spoken right, 'tis true.
70 The wheel is come full circle; I am here.

ALBANY

Methought thy very gait did prophesy
A royal nobleness; I must embrace thee.
Let sorrow split my heart, if ever I
Did hate thee or thy father.

EDGAR

Worthy prince, I know't.
75

ALBANY

Where have you hid yourself?
How have you known the miseries of your father?

EDGAR

By nursing them, my lord. List a brief tale;
And when 'tis told, O that my heart would burst!
80 The bloody proclamation to escape
That followed me so near (O our lives' sweetness,
That we the pain of death would hourly die
Rather than die at once) taught me to shift

---

167. *vices* Q has "vertues".
171. *wheel* the wheel of Fortune, on the lowest part of which Edmund
begins and ends.
182. *we* Q has "with".

Into a madman's rags, t' assume a semblance
185 That very dogs disdained; and in this habit
Met I my father with his bleeding rings,
Their precious stone new lost; became his guide,
Led him, begged for him, saved him from despair;
Never (O fault) revealed myself unto him
190 Until some half-hour past, when I was armed;
Not sure, though hoping, of this good success,
I asked his blessing, and from first to last
Told him our pilgrimage; but his flawed heart
(Alack, too weak the conflict to support)
195 'Twixt two extremes of passion, joy and grief,
Burst smilingly.

EDMUND

This speech of yours hath moved me
And shall perchance do good, but speak you on;
You look as you had something more to say.

ALBANY

If there be more, more woeful, hold it in;
200 For I am almost ready to dissolve,
Hearing of this.

EDGAR

This would have seemed a period
To such as love not sorrow; but another,

---

189. *fault*   See IV.i.38–9 (though "fault" also = "misfortune"). Q has "Father".

191. *success*   outcome; compare *All's Well that Ends Well*, I.iv.238: "But give me leave to try success . . ." See Appendix C, p. 222.

193. *our*   Q has "my". *flawed*   damaged; but there must be some cross-association with the noun "flaw" = "squall," "outburst of feeling" (as in *Measure for Measure*, II.iii.10–12: "a gentlewoman . . . Who, falling in the flaws of her own youth, Hath blister'd her report"). See Appendix B, p. 222.

201–18. *This . . . slave.*   Q; not in F; wrongly divided into lines and with the first sentence perhaps corrupt; it appears to mean that Gloucester's death would have seemed the limit to those who do not love sorrow: merely one

To amplify too much, would make much more,
And top extremity.

205 Whilst I was big in clamour, came there in a man
Who, having seen me in my worst estate,
Shunned my abhorred society; but then, finding
Who 'twas that so endured, with his strong arms
He fastened on my neck, and bellowed out

210 As he'd burst heaven, threw him on my father,
Told the most piteous tale of Lear and him
That ever ear received, which in recounting
His grief grew puissant, and the strings of life
Began to crack. Twice then the trumpets sounded,

215 And there I left him tranced.

ALBANY

But who was this?

EDGAR

Kent sir, the banished Kent, who in disguise
Followed his enemy King and did him service
Improper for a slave.

Enter a Gentleman, *with a bloody knife.*

GENTLEMAN

Help, help, O help!

EDGAR

What kind of help?

---

further incident of this kind, increasing the sorrow too much, would come to
a great deal more, and pass the extreme. The sentence comments (like III.i.7–
15, also omitted from F) upon the action, in its continued intensification of
suffering when it seems already intolerable (see Introduction, p. xii).

206. *estate* state, condition.

210. *As he'd* as if he would. *him* Theobald; Q has "me".

213. *puissant* strong. *strings of life* heartstrings; compare *King John*,
V.vii.55: "My heart hath one poor string to stay it by . . ."

215. *tranced* insensible.

217. *enemy* ill-disposed, hostile.

218. S.D. *with . . . knife* Q; not in F.

ALBANY

> Speak man.

EDGAR

220 What means this bloody knife?

GENTLEMAN

> 'Tis hot, it smokes;
It came even from the heart of—O, she's dead.

ALBANY

Who dead? speak man.

GENTLEMAN

Your lady sir, your lady; and her sister
By her is poisoned: she confesses it.

EDMUND

225 I was contracted to them both; all three
Now marry in an instant.

EDGAR

> Here comes Kent.
> *Enter* KENT.

ALBANY

Produce the bodies, be they alive or dead;   [*Exit* Gentleman.]
This judgment of the heavens that makes us tremble
Touches us not with pity.—[*To Kent, who comes forward*]
> O, is this he?
230 The time will not allow the compliment
Which very manners urges.

219–20. *What . . . knife?*   Q has "*Alb.* What . . . helpe, what meanes that bloudy knife?"

221–2. *of . . . man*   Q has "of—*Alb.* Who man, speake?"

226. *Here comes Kent*   after "pity", line 229, Q, which continues "O tis he . . ."

228. *judgment*   Q has "Justice".

231. *manners urges*   Compare *Romeo and Juliet*, V.iii.213: "What manners is in this . . .?" Contrast I.iv.148.

KENT

I am come
To bid my King and master aye good night;
Is he not here?

ALBANY

Great thing of us forgot!
Speak Edmund, where's the King? and where's Cordelia?
The bodies of GONERIL *and* REGAN *are brought in.*
35   Seest thou this object, Kent?

KENT

Alack, why thus?

EDMUND

Yet Edmund was beloved:
The one the other poisoned for my sake
And after slew herself.

ALBANY

Even so. Cover their faces.

EDMUND

40   I pant for life; some good I mean to do
Despite of mine own ⌈nature.⌋ Quickly send—
Be brief in it—to th' castle, for my writ
Is on the life of Lear and on Cordelia;
Nay, send in time.

ALBANY

Run, run, O run!

EDGAR

45   To who my lord?—[*To Edmund*] Who has the office? send
Thy token of reprieve.

---

232. *To . . . good night*   referring to Kent's own death, not Lear's; compare lines 213–14 above.
234. S.D.   Q after "Seest . . . Kent?"; F has "*Gonerill and Regans bodies
brought out*" after line 227.
245. *Who . . . office?*   Who has been given this duty? Compare II.i.104.

EDMUND

Well thought on; take my sword,
Give it the captain.

ALBANY

Haste thee for thy life.   [*Exit* EDGAR.]

EDMUND

He hath commission from thy wife and me
250 To hang Cordelia in the prison and
To lay the blame upon her own despair,
That she fordid herself.

ALBANY

The gods defend her!

Bear him hence awhile.   [EDMUND *is borne off*.]
[*Re-*]*enter* LEAR *with* CORDELIA *in his arms* [, EDGAR, Captain].

LEAR

Howl, howl, howl! O you are men of stones:
255 Had I your tongues and eyes, I'd use them so
That heaven's vault should crack. She's gone for ever.
I know when one is dead and when one lives;
She's dead as earth. Lend me a looking-glass;
If that her breath will mist or stain the stone,
260 Why then she lives.

KENT

Is this the promised end?

---

248. *Haste . . . life*   Assigned to "*Duke*" in Q, "*Edg.*" in F.

252. *fordid*   killed. See Introduction, p. ix, and Appendix B, pp. 217–18.

253. Edmund is borne off at one door as Lear re-enters by the other. So once more "The same company are here [as in I.i.] or all but the same, and they await his [Lear's] pleasure" (Granville-Barker, p. 277).

254. *men of stones*   Compare *Richard III*, III.vii.24–6: ". . . they spake not a word; But, like dumb statuës or breathing stones, Star'd each on other, and look'd deadly pale."

259. *stone*   transparent metal used as glass; compare *O.E.D.*, "specular," 1, 1627: "Specular stone that was transparent as glass."

260. *promised end*   the Last Judgment, promised by prophecy.

EDGAR

Or image of that horror.

ALBANY

Fall and cease.

LEAR

This feather stirs; she lives! if it be so,
It is a chance which does redeem all sorrows
That ever I have felt.

KENT [*kneeling*]

O my good master!

LEAR

65   Prithee, away.

EDGAR

'Tis noble Kent, your friend.

LEAR

A plague upon you, murderers, traitors all!
I might have saved her; now she's gone for ever.
Cordelia, Cordelia, stay a little. Ha!
What is't thou say'st? Her voice was ever soft,
70   Gentle, and low, an excellent thing in woman.
I killed the slave that was a-hanging thee.

CAPTAIN

'Tis true my lords, he did.

LEAR

Did I not fellow?
I have seen the day, with my good biting falchion

---

261. *Or . . . horror* Or a representation of it; compare *Macbeth*, II.iii.76:
"The great doom's image". *Fall and cease* Either "[The image of] the fall
of the heavens and the cessation of all things"; or "Let the heavens fall and
all things cease."
    273. *falchion* sword (properly one "curved, with the edge on the convex
side", *O.E.D.*).

I would have made them skip: I am old now,
275   And these same crosses spoil me.—Who are you?
Mine eyes are not o' th' best; I'll tell you straight.

KENT

If fortune brag of two she loved and hated,
One of them we behold.

LEAR

This is a dull sight. Are you not Kent?

KENT

The same;
280   Your servant Kent. Where is your servant Caius?

LEAR

He's a good fellow, I can tell you that;
He'll strike, and quickly too. He's dead and rotten.

KENT

No my good lord; I am the very man—

LEAR

I'll see that straight.

KENT

285   That from your first of difference and decay,
Have followed your sad steps—

---

274. *them*   Q, F has "him".

275. *these . . . me*   These very troubles (or all these thwartings of my will) spoil me as a swordsman.

276. *I'll . . . straight*   I'll distinguish you in a moment.

277. *brag . . . and*   Q has "bragd . . . or".

278. *One . . . behold*   Each looking at the other sees one of the two most extraordinary objects of Fortune's love and her hate. "It is an appeal for understanding . . . , in the name of their fellowship . . . in suffering" (New Cambridge).

279. *This . . . sight*   My eyesight is feeble (following line 276); not in Q.

284. *see*   attend to; compare *Richard II*, II.i.217: "To see this business".

285. *your . . . decay*   your first step in alteration and decline. Q has "your life of".

LEAR

            You are welcome hither.

KENT

Nor no man else. All's cheerless, dark, and deadly:
Your eldest daughters have fordone themselves
And desperately are dead.

LEAR

            Ay so I think.

ALBANY

290   He knows not what he says, and vain is it
That we present us to him.

EDGAR

            Very bootless.

Enter a Messenger.

MESSENGER

Edmund is dead my lord.

ALBANY

            That's but a trifle here.

You lords and noble friends, know our intent:
What comfort to this great decay may come
295   Shall be applied; for us, we will resign
During the life of this old Majesty,

---

287. *Nor . . . else* This completes the sentence begun at line 283 and
continued in lines 285–6 (despite F and Q punctuation "man." "steps."); i.e.,
"I am Caius and no one else."

289. *desperately* (a) in despair (Goneril); (b) wretchedly (Regan);
compare *O.E.D.*, 2, 1630: "The descendants of them, that have . . . been
condemned by the Inquisition . . . live in Spain most desperately."

290. *says* Q has "sees".

291. *bootless* useless; compare line 298 below. S.D. F after "him"; Q
has "*Enter Captaine*" after "bootlesse."

293. *our intent* Compare I.i.33 and its context. "The play ends as it began, with a resignation of the throne" (New Cambridge).

294. *this great decay* Lear; Q has "this decay".

To him our absolute power;—[*To Edgar and Kent*] you to
    your rights,
With boot and such addition as your honours
Have more than merited. All friends shall taste
300 The wages of their virtue, and all foes
The cup of their deservings. O, see, see!

LEAR

And my poor fool is hanged! No, no, no life!
Why should a dog, a horse, a rat, have life,
And thou no breath at all? Thou'lt come no more,
305 Never, never, never, never, never.
Pray you undo this button. Thank you sir.
Do you see this? Look on her, look, her lips,
Look there, look there!   *He dies.*

EDGAR

He faints. My lord, my lord!

KENT

Break heart, I prithee break.

EDGAR

Look up, my lord.

KENT

310 Vex not his ghost, O let him pass; he hates him

297–301. *you . . . deservings*   The attempt to re-establish order (as Malcolm does at the end of *Macbeth*, V.viii.60ff.) is defeated by Lear's death.

298. *boot*   Compare IV.vi.218. *addition*   Compare I.i.131.

302. *fool*   Cordelia. As a term of affection, "fool" is applied, for instance, by Hermione to her faithful attendants (*Winter's Tale*, II.i.118), by Beatrice to her own heart (*Much Ado About Nothing*, II.i.283), or by Henry VI to the ewes he wishes he had care of (Part 3, II.v.36).

306. *Pray . . . button*   to relieve his sense of suffocation.

307–8. *Do . . . there*   Q has merely "O,o,o,o." Critics are divided as to whether Lear sees signs of life (as in line 262) or a confirmation of her death (as in line 267). If he believes her breath stirs, he presumably dies, like Gloucester, of joy; compare Sidney, Appendix B, p. 222.

That would upon the rack of this tough world
Stretch him out longer.

EDGAR

He is gone indeed.

KENT

The wonder is he hath endured so long;
He but usurped his life.

ALBANY

15   Bear them from hence. Our present business
Is general woe.—[*To Kent and Edgar*] Friends of my soul,
     you twain
Rule in this realm, and the gored state sustain.

KENT

I have a journey, sir, shortly to go;
My master calls me, I must not say no.

EDGAR

20   The weight of this sad time we must obey;
Speak what we feel, not what we ought to say.
The oldest hath borne most; we that are young
Shall never see so much, nor live so long.

Exeunt with a dead march.

---

311. *rack* F and Q have "wracke".
314. *usurped* (took and) kept by force; compare IV.ii.28.
317. *gored* wounded.
320–3. *The weight . . . long* Assigned to Albany in Q. But he has resigned the throne to Kent and Edgar, each of whom should make a reply.
Edgar's is sad and submissive, in contrast to Albany's more hopeful lines,
293–301 (see John Shaw, *Essays in Criticism*, XVI [1966], 261–7).

203

APPENDIX A

A Shakespeare Chronology

Some important Dates relating to Shakespeare's Life, and to KING LEAR in particular

1558   November 17. Accession of Queen Elizabeth.

1559   *The Mirror for Magistrates* published; republished with additions, including the story of "Cordila," 1563–87. (Shakespeare appears to have used the editions of 1574 and 1581.)

1564   April 26. William Shakespeare christened.

1577   Holinshed, *Chronicles of England, Scotland, and Ireland* published; 3 vols. 1587.

1582   November 27. License for Shakespeare's marriage.

1583   The Queen's Master of the Revels selects a body of players for her service: the Queen's Men.

1590   Spenser, *The Faerie Queene* Books I–III, Sidney *Arcadia* published (see Appendix B).

1592   A play of *Henry VI* performed by Lord Strange's men at a theater run by Henslowe. Death of the dramatist and poet, Robert Greene; a parody of a line from Shakespeare's *Henry VI, Part 3* appears in *Greenes Groat-sworth of Wit.*

1593   Shakespeare's first poem, *Venus and Adonis*, published. Death of Marlowe.

1594   A play of *King Leir* performed by the Queen's Men or by the Earl of Sussex's. It is entered in the Stationers' Register on May 14 but not published—see 1605. First record of Shakespeare, along with William Kempe and Richard Burbage, as a member of the Lord Chamberlain's Men, one of the two companies after the actors regroup in 1592–4. (Since Shakespeare is one of the three to whom payment is made for performances at Court, he is probably a sharer in the company.) *Titus Andronicus* is performed by this company—it had come to them (with Shakespeare?) from the Earl of Pembroke's Men.

1595   *Richard II* performed, the first of Shakespeare's second group of four history plays (*Richard II, I Henry IV, 2 Henry IV, Henry V*).

1597   Shakespeare buys New Place, a large house in Stratford-on-Avon.

1599   Globe Theater built for the Lord Chamberlain's Men. Richard and Cuthbert Burbage have half a share in it; the other half is divided amongst Shakespeare and four other actors, Phillips, Pope, Heminge, and Kempe.

1600–8   Shakespeare's principal tragedies written, probably in the order: *Hamlet, Othello, King Lear, Macbeth, Antony and Cleopatra.*

1603   March 24. Death of Queen Elizabeth. With the accession of James I the Lord Chamberlain's Men become the King's Men.

1605   *The True Chronicle History of King Leir* . . . published—see 1594.

1606   December 26. Shakespeare's *King Lear* performed at Court.

1607   November 26. *King Lear* entered in the Stationers' Register.

1608   *King Lear* published (first Quarto). The King's Men acquire the Blackfriars theater. Conditions in this theater, which is roofed and artificially lit, affect Shakespeare's "romances": *Pericles, Cymbeline, The Winter's Tale* and *The Tempest,* 1608–11.

1613   July 2. The Globe burns down during a performance of *Henry VIII.*

1616   April 23. Death of Shakespeare. April 25. Burial in Holy Trinity Church, Stratford-on-Avon.

1619   Second Quarto of *King Lear* published.

1623   First Folio edition of Shakespeare's *Comedies, Histories, & Tragedies* published.

APPENDIX B

Sources for KING LEAR

1. *The True Chronicle History of King Leir and his Three Daughters* . . . (1605) [Text modernized from the Malone Society reprint of 1907, the line numbering of which is followed. Some direct comparisons with *King Lear* are noted in square brackets.]

The play opens at Leir's court in Troynovant, i.e., London.

LEIR

21   A son we want for to succeed our crown,

And course of time hath cancellèd the date
Of further issue from our withered loins:
One foot already hangeth in the grave,
25 And age hath made deep furrows in my face;
The world of me, I of the world am weary;
And I would fain resign these earthly cares. . . . [I.i.33–6]

SKALLIGER

35 I censure thus: Your majesty, knowing well
What several suitors your princely daughters have,
To make them each a jointure, more or less
As is their worth, to them that love profess. . . . [I.iv.121–2]

LEIR

81 This granted, when they jointly shall contend,
Each to exceed the other in their love,
Then at the vantage will I take Cordella:
Even as she doth protest she loves me best,
85 I'll say, "Then, daughter, grant me one request
To show thou lov'st me as thy sisters do:
Accept a husband whom myself will woo."
This said, she cannot well deny my suit,
Although, poor soul, her senses will be mute.
90 Then will I triumph in my policy,
And match her with a king of Brittany. . . .

LEIR

224 Dear Gonorill, kind Ragan, sweet Cordella,
Ye flourishing branches of a kingly stock,
Sprung from a tree that once did flourish green,
Whose blossoms now are nipped with winter's frost,
And pale grim death doth wait upon my steps,
And summons me unto his next assizes.
230 Therefore, dear daughters, as ye tender the safety
Of him that was the cause of your first being,
Resolve a doubt which much molests my mind,
Which of you three to me would prove most kind—
Which loves me most, and which at my request
235 Will soonest yield unto their father's hest.

GONORILL

I hope my gracious father makes no doubt
Of any of his daughters' love to him.
Yet for my part, to show my zeal to you,

Which cannot be in windy words rehearsed,
240　I prize my love to you at such a rate
I think my life inferior to my love.
Should you enjoin me for to tie a millstone
About my neck and leap into the sea,
At your command I willingly would do it.
245　Yea, for to do you good I would ascend
The highest turret in all Brittany,
And from the top leap headlong to the ground.
Nay, more. Should you appoint me for to marry
The meanest vassal in the spacious world,
250　Without reply I would accomplish it.
In brief, command whatever your desire,
And if I fail, no favor I require.

LEIR

O, how thy words revive my dying soul!

CORDELLA

[*Aside*] O, how I do abhor this flattery!

LEIR

255　But what saith Ragan to her father's will?

RAGAN

O, that my simple utterance could suffice
To tell the true intention of my heart,
Which burns in zeal of duty to your grace,
And never can be quenched but by desire
260　To show the same in outward forwardness.
Oh, that there were some other maid that durst
But make a challenge of her love with me!
I'd make her soon confess she never loved
Her father half so well as I do you.
265　Ay, then my deeds should prove in plainer case,
How much my zeal aboundeth to your grace;
But for them all, let this one mean suffice
To ratify my love before your eyes:
I have right noble suitors to my love,
270　No worse than kings, and haply I love one.
Yet, would you have me make my choice anew,
I'd bridle fancy, and be ruled by you.

LEIR

Did never Philomel sing so sweet a note!

CORDELLA

[*Aside*] Did never flatterer tell so false a tale!

LEIR

275   Speak now, Cordella, make my joys at full,
And drop down nectar from thy honey lips.

CORDELLA

I cannot paint my duty forth in words;
I hope my deeds shall make report for me.
But look: what love the child doth owe the father,
280   The same to you I bear, my gracious lord.

GONORILL

Here is an answer answerless indeed:
Were you my daughter, I should scarcely brook it.

RAGAN

Dost thou not blush, proud peacock as thou art,
To make our father such a slight reply?

LEIR

285   Why, how now, minion, are you grown so proud?
Doth our dear love make you thus peremptory?
What, is your love become so small to us
As that you scorn to tell us what it is?
Do you love us, as every child doth love
290   Their father? True indeed, as some
Who by disobedience short their father's days—
And so would you! Some are so father-sick
That they make means to rid them from the world—
And so would you! Some are indifferent
295   Whether their agèd parents live or die,
And so are you! But, didst thou know, proud girl,
What care I had to foster thee to this,
Ah, then thou wouldst say as thy sisters do:
Our life is less than love we owe to you.

CORDELLA

300   Dear father, do not so mistake my words,
Nor my plain meaning be miscónstruèd;
My tongue was never used to flattery.

GONORILL

You were not best say I flatter; if you do,

My deeds shall show I flatter not with you.
5   I love my father better than thou canst.

CORDELLA

The praise were great, spoke from another's mouth;
But it should seem your neighbors dwell far off.

RAGAN

Nay, here is one, that will confirm as much
As she hath said, both for myself and her.
10 I say, thou dost not wish my father's good.

CORDELLA

Dear father—

LEIR

Peace, bastard imp, no issue of King Leir;
I will not hear thee speak one tittle more.
Call not me father, if thou love thy life,
15 Nor these thy sisters once presume to name.
Look for no help henceforth from me nor mine;
Shift as thou wilt, and trust unto thyself.
My kingdom will I equally divide
'Twixt thy two sisters to their royal dower.
20 And will bestow them worthy their deserts;
This done, because thou shalt not have the hope
To have a child's part in the time to come,
I presently will dispossess myself
And set up these upon my princely throne.

GONORILL

25 I ever thought that pride would have a fall.

RAGAN

Plain-dealing, sister! Your beauty is so sheen
You need no dowry to make you be a queen. . . .

LEIR

5   Cease, good my lords, and sue not to reverse
Our censure, which is now irrevocable. [I.i.144]
We have dispatchèd letters of contact
Unto the kings of Cambria and Cornwall;
Our hand and seal will justify no less.
10 Then do not so dishonor me, my lords,
As to make shipwreck of our kingly word.
I am as kind as is the pelican, [III.iv.67]

That kills itself to save her young one's lives;
And yet as jealous as the princely eagle

515 That kills her young ones, if they do but dazzle
Upon the radiant splendor of the sun. . . . [I.i.104]

547 What resteth then, but that we consummate
The celebration of these nuptial rites?
My kingdom I do equally divide.

550 Princes, draw lots, and take your chance as falls.
Then they draw lots.

These I resign as freely unto you
As erst by true succession they were mine.
And here I do freely dispossess myself

555 And make you two my true adopted heirs.
Myself will sojourn with my son of Cornwall. . . .

PERILLUS

562 I have been silent all this while, my lord,
To see if any worthier than myself
Would once have spoke in poor Cordella's cause;
But love or fear ties silence to their tongues.
Oh hear me speak for her, my gracious lord,
Whose deeds have not deserved this ruthless doom, [I.i.144, Q]
As thus to disinherit her of all.

LEIR

Urge this no more, and if thou love thy life. [I.i.149]

570 I say she is no daughter, that doth scorn
To tell her father how she loveth him.
Whoever speaketh hereof to me again
I will esteem him for my mortal foe.
Come, let us in to celebrate with joy

575 The happy nuptials of these lovely pairs.

Exeunt omnes; manet Perillus.

PERILLUS

Ah, who so blind as they that will not see
The near approach of their own misery?
Poor lady, I extremely pity her;

580 And whilst I live, each drop of my heart blood
Will I strain forth, to do her any good.   *Exit.*

Cordella marries the King of Gallia (France). Leir is ill-treated by
Gonorill, who intercepts his letters to Ragan, 991–1020. He fares no
better with Ragan and flees with Perillus, but is pursued by a murderer
in her pay. They are saved by the murderer's fear of thunder and light-

ning, 1634, 1740 [III.ii.47–57], and escape to Gallia, where they meet
Cordella and her husband on their way, in disguise, to Britain to
help him.

CORDELLA

60   Alack, that ever I should live to see
     My noble father in this misery.

KING

Sweet love, reveal not what thou art as yet,
Until we know the ground of all this ill.

CORDELLA

O, but some meat, some meat! Do you not see
65   How near they are to death for want of food?

PERILLUS

Lord, which didst help thy servants at their need,
Or now or never send us help with speed.
Oh comfort, comfort! Yonder is a banquet,
And men and women, my lord; be of good cheer,
70   For I see comfort coming very near.
O my lord, a banquet, and men and women!

LEIR

O, let kind pity mollify their hearts,
That they may help us in our great extremes.

PERILLUS

God save you, friends, and if this blessed banquet
75   Affordeth any food or sustenance,
Even for his sake that saved us all from death,
Vouchsafe to save us from the gripe of famine.
                         She bringeth him to the table.

CORDELLA

Here father, sit and eat; here sit and drink;
And would it were far better for your sakes.
80   *Perillus takes Lier by the hand to the table.*

PERILLUS

I'll give you thanks anon; my friend doth faint
And needeth present comfort.   *Leir drinks.*

MUMFORD

I warrant, he ne'er stays to say grace.
O, there's no sauce to a good stomach!

PERILLUS

2185 The blessed God of heaven hath thought upon us.

LEIR

The thanks be his, and these kind courteous folk,
By whose humanity we are preserved.

They eat hungerly. Leir drinks.

CORDELLA

And may that draught be unto him, as was
That which old Aeson drank, which did renew
2190 His withered age, and make him young again.
And may that meat be unto him as was
That which Elias ate, in strength whereof
He walkèd forty days and never fainted.
Shall I conceal me longer from my father?
2195 Or shall I manifest myself to him?

KING

Forbear a while, until his strength return,
Lest, being overjoyed with seeing thee,
His poor weak senses should forsake their office,
And so our cause of joy be turned to sorrow. ....

[IV.vii.79–82, V.iii.193–6]

CORDELLA

2297 But look, dear father, look; behold and see
Thy loving daughter speaketh unto thee.

She kneels.
[IV.vii.57ff.]

LEIR

O, stand thou up! It is my part to kneel
And ask forgiveness for my former faults.

He kneels.

CORDELLA

2301 O, if you wish I should enjoy my breath,
Dear father rise, or I receive my death.

He riseth.

LEIR

Then I will rise, to satisfy your mind,
But kneel again, till pardon be resigned.

He kneels.

CORDELLA

2305 I pardon you? The word beseems not me,
But I do say so, for to ease your knee.
You gave me life, you were the cause that I
Am what I am, who else had never been.

LEIR

But you gave life to me and to my friend,
Whose days had else had an untimely end.

CORDELLA

You brought me up whenas I was but young
And far unable for to help myself.

LEIR

I cast thee forth whenas thou wast but young
And far unable for to help thyself.

CORDELLA

God, world, and nature say I do you wrong
That can endure to see you kneel so long.

KING

Let me break off this loving controversy,
Which doth rejoice my very soul to see.
Good father, rise; she is your loving daughter   *He riseth.*
And honors you with as respective duty
As if you were the monarch of the world.

CORDELLA

But I will never rise from off my knee   *She kneels.*
Until I have your blessing, and your pardon
Of all my faults committed any way
From my first birth unto this present day.

LEIR

The blessing which the God of Abraham gave
Unto the tribe of Judah, light on thee
And multiply thy days, that thou mayst see
Thy children's children prosper after thee.
Thy faults, which are just none that I do know,
God pardon on high, and I forgive below.   *She riseth.*

CORDELLA

Now is my heart at quiet, and doth leap
Within my breast for joy of this good hap;
And now, dear father, welcome to our court;
And welcome, kind Perillus, unto me—
Mirror of virtue and true honesty.

LEIR

O, he hath been the kindest friend to me
That ever man had in adversity.

PERILLUS

My tongue doth fail, to say what heart doth think,
2340   I am so ravished with exceeding joy.

KING

All you have spoke; now let me speak my mind
And in few words much matter here conclude: *He kneels.*
If e'er my heart do harbor any joy
Or true content repose within my breast
2345   Till I have rooted out this viperous sect
And repossessed my father of his crown,
Let me be counted for the perjuredst man
That ever spake word since the world began.   *Rise.*

MUMFORD

Let me pray too, that never prayed before: *Mumford kneels.*
2350   If e'er I re-salute the British earth
(As, ere 't be long, I do presume I shall)
And do return from thence without my wench,
Let me be gelded for my recompense.   *Rise.*

KING

Come, let's to arms for to redress this wrong;
Till I am there, methinks the time seems long.   *Exeunt.*

After this reconciliation, the King of Gallia invades Britain and Leir is
restored to his kingdom.

2. Raphael Holinshed, *Chronicles of England, Scotland, and Ireland* (1587)

Leir the son of Baldud was admitted ruler over the Britains in the year
of the world 3105, at what time Joas reigned in Juda. This Leir was a
prince of right noble demeanor, governing his land and subjects in
great wealth. He made the town of Caerleir now called Leicester, which
standeth upon the river of Sore. It is written that he had by his wife
three daughters without other issue, whose names were Gonorilla,
Regan, and Cordeilla, which daughters he greatly loved, but specially
Cordeilla the youngest far above the two elder. When this Leir therefore was come to great years, and began to wax unwieldy through age,
he thought to understand the affections of his daughters towards him,
and prefer her whom he best loved, to the succession over the kingdom.
Whereupon he first asked Gonorilla, the eldest, how well she loved

him: who calling her gods to record protested that she "loved him more than her own life, which by right and reason should be most dear unto her." With which answer the father being well pleased, turned to the second, and demanded of her how well she loved him: who answered (confirming her sayings with great oaths) that she loved him "more than tongue could express, and far above all other creatures of the world."

Then called he his youngest daughter Cordeilla before him, and asked of her what account she made of him, unto whom she made this answer as followeth: "Knowing the great love and fatherly zeal that you have always borne towards me (for the which I may not answer you otherwise than I think, and as my conscience leadeth me) I protest unto you that I have loved you ever and will continually (while I live) love you as my natural father. And if you would more understand of the love that I bear you, ascertain yourself that so much as you have, so much you are worth, and so much I love you, and no more." The father, being nothing content with this answer, married his two eldest daughters, the one unto Henninus, the duke of Cornwall, and the other unto Maglanus, the duke of Albania, betwixt whom he willed and ordained that his land should be divided after his death, and the one half thereof immediately should be assigned to them in hand: but for the third daughter Cordeilla he reserved nothing.

Nevertheless it fortuned that one of the princes of Gallia (which now is called France) whose name was Aganippus, hearing of the beauty, womanhood, and good conditions of the said Cordeilla, desired to have her in marriage, and sent over to her father, requiring that he might have her to wife; to whom answer was made, that he might have his daughter, but as for any dowry he could have none, for all was promised and assured to her other sisters already. Aganippus notwithstanding this answer of denial to receive anything by way of dowry with Cordeilla, took her to wife, only moved thereto (I say) for respect of her person and amiable virtues. This Aganippus was one of the twelve kings that ruled Gallia in those days, as in the British history it is recorded. But to proceed.

After that Leir was fallen into age, the two dukes that had married his two eldest daughters, thinking it long ere the government of the land did come to their hands, rose against him in armor and reft from him the governance of the land, upon conditions to be continued for term of life: by the which he was put to his portion, that is, to live after a rate assigned to him for the maintenance of his estate, which in process of time was diminished as well by Maglanus as by Henninus. But the greatest grief that Leir took was to see the unkindness of his daughters, which seemed to think that all was too much which their father had, the same being never so little: insomuch that going from the one to the other, he was brought to that misery, that scarcely they would allow him one servant to wait upon him.

In the end, such was the unkindness, or (as I may say) the unnaturalness which he found in his two daughters, notwithstanding their fair and pleasant words uttered in time past, that being constrained of necessity, he fled the land and sailed into Gallia, there to seek some comfort of his youngest daughter, Cordeilla, whom before time he hated. The lady Cordeilla hearing that he was arrived in poor estate, she first sent to him privily a certain sum of money to apparel himself withal, and to retain a certain number of servants that might attend upon him in honorable wise, as appertained to the estate which he had borne. And then so accompanied, she appointed him to come to the court, which he did, and was so joyfully, honorably, and lovingly received, both by his son-in-law Aganippus and also by his daughter Cordeilla, that his heart was greatly comforted: for he was no less honored, than if he had been king of the whole country himself.

Now when he had informed his son-in-law and his daughter in what sort he had been used by his other daughters, Aganippus caused a mighty army to be put in a readiness, and likewise a great navy of ships to be rigged, to pass over into Britain with Leir, his father-in-law, to see him again restored to his kingdom. It was accorded that Cordeilla should also go with him to take possession of the land, the which he promised to leave unto her, as the rightful inheritor after his decease, notwithstanding any former grant made to her sisters or to their husbands in any manner of wise.

Hereupon, when this army and navy of ships were ready, Leir and his daughter Cordeilla with her husband took the sea, and arriving in Britain fought with their enemies and discomfited them in battle, in the which Maglanus and Henninus were slain; and then was Leir restored to his kingdom which he ruled after this by the space of two years, and then died forty years after he first began to reign. His body was buried at Leicester in a vault under the channel of the river of Sore beneath the town.

Cordeilla, the youngest daughter of Leir, was admitted Queen and supreme governess of Britain in the year of the world 3155, before the building of Rome 54, Uzziah then reigning in Juda, and Jeroboam over Israel. This Cordeilla after her father's decease ruled the land of Britain right worthily during the space of five years, in which meantime her husband died. And then about the end of those five years her two nephews, Margan and Cunedag, sons to her aforesaid sisters, disdaining to be under the government of a woman, levied war against her, and destroyed a great part of the land, and finally took her prisoner, and laid her fast in ward, wherewith she took such grief, being a woman of a manly courage, and despairing to recover liberty, there she slew herself when she had reigned (as before is mentioned) the term of five years.

3. Edmund Spenser, *The Faerie Queene*, Book II, Canto 10 (1590)

xxvii

Next him king *Leyr* in happie peace long raind,
  But had no issue male him to succeed,
  But three faire daughters, which were well uptraind,
  In all that seemed fit for kingly seed:
  Mongst whom his realme he equally decreed
  To have divided. Tho when feeble age
  Nigh to his utmost date he saw proceed,
  He cald his daughters; and with speeches sage
Inquyrd, which of them most did love her parentage.

xxviii

The eldest *Gonorill* gan to protest,
  That she much more than her owne life him lov'd:
  And *Regan* greater love to him profest,
  Then all the world, when ever it were proov'd;
  But *Cordeill* said she lov'd him, as behoov'd:
  Whose simple answer, wanting colours faire
  To paint it forth, him to displeasance moov'd,
  That in his crowne, he counted her no haire,[1]
But twixt the other twaine his kingdome whole did shaire.

xxix

So wedded th'one to *Maglan* king of Scots,
  And th'other to the king of *Cambria*,
  And twixt them shayrd his realme by equall lots:
  But without dowre the wise *Cordelia*
  Was sent to *Aganip* of *Celtica*.
  Their aged Syre, thus eased of his crowne,
  A private life led in *Albania*,
  With *Gonorill*, long had in great renowne,
That nought him griev'd to bene from rule deposed downe.

[1] heir

xxx

But true it is, that when the oyle is spent,
    The light goes out, and weeke[2] is throwne away;
    So when he had resigned his regiment,
    His daughter gan despise his drouping day,
    And wearie waxe of his continuall stay.
    Tho[3] to his daughter *Regan* he repayrd,
    Who him at first well used every way;
    But when of his departure she despayrd,
Her bountie she abated, and his cheare empayrd.[4]

xxxi

The wretched man gan then avise[5] too late,
    That love is not, where most it is profest,
    Too truely tryde in his extreamest state;
    At last resolv'd likewise to prove the rest,
    He to *Cordelia* him selfe addrest,
    Who with entire affection him receav'd,
    As for her Syre and king her seemed best;
    And after all an army strong she leav'd,
To war on those, which him had of his realme bereav'd.

xxxii

So to his crowne she him restor'd againe,
    In which he dyde, made ripe for death by eld,[6]
    And after wild,[7] it should to her remaine:
    Who peaceably the same long time did weld:
    And all mens harts in dew obedience held:
    Till that her sisters children, woxen[8] strong
    Through proud ambition, against her rebeld,
    And overcommen kept in prison long,
Till wearie of that wretched life, her selfe she hong.

4. Sir Philip Sidney, *Arcadia*, Book II, Chapter 10 (1590)

The pitiful state and story of the Paphlagonian unkind King, and his kind son, first related by the son, then by the blind father.

2 wick
3 then
4 lessened his entertainment
5 consider
6 old age
7 willed
8 grown

It was in the kingdom of Galacia, the season being (as in the depth of winter) very cold, and as then suddenly grown to so extreme and foul a storm, that never any winter (I think) brought forth a fouler child: so that the princes were even compelled by the hail, that the pride of the wind blew into their faces, to seek some shrouding place within a certain hollow rock offering it unto them, they made it their shield against the tempest's fury. And so staying there, till the violence thereof was passed, they heard the speech of a couple, who not perceiving them (being hid within that rude canopy) held a strange and pitiful disputation which made them step out; yet in such sort as they might see unseen. There they perceived an aged man, and a young, scarcely come to the age of a man, both poorly arrayed, extremely weather-beaten; the old man blind, the young man leading him: and yet through all those miseries, in both these seemed to appear a kind of nobleness, not suitable to that affliction. But the first words they heard were these of the old man. "Well Leonatus," said he, "since I cannot persuade thee to lead me to that which should end my grief, and thy trouble, let me now entreat thee to leave me: fear not, my misery cannot be greater than it is, and nothing doth become me but misery; fear not the danger of my blind steps, I cannot fall worse than I am. And do not I pray thee, do not obstinately continue to infect thee with my wretchedness. But fly, fly from this region, only worthy of me." "Dear father," answered he, "do not take away from me the only remnant of my happiness: while I have power to do you service, I am not wholly miserable." "Ah my son," said he, and with that he groaned, as if sorrow strove to break his heart, "how evil fits it me to have such a son, and how much doth thy kindness upbraid my wickedness?" These doleful speeches, and some others to like purpose (well showing they had not been born to the fortune they were in) moved the princes to go out unto them, and ask the younger what they were. "Sirs," answered he, with a good grace, and made the more agreeable by a certain noble kind of piteousness, "I see well you are strangers, that know not our misery, so well here known that no man dare know but that we must be miserable. Indeed our state is such as though nothing is so needful unto us as pity, yet nothing is more dangerous unto us than to make ourselves so known as may stir pity. But your presence promiseth that cruelty shall not overrun hate. And if it did, in truth our state is sunk below the degree of fear.

"This old man (whom I lead) was lately rightful prince of this country of Paphlagonia, by the hardhearted ungratefulness of a son of his, deprived, not only of his kingdom (whereof no foreign forces were ever able to spoil him) but of his sight, the riches which Nature grants to the poorest creatures. Whereby, and by other his unnatural dealings, he hath been driven to such grief, as even now he would have had me to have led him to the top of this rock, thence to cast himself headlong to death: and so would have made me (who received my life of him) to be the worker of his destruction. But noble gentlemen," said he, "if either of you have a father, and feel what dutiful affection is engraffed in a son's heart, let me entreat you to convey this afflicted prince to some place of rest and security. Amongst your worthy acts it shall be none of the least that a King, of such might and fame and so unjustly oppressed, is in any sort by you relieved."

But before they could make him answer, his father began to speak, "Ah my son," said he, "how evil an historian are you that leave out the chief note of all the discourse! My wickedness, my wickedness. And if thou doest it to spare my ears (the only sense now left me proper for knowledge) assure thyself thou dost mistake me. And I take witness of that sun which you see" (with that he cast up his blind eyes, as if he would hunt for light) "and wish myself in worse case than I do wish myself, which is as evil as may be, if I speak untruly; that nothing is so welcome to my thoughts as the publishing of my shame. Therefore know you gentlemen (to whom from my heart I wish that it may not prove ominous foretoken of misfortune to have met with such a miser as I am) that whatsoever my son (O God, that truth binds me to reproach him with the name of my son) hath said, is true. But besides those truths, this also is true, that having had in lawful marriage, of a mother fit to bear royal children, this son (such one as partly you see, and better shall know by my short declaration) and so enjoyed the expectations in the world of him, till he was grown to justify their expectations (so as I needed envy no father for the chief comfort of mortality, to leave another oneself after me) I was carried by a bastard son of mine (if at least I be bound to believe the words of that base woman, my concubine, his mother) first to mislike, then to hate, lastly to destroy, to do my best to destroy, this son (I think you think) undeserving destruction. What ways he used to bring me to it, if I should tell you, I should tediously trouble you with as much poisonous hypocrisy, desperate fraud, smooth malice, hidden ambition, and smiling envy, as in any living person could be harbored. But I list it not, no remembrance, (no, of naughtiness) delights me but mine own; and methinks the accusing his trains might in some manner excuse my fault, which certainly I loathe to do. But the conclusion is that I gave order to some servants of mine, whom I thought as apt for such charities as myself, to lead him out into a forest and there to kill him.

"But those thieves (better natured to my son than myself) spared his life, letting him go, to learn to live poorly: which he did, giving himself to be a private soldier in a country hereby. But as he was ready to be greatly advanced for some noble pieces of service which he did, he heard news of me: who (drunk in my affection to that unlawful and unnatural son of mine) suffered myself so to be governed by him that all favors and punishments passed by him, all offices and places of importance distributed to his favorites; so that ere I was aware, I had left myself nothing but the name of a king: which he shortly weary of too, with many indignities (if any thing may be called an indignity which was laid upon me) threw me out of my seat, and put out my eyes; and then (proud in his tyranny) let me go, neither imprisoning nor killing me: but rather delighting to make me feel my misery; misery indeed, if ever there were any; full of wretchedness, fuller of disgrace, and fullest of guiltiness. And as he came to the crown by so unjust means, as unjustly he kept it, by force of stranger soldiers in citadels, the nests of tyranny and murderers of liberty, disarming all his own countrymen, that no man durst show himself a well-willer of mine: to say the truth (I think) few of them being so (considering my cruel folly to my good son, and foolish kindness to my unkind bastard): but if there were any who fell to pity of so great a fall and had yet any sparks of unstained duty left in them towards me, yet durst they not show it, scarcely with giving me alms at their doors; which yet was the only sustenance of my distressed life, nobody daring to show so much charity, as to lend me a hand to guide my dark steps: Till this son of mine (God knows, worthy of a more virtuous and more fortunate father) forgetting my abominable wrongs, not recking danger, and neglecting the present good way he was in doing himself good, came hither to do this kind office you see him perform towards me, to my unspeakable grief; not only because his kindness is a glass even to my blind eyes, of my naughtiness, but that, above all griefs, it grieves me he should desperately adventure the loss of his soul-deserving life for mine, that yet owe more to fortune for my deserts, as if he could carry mud in a chest of crystal. For well I know, he that now reigneth, how much soever (and with good reason) he despiseth me, of all men despised; yet he will not let slip any advantage to make away him whose just title (ennobled by courage and goodness) may one day shake the seat of a never secure tyranny. And for this cause I craved of him to lead me to the top of this rock, indeed I must confess, with meaning to free him from so serpentine a companion as I am. But he finding what I purposed, only therein since he was born, showed himself disobedient unto me. And now, gentlemen, you have the true story, which I pray you publish to the world, that my mischievous proceedings may be the glory of his filial pity, the only reward now left for so great a merit. And if it may be, let me obtain that of you which my son denies me: for never was there more pity in saving any, than in ending me; both because therein my agonies shall end, and so shall you preserve this excellent young man who else wilfully follows his own ruin." [The bastard son, Plexirtus, appears "with forty horse . . . to murder his brother." Leonatus defends himself without betraying his identity. General fighting ensues. Eventually] the blind King (having, in the chief city of his realm, set the crown upon his son Leonatus' head) with many tears (both of joy and sorrow) setting forth to the whole people his own fault and his son's virtue, after he had kissed him, and forced his son to accept honor of him (as of his new-become subject) even in a moment died, as it should seem: his heart broken with unkindness and affliction, stretched so far beyond his limits with this excess of comfort, as it was able no longer to keep safe his royal spirits.

APPENDIX C

A Note on Shakespeare's English

The English language has changed a great deal since *King Lear* was written, over three hundred and fifty years ago, but the play's intrinsic interest will often enable an audience in a theater to respond even though they do not grasp the language in detail. Usually in fact they take what seems current English and disregard the rest, so that the economical exposition in the first lines of *King Lear* concerning the division of the kingdom seems mere court chatter and the fact that Edmund has been abroad ("out") and must go again is missed, although it suggests that Edmund has only this one opportunity to outwit his brother. Students of the play must be more wary. It has to be recognized that Shakespeare's language is nearer in time to Chaucer's than to ours. Therefore, in III.vii.37, "quicken" means to come to life, from the older sense of "quick," living, also present in "quickly," at IV.i.67, where the point is that the man who lives in comfort should be made to feel Heaven's power in a lively fashion and not merely with speed. "Speed" in turn refers, as in Old English, to being successful rather than swift, when it appears as a verb in I.ii.19, and IV.vi.200; and to "succeed" (I.ii.129) means to follow, so that "success" means outcome (V.iii.191). "Angering" (IV.i.39), too, seems to keep its older meaning, afflicting or distressing. It is likely that "stelled" (III.vii.58) comes in form and sense from O.E. *stellan*, to place or set, which like "moe" (I.v.28), meaning greater in number (O.E. *mā*), and "gallow" (III.ii.42), has not survived into our time.

Sometimes the problem is that words which are differentiated in spelling in modern English are not so differentiated in the language of Shakespeare or of earlier writers. Two examples of this fact are found side by side in I.i.64–5, "metal" and "prize." Modern English distinguishes the concrete and abstract senses of "metal" by spelling; Shakespeare can here use "metal" so as to keep both kinds of meaning in view at once. In the case of "prize," and "price" (II.i.118), both variants go back, together with "praise," to a common ancestor, O.F. *preisier*: the senses of the whole group are not yet consistently distinguished by spelling, so that any one form may bear any one of the meanings of the whole group. There is a similar relation between "plight" (I.i.275), "plait," and "pleat."

Because *King Lear* is written at a time when large numbers of words are being imported into English, other languages have to be taken into account, for many of the imported words have not yet been given native senses by repeated use in native contexts. So we have meanings much nearer to the Latin in the case of "curious" (I.iv.29) or "curiosity" (I.i.5, I.ii.4, I.iv.59), "enormous" (II.ii.157), "provision" (II.iv.199, III.vi.89), "office" (II.i.104, II.iv.172, V.iii.245), "prevent" (III.iv.143), "speculations" (III.i.24), to mention those where the modern sense would be most misleading. Where the form of the word looks odd, as with "compact" (II.ii.107) from the Latin past participle *compactus,* instead of an English form in -ed, or "cadent" (I.iv.261) from a Latin present participle (which we do not at once connect with "cadence," the only modern word which preserves the stem *cad-*), the oddity sends us to the notes or a dictionary: the insidious cases are those where the word is familiar to us today but, as with "office," in a sense much further away from the Latin than Shakespeare's.

It is the same with a number of words from French and Italian. Sometimes they stand out because of their form, as with the French "moiety" (I.i.6), "meiny" (II.iv.34), or "caitiff" (III.ii.53), but repeatedly they look familiar and may gull us with apparent intelligence. So "garb" (II.ii.87) never refers to dress in Shakespeare, but only to the style or fashion of doing something (from Italian *garbo,* grace, elegance), and Edmund's "alarumed spirits" (II.i.51) are not scared but called to arms, Italian *all' arme.* Where English and French share a word form, though derived from a different word in each case, Shakespeare is not above punning on the English and French sense at once, as with "rest" in I.i.118.

Other cases of meaning change are not so easily to be related to general tendencies in Elizabethan and Jacobean English. There is, for instance, the question of different emotional overtones in Shakespeare's use of a word and in ours. Sometimes, as with "goodman" (II.ii.37), "villain" (III.vii.75), and "peasant" (III.vii.77), an unfavorable sense may arise from class consciousness of a kind an historian might deal with, but more frequently there is no simple "explanation" of this sort.

A persistent example in *King Lear* is "practice" (I.ii.164, II.i.71, 105, II.iv.110, V.iii.148) which means a stratagem, and has overtones of scheming and trickery which it has lost in modern English. Similarly, "fond" means foolish (I.iv.277) and the apparently neutral word "note" (II.i.81) has overtones of stigma or reproach, while "suggestion" (II.i.71), equally neutral to us, is repeatedly used in contexts where prompting or urging to *evil* is in question. Conversely, Shakespeare's sense may avoid the unfavorable suggestions of ours, as in "catastrophe" (to a comedy, I.ii.121), "knave" (I.i.16, I.iv.38, though not in II.ii.17), or "censure" (III.v.2), and may even add other favorable suggestions to those we expect, as with "royal" (I.i.236) or "generous" (I.ii.8).

Shakespeare's word may carry a sense which is more specialized than the principle modern sense or, on the other hand, more general: so there is a legal specialization of the sense of "interest" in I.i.145, and a restriction of the sense of "go" to going on *foot* in I.iv.104; on the other hand "dieted" in IV.i.65 may contain a more general sense of "diet," referring to the whole of a man's way of living, just as "wit" in I.iv.164 means understanding or intelligence in general (even though in I.ii.165 it seems to bear the more special sense, which has not survived, of an ingenious plan). Or it may be that Shakespeare can expect a strong response to a word which is much weakened for us, as with "saucy" (II.ii.87), "naughty" (III.iv.98, III.vii.35), or "dreadful" (III.ii.57).

The grammar of the language has changed almost as much since Shakespeare's time as word-meaning has. The selection of a verb form without "s" to go with a plural subject is not yet a fixed habit for Shakespeare, so that he may write "regards that stands" (I.i.234) or "our businesses . . . craves" (II.i.125–6, where we tend to misunderstand by linking the verb with the nearest singular noun, "counsel"). This license goes back to an earlier stage of the language, as does the ability to set one sentence beside another without subordinating it grammatically even though it is subordinated in sense, as with "Let him fly far" at II.i.54. The old adverbial genitive survives in "ways" (II.ii.32; compare the American usage "nights" for "at night"); the old use of "his" as the genitive of "it" is in II.ii.88, although I.iv.193 uses "it" for this function; our form "its" does not occur yet. In "you were

Appendix

best" (I.iv.83), and "thou wert better" (III.iv.90) the pronoun is properly not the subject of the verb but the remains of an old dative with
an impersonal verb, so that the sense is "it would be better or best for
you." The impersonal use of "like" at I.i.195 or II.ii.80 may give similar
trouble, for the noun or pronoun following the verb indicates the person whom the subject of the verb pleases. Modern English turns "to
like" into a personal verb but preserves the older impersonal construction with "to please." Another kind of difficulty with pronoun and verb
is found in I.ii.89 "wind me into him," where "me" is not the object
of the verb but indicates the person who has an interest in the action
(the so-called ethic dative), so that the sense is "Wind yourself into
him for me, or on my account." The same construction is involved in
the quibbling sense of "conceive you" in I.i.10. With the verbs "ask"
and "cry," a pronoun may stand as a second object, as in "cry you
mercy" or "ask me blessing" (III.iv.155, vi.47 and V.iii.10; compare
III.ii.56–7). Sometimes it is a question of the older, fuller sense of
an auxiliary verb, as with "shall" in I.i.27 and V.iii.22 (compare
II.iv.200), or the exact use of a subjunctive, for instance after "if," when
the action is merely considered, not asserted to have taken place: "If
she have . . ." II.iv.136–7. Conjunctions like "and" and "that" may do
more work than in Modern English: "and" is repeatedly equivalent to
"if," and "that" to some other conjunction, such as "when" in II.i.43
or "seeing that" in I.i.163 (compare "though that" IV.vi.207, "if that"
IV.ii.46; V.iii.259). An adverbial clause may be introduced by a relative
pronoun in V.iii.49, where Edmund is giving his reason for imprisoning
the King: "Whose age . . ." is equivalent to "because his age . . ." Per-
sistently the long-standing distinction, which we have lost, between
"thou" and "you" affects the tone of the dialogue. The common form
is "you," while "thou" is used with overtones either of affection
towards intimates, or of well-disposed superiority towards social inferiors, or of enmity towards strangers of the speaker's own rank. One
can observe the change from the common "you" to the affectionate
"thou," and back again, as Lear addresses Regan in II.iv.123ff. (she replies, of course, with the respectful "you"), or Goneril Edmund in
IV.ii.22–3; in the quarrel which follows between Goneril with her husband, he begins with the more distant form "you" but they fall to
"thou" as matrimonial acrimony grows (lines 50–67). The form of
address to inferiors shows clearly in the contrast between Edgar's
"Now fare ye well, good sir" and Gloucester's "Now fellow, fare thee
well" (IV.vi.32–41). The enmity in "thou" between social equals appears, for instance, between Edgar and Edmund before the duel
(V.iii.123–47).

Besides these grammatical niceties which the language has discarded, there is a certain amount of looser grammar such as the double comparatives and superlatives (I.i.206, II.ii.92, 136, II.iii.7, II.iv.105, III.ii.62), or the use of "whom" instead of "who" (I.i.209) or of "who" instead of "whom" (V.iii.245); two constructions may be confused, as in IV.vi.33–4 or V.i.67–8, or part of a construction elided, as in II.iv.41, 284, IV.vi.251, and V.iii.117. Adverbs like "here" and "where" may be turned into nouns in I.i.256, adjectives into verbs, like "worthied" II.ii.110, or nouns into verbs, as in "He childed as I fathered" (III.vi.103 = He had children as cruel as my father).

Shakespearian pronunciation is too complicated a matter to be discussed here: the notes to I.iv.296–7, 323; I.v.42; II.i.93, and II.ii.72 refer to specific points in justification of rhyme, reading or interpretation. An idea of what the language may have sounded like in the seventeenth century may be gained from *Shakespeare's Pronunciation: A Selection of Readings* by Helge Kökeritz (a Yale University Press Recording— TV·19233) or *A Thousand Years of English Pronunciation*, a selection of readings by Helge Kökeritz (Lexington Records—LE·7650/55).

APPENDIX D

The Play's Theatrical History

The performance recorded on the title page of the Quarto (see p. 1), one by a group of Yorkshire players at Gowthwaite Hall, Nidderdale, in 1610 (see *RES*, XVIII (1942), 129–143), and those vaguely mentioned by Downes in *Roscius Anglicanus* (1708) as having taken place "from 1662 to 1665" are the only performances—with the possible exception of one in 1675 (Summers's edition of Downes, 1928, p. 188)—before the play began to be refashioned to give more scope to actresses. Tate's version of the play which began to be acted in 1681 omits the Fool, France, and Burgundy, and makes Edgar the man who wins Cordelia. She makes her brusque reply to her father in order to avoid being married off to Burgundy, and Edgar adopts his disguise in order to be "near to wait upon her Fortune." The intrigues of the other two sisters with Edmund are developed; but all ends with the success of "Truth and Virtue." It is virtually a new play with occasional speeches by Shakespeare. This version was acted frequently in the next century, with Betterton as Lear until 1710, or with Quin and Delane in the thirties and early forties. Garrick supplanted the latter from 1742 and was responsible, from 1756, for restoring most of the Shakespearian dialogue which would fit into the story as refashioned by Tate. George Colman the Elder went further in his version of 1768, which was not quite independent of Tate, but did cut out the love-scenes (though also Gloucester's attempted suicide). The Fool was still cut; the happy ending remained. In this form, the main part was acted by Powell. The version did not survive the season of 1770–71. Garrick continued to play in his version until he retired in 1776.

The early Cordelias had included Mrs. Bracegirdle, who played opposite Betterton, but the greatest eighteenth-century actress to take the part was Mrs. Siddons, with her brother J. P. Kemble as Lear, in 1788, 1792–93, 1795 and 1801—in Garrick's version in 1788 but in one which was predominately Tate's thereafter. After Kemble (who continued to play Lear without his sister), the great early nineteenth century Lears were Kean, 1820–30, and Macready, 1834–51. In 1823 Kean restored the tragic ending while keeping the love story. Macready played Shakespeare not Tate, though with cuts (including the Fool) and transpositions. Eventually in 1838 he restored the Fool, played by a girl. From now on, something like Shakespeare's play is the rule, although it was not until Phelps's Lear, 1845–61, that Shakespeare's order of scenes was restored, along with more of his text. The main omission was now the blinding of Gloucester (which Tate had staged but Colman merely narrated) and this was still omitted by Irving in 1892–93. Irving as Lear was quite overshadowed by Ellen Terry as Cordelia; but his production was the climax of nineteenth-century scenic splendor. He placed the action in Britain shortly after the Romans had left: his most notable predecessor in this respect, Charles Kean in 1858, had used settings and costumes recalling Anglo-Saxon England of the eighth century.

In the present century William Poel and Harley Granville-Barker have worked for a better understanding of the plays as written for Shakespeare's theater, leading to the simplifying of scenes, the reduction of scene divisions, and the restoration of a full text. Poel's productions without scenery for the Elizabethan Stage Society led to those of Nugent Monck at the Maddermarket in Norwich (*King Lear*, 1926) on a stage modeled on Shakespeare's. Rarely performed on the commercial stage this century before World War I, the play was much revived between the wars: with Russell Thorndike as Lear and Sybil Thorndike as the Fool in 1918, or with Robert Atkins in 1920–21, playing in a version with hardly any cuts, like that which Granville-Barker and Lewis Casson produced in 1940 with Gielgud as Lear. Gielgud has given his record of the rehearsals for this latter production, the second in which he had appeared as Lear, in chapter 5 and appendix 1 of his book *Stage Directions,* 1963. He again took the part in 1950 and 1955. Jessica Tandy, Peggy Ashcroft, Claire Bloom and Mary Watson have all played opposite to him as Cordelia. His main rivals in the part have been Donald Wolfit, 1942–53, Laurence Olivier, 1946, Michael Redgrave, 1953, Charles Laughton, 1959, and Paul Scofield, 1962–63. The principal directors have been Nugent Monck, 1942, Olivier, 1946, Gielgud, 1950, Hugh Hunt, 1952, Douglas Seale, 1958, Byam Shaw, 1959, and Peter Brook, 1962. Brook's assistant director, Charles Marowitz, has published his "Log" of the rehearsals in *The Tulane Drama Review* for 1963 (see Introduction, p. xix above).

In New York, actors taking the part of Lear have included Malone in 1754, J. B. Booth in 1821–52, Edwin Forrest 1826–70, and Edwin Booth 1875–88. Tate's version was presented until Macready's visit of 1844. The outstanding Lear of the early twentieth century was Robert Mantell. The German director Edwin Piscator presented an experimental *King Lear* in 1940, the same year as Louis Calhern took the part at the National Theater, directed by John Houseman. Following Orson Welles (directing and playing Lear) in 1956 and the 1959 production by the Players Theater Company, the New York Shakespeare Festival staged the play in Central Park in 1962. Paul Scofield acted in Brook's production in 1964. At the American Shakespeare Festival Theater, Stratford, Connecticut, Allen Fletcher directed Morris Carnovsky in outstanding performances of an almost uncut text in 1963 and 1965. In 1963 Herbert Blau of the San Francisco Actor's Workshop attempted, like Brook, to relate the play to Beckett, and also to Genet; Blau's account of the production is also in *The Tulane Drama Review* for 1963.

In Canada the theater at Stratford, Ontario, has attempted since 1952 to reproduce Elizabethan acting conditions on a stage jutting out into the audience, with a tarras on top of a pillared booth and with entry doors to the latter and to left and right of the back of the main platform. John Colicos played Lear in the tercentenary celebrations here in 1964.

APPENDIX E

The Transmission of the Text

Both F and Q of *King Lear* seem to be at several removes from Shakespeare's autograph.

F gives the play in a form which would work in the theatre: entrances and exits are almost complete, other stage directions are terse and practical, and speakers' names (except for the use of both *Edmund* and *Bastard* for the same character) are in consistent forms.

Q, on the other hand, leaves out many necessary entrances and exits, or else has them in vague or incomplete form, e.g., *"Enter Gloster brought in by two or three"* (III.vii.25), or merely *"Enter King"* (II.iv.) when the Fool and a Gentleman are to enter with him. Other stage directions are fuller than in F and more visual, e.g., the form adopted in this text when Lear first comes in (I.i.28). The speakers' names are inconstant or ambiguous: *"Duke"* for either Cornwall or Albany, for Oswald *"Gentleman"* and *"Steward"* as well as his name. Such a form of the play would not serve on the stage.

Q is about 300 lines longer than F; F in turn prints some 100 lines which are not found in Q. Many of the F omissions are tidily made (e.g., with the meter mended as at II.ii.133) and for a theatrical purpose, such as to reduce the number of speaking roles (III.vii.97ff.). The briefer Q omissions, on the other hand, look more like the result of carelessness; for instance at III.iv.17–18 both the beginning and the end of the omission would make a hasty compositor think he had set line 18 when he had not, for the line and a half which is omitted begins with the very words "in such a night" which immediately follow the omission, and ends with the syllable "-ure" with which the line preceding it ends (in Q) as well. Moreover, these omissions often leave noticeable gaps, as when part of IV.i.6 is dropped, and all of the next three lines 7–9, so that line 10 has to be lengthened with "Who's here". Omissions from F, then, look like theatrical cuts, omissions from Q like the mistakes of a copyist or compositor. These features strengthen the case for regarding F as depending upon a manuscript which had been used in the theatre.

If, then, what is called the prompt copy of the play lies behind F, does the rather fuller Q version take us any nearer to the author's manuscript? It does not seem very likely, for nearly a quarter of the play is wrongly divided into verse lines and nearly a fifth is printed as prose instead of verse; there is very little punctuation apart from commas, often to the gross detriment of the sense, and there is some extraordinary phonetic spelling which looks like the work of somebody who did not understand the text (for instance, "a dog's obeyed in office" appears as "a dogge, so bade in office" at IV.vi.152). It may just be possible that these characteristics are the fault of the compositor, as the printing of some nonsense clearly is ("a nellthu night more" corrected in some copies to "he met the night mare" at III.iv.107). But if they represent any features of the manuscript, it is unlikely to have been from Shakespeare's hand.

Moreover, Q seems at many points, when it is compared with F, to give words which either anticipate or recall words used elsewhere in the play. There is more of this interplay in the first act than later on, but it persists throughout the play; more than anything else it damages the claim of Q to be taken as an authoritative text. A glance at the variants in the notes to I.i.34–38 will readily show what this means at its worst: line 34 is made imperfect in sense through the anticipation, in "cares . . . of state," of line 45—which is then left out, along with line 44, from its proper place; the contrast between "age" and "younger" and between "strengths" and "unburdened" is lost (as Duthie points out); while "confirming" seems wrong as early as line 35 because it means "ratifying, making valid what has already been instituted" and this is the first time official mention has been made of the transfer of executive authority, so that the word is more likely to be an anticipation of line 133; finally, the omission of the important word "nature", and the consequent reorganization of the clause, greatly reduce the point of the conclusion to the speech. This kind of corruption suggests that the copy for the printer had been put together by someone whose memory of the play interfered with his transmission of it. In the rest of the play, he frequently gets phrases wrong by confusion with others like them: in III.iv.20 "your . . . father who gave you all" instead of "gave all" because he is thinking of II.iv.244 "I gave you all", or II.ii.79 and 103, which are confused to give "what's his offence" and "What's the offence" instead of "What is his fault" and "What was th' offence". When, in addition, we find exclamations like "look" (II.iv.7) or familiar vocatives like "my good boy" (III.ii.76), such as might well be added by an actor, it does look as if the person whose memory is corrupting the text knew the play from repeated performances or rehearsals. But it is less important here to try to explain how this corruption occurred than to recognize that it is of a kind which makes Q unreliable, even though, of course, Q might none the less preserve the right reading in particular cases and a tenable theory of its origin might help us to tell which these cases were.

This unreliability, together with the fact that, when Q differs from F, F seems more often to be right, might lead us to neglect Q and take F as the only authoritative text. But there is an important complication. From a number of errors common to both texts (like "bare" for "bar", V.iii.86), it appears that the printer of F was working from an actual copy of Q, though a copy which had been carefully, but not impeccably, edited. The strongest evidence arises from the fact that, Q itself having

been proofread and corrected in certain places, both corrected and uncorrected sheets were then bound up together without discrimination.
In a number of instances F clearly follows the uncorrected Q readings,
particularly those in sheets H and K, as with "seemes" (IV.ii.60) or
"Iustices" (IV.ii.79). There is a great deal of such evidence, brought
together in Greg, strengthening the case for the use of an edited Q as
printer's copy for F.

At some points it looks as if what was edited for the printer was a
copy of Q2 rather than Q1. The evidence (discussed by A. S. Cairncross, *RES*, N.S., VI (1955), 252ff., as well as by Doran, pp. 109–21) in-
volves details, mainly of spelling and punctuation, significantly grouped
on certain Q pages so as to suggest that there was some alternation in
the use of Q1 and Q2 as copy. Where F follows Q2 in an error, the
evidence is strongest—as in II.i.55–6 where the mispunctuation "uncaught and found;" is that of Q2—or where an error in F seems
otherwise traceable to Q2, as with the mistaken catchword (in some
copies of F only, i.e., subsequently corrected) "Gainst" for "But" in
II.i.43. It seems to me possible that this was caused by the appearance
of "gainst" in the last line of the Q2 page, immediately above the signature D (whereas in Q1 the line is about a third of the way down the
page, and "gainst" is in no way conspicuous). I find Cairncross's article
puzzling in some respects, but the results of my own collation tend to
confirm his. Moreover, now that Charlton Hinman has established
which parts of *King Lear* in F were set by each of the two compositors
he calls B and E, it can be seen that the F pages which show evidence
of having been set from a corrected copy of Q2 (like pp. 290–1, on
which the examples just noted occur) are nearly all of them the work
of compositor E. The evidence is perhaps most striking in the section
of the play from II.ii.146 to IV.vi.272, that is in the group of twelve
pages, 293–304, forming a quire and marked with the signature rr.
Only three and a half of these were set by E, 293, 294a, 295, and 297,
and it is on these that indications of Q2 copy tend to be present—a
mispunctuation like "mind," at the end of III.iv.12 on p. 297, or the
correct use of brackets in II.iv.241 and of the dash after "shall" in
II.iv.274 on p. 295—whereas contrary indications of Q1 copy are
plentiful in the long section set by B, following p. 297. If the use of
Q2 rather than Q1 goes with the work of one compositor rather than
another, the case for a direct connection between F and the Qq is
strengthened.

By the same token, the case for an indirect connection, by means of
an intervening transcript, is weakened. Indeed some of the evidence
adduced for a transcript itself correlates with the change of compositor

and so reinforces the case for a direct link between F and the Qq. For instance, Philip Williams argued for such a transcript in *Shakespeare Quarterly*, IV (1953), 451–60, because the printing of certain characters' names in the text (not as speech-headings) in F varied between roman and italic type in a fashion which did not correlate with Q1, but seemed to suggest variation in an intervening manuscript where these names appeared in italic script only in certain stretches of it. But in fact, of the forms quoted (p. 459) as showing roman type where Q1 has italic, all but two come from the work of compositor B; and of the two from compositor E, one is in a part of the play (V.iii.122) for which there is other evidence to suggest that Q2 was used as copy for F—and it duly appears in Q2 as roman ("Gloster", not "*Gloster*" as in Q1). So the change to roman type seems to be due to B's habit and E's copy rather than to any peculiarity of a transcript.

The fact that, throughout the work of both compositors in F, the spelling of "Gonerill" is used, whereas the Qq use "Gonorill", may tell against the theory that the latter were used as copy—at least, if we cannot believe that someone collating them with the promptbook would make such a small change in every case. But it does not seem implausible that the experienced compositor, B, should make the change throughout and that the change should be marked in the copy (of Q2) for E. Moreover J. K. Walton's discussion of this kind of evidence, in the appendix to *The Copy for the Folio Text of Richard III* (Auckland, 1955) shows clear links between the speech headings of Q and F. Conceivably such links, or those between F and the uncorrected pages of Q1 for that matter, might be preserved via a transcript, but, to satisfy the other evidence, this would have to be a transcript of a prompt book made up of manuscript pages and of pages from both quartos.

The theory that F was set from a corrected earlier print seems, then, to be reinforced in the light of recent evidence; even those who argue for an intervening transcript accept the eventual dependence of F upon Q. It follows that, where F and Q agree, there is no means of being sure that what they agree in is the right reading. Where they differ, of course, an editor can judge between what they offer, bearing in mind that F can be traced to the prompt book, whereas the nature of the copy for Q is not so clear. That is to say, where F corrects Q (as with "ballow" or "English," IV.vi.233, 240) the correction is likely to have been made by reference to the prompt book.

There is an important group of cases where F gives a weaker, more ordinary word for a bolder, more original word in Q. Two famous examples are in III.vii: "sticke" in F for the much more expressive and unusual verb "rash" in Q, at line 55, or "sterne" in F for "dearne" in Q, at line 60. The possibility of this sort of "sophistication" means that the closeness of F to theatrical copy gives no guarantee that it is more reliable than Q, despite all Q's deficiencies.

APPENDIX F

Bibliography

A full range of work on Shakespeare is displayed in vol. I. of *The Cambridge Bibliography of British Literature*, ed. F. W. Bateson (4 vols., New York, 1941), pp. 539ff., and in the *Supplement*, ed. G. W. Watson (1957), pp. 257ff. These are kept up to date by the Annual Bibliographies of the *Shakespeare Quarterly* and the *PMLA* (Publications of the Modern Language Association of America) and by the annual surveys in *The Year's Work in English Studies* and in *Shakespeare Survey*. There is a selective bibliography of criticism of *King Lear* in Helmut Bonheim, *The King Lear Perplex* (Belmont, Calif., 1960), pp. 179–189. Only a few of the vast number of books directly or indirectly useful to the student of *King Lear* can be mentioned here.

On the social and historical background of the plays *Shakespeare's England*, edited by Sidney Lee and C. T. Onions (Oxford, 1916) presents a number of specialized essays. Useful smaller books like M. St. Clare Byrne's *Elizabethan Life in Town and Country* (Seventh edition, revised, London, 1954) or J. Dover Wilson's *Life in Shakespeare's England: A Book of Elizabethan Prose* (London, 1911) are available in paperback editions. The large work of E. K. Chambers, *William Shakespeare: a Study of Facts and Problems* (Oxford, 1930), gives full information on Shakespeare's life and summarizes the state of scholarship in 1930 with reference to each of the plays and poems. The same author's *The Mediaeval Stage* and *The Elizabethan Stage* (Oxford, 1903, 1923) are exhaustive on the development of the theater. For Shakespeare's stage there are readable and no less scholarly books in A. Nagler, *Shakespeare's Stage* (New Haven, 1958), Bernard Beckerman, *Shakespeare at the Globe 1599–1609* (New York, 1964), and J. L. Styan, *Shakespeare's Stagecraft* (Cambridge, England, 1967). The staging of *King Lear* in particular is considered by W. W. Greg, "The Staging of *King Lear*," *RES*, XVI (1940), 300–303, and, from a modern point of view, by Charles Marowitz, "Lear Log," *Tulane Drama Review*, VIII (Winter, 1963), 103–121; the latter is influenced by a chapter, "*King Lear* or *Endgame*," in Jan Kott's over-praised *Shakespeare our Contemporary* (London, 1964).

Appendix

The standard books on the problems of the text are by W. W. Greg (*The Editorial Problem in Shakespeare: A Survey of the Foundations of the Text*, Oxford, 1942; *The Shakespeare First Folio: Its Bibliographical and Textual History*, Oxford, 1955) and Alice Walker (*Textual Problems of the First Folio*, Cambridge, England, 1953). Detailed work on the compositors and the order of printing of the First Folio has been done by Charlton Hinman, *The Printing and Proof-Reading of the First Folio of Shakespeare*, 2 vols. (Oxford, 1963). Hinman's assumptions and his conclusion that only a small proportion of F pages were proofread, and even these without reference to copy, are challenged by D. F. McKenzie in *Studies in Bibliography*, XXII (1969), 1–75.

Eighteenth-century criticisms of *King Lear* are reprinted by D. Nichol Smith in *Shakespeare Criticism, a Selection* [1623–1840] (London, 1916)—for instance Dr. Johnson's important "General Observations" on the play in his edition of Shakespeare (London, 1765). Coleridge's discussion is in the *Lectures and Notes on Shakespeare and other English Poets*, collected by T. Ashe in 1883 and by T. M. Raysor, *Coleridge's Shakespearean Criticism* (London, 1930). Hazlitt writes with his usual verve on the play and productions of it which he had seen in vol. XVIII of his *Complete Works* edited by P. P. Howe (London, 1930–4; pp. 316–338, "The Drama," Nos. v–vi).

The most inclusive nineteenth-century view, that of A. C. Bradley in *Shakespearean Tragedy* (London, 1904), has been repeatedly challenged in the present century. The best of this work modifies Bradley but leaves him still important. William Empson, for instance, in chapter 6, " 'Fool' in *Lear*," of *The Structure of Complex Words* (London, 1951), shows that "If you assume that a key word, or . . . a whole pattern of related key words, is the proper thing to follow in considering a poetic drama, you get a noticeably different result in this play from the result of the Victorian [i.e., Bradleyan] assumption that the characters ought to be followed separately"; but he remains at the end surprised at the amount he has owed to Bradley. G. Wilson Knight who has studied Shakespeare as if the whole of a play could be laid out to the view at once, rather than in the time sequence of the theater, regards his work on the themes and images of the plays as an extension of Bradley's; he writes on *King Lear* in *The Wheel of Fire* (London, 4th ed., 1949): "The *Lear* Universe," pp. 177–206, "*King Lear* and the Comedy of the Grotesque," pp. 160–176. Poetic imagery in isolation from the visual imagery of the stage and the sequence of the plot is studied by Caroline Spurgeon in her Shakespeare Association Lecture of 1930 and in *Shakespeare's Imagery and What it tells us* (Cambridge,

England, 1935). Her most important successor is W. H. Clemen, in *The Development of Shakespeare's Imagery* (Cambridge, Mass., 1951). The most elaborate of such studies in relation to *King Lear* is R. B. Heilman's *This Great Stage: Image and Structure in "King Lear"* (Baton Rouge, La., 1948). The themes as distinct from the images of the play are the concern of critics like J. F. Danby who in *Shakespeare's Doctrine of Nature, a Study of "King Lear"* (London, 1949), works out the opposition of "The benignant Nature of Bacon, Hooker, and Lear" to "The malignant Nature of Hobbes, Edmund, and the Wicked Daughters." L. C. Knights in *Some Shakespearean Themes* (London, 1959) builds up from here a sophisticated neo-Christian view of the play. The whole tendency to treat the plays as embodying abstract moral themes is attacked in W. R. Keast's essay "The 'New Criticism' and *King Lear*" in *Critics and Criticism*, ed. R. S. Crane (Chicago, 1952) and by John Holloway in *The Story of the Night; Studies in Shakespeare's Major Tragedies* (London, 1961). Arthur Sewell's book *Character and Society in Shakespeare* (Oxford, 1951) makes an important attempt to reconcile the study of character with the identification, in moral terms, of "the comprehensive vision of the play." The way in which "the pursuit of [moral] abstraction kills the actuality" of the play is the subject of two important articles by Barbara Everett in *The Critical Quarterly*, II: "The Figure in Professor Knights's Carpet," (Summer, 1960), pp. 171–76, and "The New King Lear," (Winter, 1960), pp. 325–339. William Empson, Kenneth Muir, John F. Danby and Emrys Jones reply in III (Spring, 1961), pp. 67–75.

Christian interpretations of the play like that of R. W. Chambers in his W. P. Ker Memorial Lecture (University of Glasgow, 1940) or O. J. Campbell's more extravagant article, "The Salvation of Lear," in *ELH*, XV (June, 1948), 93–109, are challenged in W. R. Elton's book, *"King Lear" and the Gods* (San Marino, California, 1966) and by N. S. Brooke in *Shakespeare: "King Lear"* (London, 1963), a notable commentary on the whole play. Other contributions to this controversy can be found in, for instance, Norman Rabkin's *Approaches to Shakespeare* (New York, 1964): R. W. Battenhouse on "Shakespearean Tragedy: a Christian Approach," pp. 203–216, answered by Sylvan Barnet, "Some Limitations of a Christian Approach to Shakespeare," pp. 217–229. Helen Gardner in her John Coffin Memorial Lecture of 1966 (University of London, 1967) develops, by reference to our experience of the play, the view that Shakespeare was deliberate in making the world of *King Lear* neither Christian nor pagan.

J. D. Rosenberg's "King Lear and his Comforters" in *Essays in Criticism*, XVI (April, 1966), 135–146, begins "by defending Lear from the excesses of over-zealous Christians" and ends "in fear that he will be devoured by existential lions." The ways in which the play may readily be adapted to modern views, and the risks of distorting it in the process, are ably dealt with by V. A. Kolve in "The Modernity of *Lear*," *Pacific Coast Studies in Shakespeare* (Eugene, Oregon, 1966), pp. 173–189. Maynard Mack not only discusses *"King Lear" in Our Time* (Berkeley, California, 1965) but also relates the play to its predecessors—for instance, to the morality plays—as does Bernard Spivack in *Shakespeare and the Allegory of Evil* (New York, 1958). W. Farnham in *The Mediaeval Heritage of Elizabethan Tragedy* (Berkeley, California, 1936) emphasizes the shock to man's pride in *King Lear*, from the revelation of his physical repulsiveness. R. A. Fraser's *Shakespeare's Poetics in Relation to "King Lear"* (London, 1962) considers the images, found in the work of contemporaries of Shakespeare, which fix or crystallize "central motifs" of the play such as Providence, Fortune, or Redemption. The morality of the play is seen in much more specific terms than these by Jonas Barish and Marshall Waingrow in *Shakespeare Quarterly*, IX (Summer, 1958), 347–55, " 'Service' in *King Lear*."

Essays on *King Lear*, ranging all the way from costume to catharsis, occupy the whole of a special number of *Shakespeare Survey 13* (1960).

A recording of the play by the Marlowe Dramatic Society and professional players, directed by George Rylands, is issued in England by Argo (RG 280-283) and in America by London records (A•4423). In America a recording directed by Howard Sackler, with Paul Scofield as Lear, is available on Caedmon records (SRS•233).

APPENDIX G

Abbreviations, References and Editions Used in the Commentary

a.	adjective (in *O.E.D.* references).
Abbott	E. A. Abbott, *A Shakespearian Grammar* (London, 3rd ed., 1870). References are to sections, not to pages.
adv.	adverb.
Alexander	Shakespeare, *The Complete Works*, ed. P. Alexander (London, 1951).
Arden	*King Lear*, ed. K. Muir (London, 8th ed., 1952).

Arden ed. 1   *King Lear,* ed. W. J. Craig (London, 1901).

A.V.   The Bible, Authorized Version, 1611.

Bible   Unless otherwise stated, quotations are from the
              Breeches Bible, ed. of 1599.

Blau   Herbert Blau, "A Subtext Based on Nothing," *Tu-
              lane Drama Review,* VIII (Winter, 1963), 122–132.

c.   *circa* about.

Capell   *Mr. W. Shakespeare, his Comedies, Histories and
              Tragedies,* ed. E. Capell, 10 vols. (London, 1767–68).

ch.   chapter.

corr.   corrected.

Cotgrave   R. Cotgrave, *A Dictionarie of the French and En-
              glish Tongues* (London, 1611).

Coxe   M. R. Coxe, *Cinderella* (London, 1893).

Dobson   E. J. Dobson, *English Pronunciation 1500–1700* (Ox-
              ford, 1957).

Doran   M. Doran, *The Text of "King Lear"* (Palo Alto,
              Calif., 1931).

Duthie   *King Lear,* ed. G. I. Duthie (Oxford, 1949).

ed.   edited, edition, editor.

E.E.T.S.   Early English Text Society.

F   First Folio edition of Shakespeare's *Comedies, His-
              tories, & Tragedies* (London, 1623).

Feuillerat   *The Complete Works of Sir Philip Sidney,* ed. Al-
              bert Feuillerat (Cambridge, Eng., 1912).

Florio   J. Florio, *A World of Words, or most copious and
              exact Dictionarie in Italian and English* (London,
              1598). *Queen Anna's New World of Words* (Lon-
              don, 1611).

Franz   W. Franz, *Die Sprache Shakespeares* (Halle, 1939).

Granville-Barker Harley Granville-Barker, *Prefaces to Shakespeare,*
              I (Princeton, 1947).

Greg   W. W. Greg, *The Variants in the First Quarto of
              'King Lear'* (Oxford, 1940).

Harsnett   S. Harsnett, *A Declaration of Egregious Popish Im-
              postures* (London, 1603).

Hinman   Charlton Hinman, *The Printing and Proof-Reading
              of the First Folio of Shakespeare,* 2 vols. (Oxford,
              1963).

Johnson   *The Plays of Shakespeare,* ed. S. Johnson, 8 vols.
              (London, 1765).

Jonson, B.   *Bartholomew Fair,* ed. E. A. Horsman, 2nd ed. (London, 1965). *The Oxford Ben Jonson,* ed. C. H. Herford and Percy Simpson, (Oxford, 1925–52).

Kittredge   *King Lear,* ed. G. L. Kittredge (Boston, 1940).

Kyd, T.   *The Spanish Tragedy,* ed. P. Edwards (London, 1959).

Malone   *Shakespeare's Works,* ed. E. Malone, 10 vols. (London, 1790).

Maxwell   J. C. Maxwell, "The Technique of Invocation in *King Lear,*" *MLR,* XLV (1950), 142–147.

M.E.   Middle English (c. 1100–c. 1500 A.D.).

MLR   *The Modern Language Review.*

MS   Manuscript.

Muir   K. Muir, "Samuel Harsnett and *King Lear,*" *RES,* N.S. II (1951), 11–21.

Muir, *Sources*   K. Muir, *Shakespeare's Sources,* vol. I (London, 1957).

New Cambridge   *King Lear,* ed. G. I. Duthie and J. D. Wilson (Cambridge, England, 1962).

Nicol   Allardyce Nicol, " 'Passing Over the Stage,' " *Shakespeare Survey,* XII (1959), 47–55.

O.E.   Old English (before 1100 A.D.).

O.E.D.   *The Oxford English Dictionary,* ed. James A. H. Murray, H. Bradley, W. A. Craigie, and C. T. Onions (13 vols.; Oxford, 1933; first published 1888–1928 as *A New English Dictionary*).

O.F.   Old French.

Onions   C. T. Onions, *A Shakespeare Glossary* (Oxford, 1911; revised edition, 1946).

Perrett   W. Perrett, *The Story of King Lear from Geoffrey of Monmouth to Shakespeare* (Berlin, 1904).

Pope   *The Works of Shakespeare,* ed. Alexander Pope, 6 vols. (London, 1723–25).

Q   First Quarto edition of *King Lear* (London, 1608).

RES   *The Review of English Studies.*

Rowe   *The Works of Mr. William Shakespeare,* ed. N. Rowe, 6 vols. (London, 1709).

sb.   substantive, noun.

S.D.   stage direction(s).

Steevens   *The Plays of William Shakespeare . . . to which are added Notes by Samuel Johnson and George Stevens,* 4th ed. (London, 1773).

Appendix

Taylor	G. C. Taylor, *Shakespeare's Debt to Montaigne* (Cambridge, Mass., 1925).
Theobald	*The Works of Shakespeare*, ed. Lewis Theobald, 7 vols. (London, 1733).
Tilley	M. P. Tilley, *A Dictionary of the Proverbs in England in the Sixteenth and Seventeenth Centuries* (Ann Arbor, Michigan, 1950). References are to the initial letter and the number by which proverbs are listed, not to pages.
uncorr.	uncorrected.
v.	verb.
Warburton	*The Works of Shakespeare*, ed. W. Warburton, 8 vols. (London, 1747).
Wyld	H. C. Wyld, *A History of Modern Colloquial English*, 3rd ed. (Oxford, 1936).